D0554321

Taking the Environment Seriously

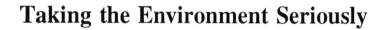

Roger E. Meiners and Bruce Yandle, Editors

The Political Economy Forum

Rowman & Littlefield Publishers, Inc.

ROWMAN & LITTLEFIELD PUBLISHERS, INC.

Published in the United States of America
by Rowman & Littlefield Publishers, Inc.
4720 Boston Way, Lanham, Maryland 20706

British Cataloging in Publication Information Available

Library of Congress Cataloging-in-Publication Data

Taking the environment seriously / Roger E. Meiners and
Bruce Yandle, editors.
p.   cm.
Includes bibliographical references and index.
1. Environmental policy—United States.
2. Environmental protection—Law and legislation—United
States.   3. Environmental risk assessment—United States.
I. Meiners, Roger E.   II. Yandle, Bruce.
GE180.T35   1993
363.7'00973—dc20   93–8830 CIP

ISBN 0–8476–7873–3 (cloth : alk. paper)

Printed in the United States of America

 ™ The paper used in this publication meets the minimum requirements of
American National Standard for Information Sciences—Permanence of
Paper for Printed Library Materials, ANSI Z39.48–1984.

Dedicated to those individuals
who have generously supported
our research for many years.

Contents

Preface

Taking the Environment Seriously:
What Do We Mean?

Roger E. Meiners and Bruce Yandle

More than twenty years' effort by the U.S. government to enhance and protect the environment has produced widespread dissatisfaction. As stated recently in the *New York Times*, "many scientists, economists, and Government officials have reached the dismaying conclusion that much of America's environmental program has gone seriously awry."[1]

Why the disappointment and frustration? How has the nation's environmental program gone astray? An examination of the record of improvements, contrasted with statements of disappointment, carries us to a paradox that suggests the entire effort has misfired. What about the record?

Though there are exceptions, such as Los Angeles, the air in most major cities is far cleaner than it was in 1970.[2] Although the auto and truck population has about doubled, lead in the atmosphere has dropped over 95 percent and carbon monoxide has dropped over 40 percent. Water quality, on average, is no worse today than when the massive efforts of the 1970s took hold. Sewage is better treated and a lot of hazardous waste has been removed. Rivers are no longer fire hazards, and it has been a long time since major factories were closed briefly to give local residents some breathing room. In addition, more than a thousand endangered species, which include animals, insects, and plants, now are guarded by federal statute.

People appreciate environmental improvements. But questions about disappointment must deal with how results match expectations. Understanding disappointment is not as simple as comparing how things are now with how they were two decades ago. Unbounded expectations are a part of the picture. Demands for ever-increasing government standards, and zealous efforts to block innovations that would accommodate cleaner economic growth and achieve stated goals, tell us there is more to the story than developing a logical set of priorities and writing cost-effective regulations.

At the outset, however, we must recognize that it is not clear just how much improvement has come from our regulatory efforts compared to how much has resulted from the effects of higher energy prices, improved technology, and the displacement of major polluting industries by the growth of the services economy. Today's economy differs significantly from the smokestack economy of the 1960s. Some aspects of the environment would have improved without any regulatory intervention.

Realizing that economic change and higher incomes may automatically bring less pollution just scratches the surface of the problem being explored. We must probe deeper. Replacing the common law protection of the environment, which is based on scientific evidence of damage, with the rule of politics, suggests we cannot consider the problem as just another effort to protect and allocate scarce and valuable resources.

Self-proclaimed environmentalists, such as Vice President Al Gore, have little interest in scientific evidence about environmental matters. Gore helped force out of office a respected scientist who was research director at the Department of Energy. The scientist had stated that there was little evidence that there was an ozone depletion problem. Politician Gore would not tolerate a deviation from his untrained views on the matter, so the scientist had to go.[3] This is not an isolated incident. As we will see in this book, scientific evidence often clashes with politically inspired legislation that is asserted to be protecting the environment.

Indeed, some environmentalists are better understood if viewed as part of a religious movement. For them, any goal short of perfection is unsatisfactory. The environment is sacred. Any effort to balance competing interests, whether by markets or politics, is still a sacrilege. As things stand now, there are more competing claims for environmental property than there are property rights. Frustration is a natural outcome.

Property Rights: A Central Issue

Environmental controversies seem to boil down to arguments about property rights, which in many cases have never been settled. Many people claim a right to clean air. Some argue they are entitled to uncontaminated beaches. And some believe they have a right to a world with no pollution, because Congress said so.

Commercial fishermen want to maintain a livelihood that depends on the effective functioning of estuaries that form the spawning grounds of fish. Coastal communities want to expand their sewage treatment works that deteriorate waters in the same estuaries. People who value flora and fauna that flourish in water-filled bottom lands want to claim protective rights to agricultural wetlands on someone else's property. And in the name of serving the American public, the U.S. Park Service wishes to claim the rights to certain view-sheds that conflict with the rights held by existing neighboring homeowners.

The definition and enforcement of property rights, which can be voluntarily traded, form a time-honored approach for resolving some of these problems in a free society. But the process that leads to the evolution of rights cannot easily be documented. Like many other complex social institutions that order our days, property rights emerge spontaneously, not by Washington edict. At the same time, long-established rights can be destroyed overnight by new statutes that promise more rights than there is property to go around. To make matters worse, the newly promised rights generally come without prices. Scarce environmental quality is asserted to be free.

The laws of economics tell us what to expect when a zero price is attached to a scarce and valuable asset, like environmental quality. The amount people seek and expect to have expands almost without limit. Perfection is the order of the day. Frustration is the result.

Regulating Inputs Not Outcomes: A Strange Paradox

Not all environmentalists seek perfection. But a strange paradox contributes to the misery of those who would be happy with something better than what we have now. Oddly, current regulatory procedures for protecting the environment pay little attention to the environment.

Consider these facts. Dozens of environmental statutes have been passed by Congress. Thousands of regulations have been written, a massive environmental bureaucracy has been formed to enforce the regulations, and hundreds of billions of dollars have been spent. Every facet of manufacturing is regulated, such as the design of automobiles, refrigerators, and lawn mowers. Practically all chemical entities must pass federal scrutiny before being released to the market. Gasoline has been reformulated and cleaner fuel is on the way. Attempts are made to control toxic substances from cradle to grave. People planning to build houses are advised by the U.S. Fish and Wildlife Service to have an environmental assessment to determine if an endangered species may be disturbed. When all other permits are obtained, foresters are advised to get one last permit before moving the soil that surrounds the roots of felled trees; soil moved on bottom land may be interpreted as discharge into navigable waters. The rules are so complex that there cannot be enough environmental police to do the job.

But notice that all of these controls relate to production inputs. None focus directly on the environment itself. Today, after more than 20 years, there is little direct effort made to protect *the environment*. And for some strange reason, no one seems to be keeping score. A set of national monitoring devices that could tell us when the air and water are better or worse is lacking. This is the paradox. Environmental outcomes are more like a by-product of a gigantic process designed to produce something else. The paradox brings us to the purpose of the book.

The Background and Purpose of the Book

Could it be that most people simply do not care about outcomes? That the demand for perfection will deny all practical efforts to enhance the biological envelope in which we all live? We don't think so. We believe ordinary people care deeply about the environment. They deserve to know what is going on.

When the search for environmental quality is better understood, people will get serious about the environment. And when we get serious, we will change the way we manage environmental use. Ordinary people, living in ordinary communities, will protect themselves from environmental damages and improve their well being while doing so.

It is time to take the environment seriously. That is what led us to organize this collection of papers by colleagues who share our concern. We hope the book will be read by scholars, teachers, students, and all who care about environmental quality.

Our effort to build this book has not been brief. The project began three years ago and included participation in national and international conferences and seminars. Along the way, we developed and taught new graduate and undergraduate courses in environmental policy, testing some of the ideas found here. We directed theses and dissertations on topics contained in the book. We have written policy papers, prepared related articles for professional journals, and engaged in countless conversations with colleagues, environmentalists, regulators, industrialists, and people in agriculture.

Reaching beyond the academic world, we have spoken to diverse audiences and considered their questions and comments. Our more isolated studies led us to reexamine the origins of environmental law, to assess America's body of common law, and to follow current episodes as they unfold on a day-to-day basis.

As we worked to understand the nation's environmental effort, we began to appreciate better some of the complexities we faced. At times we felt that the more we saw, the less we understood. No single academic discipline or set of experiences is capable of explaining why the process of protecting the environment is more important than the environment itself. Combining the views of many disciplines offers some insights.

For example, we realize that the regulatory process serves diverse interests that struggle to tilt rules one way or another. Each time legislation is written or amended, leaders of special interest groups have opportunities to stir up support among their members. Politicians benefit by offering to assist the various groups. For some groups, it seems it is better to alter the rules of the game spasmodically than to define them once and for all. As long as environmental outcomes remain a moving target, special interest groups have a reason for being. If the problem is ever resolved, the political game will end. But solutions serve only the public interest, which is never well organized.

We have also learned that considerable understanding can be gained by describing the details of major regulatory struggles. A careful ordering of events often reveals that goals once stated as the *purpose* of environmental laws have little meaning in the ensuing struggle to tilt the process in yet another direction. It is little wonder that seekers of environmental quality are disappointed with outcomes.

We have been assisted by many colleagues in our efforts to learn about the environment. Many organizations helped along the way, but we especially thank the Political Economy Research Center (PERC) in Bozeman, Montana, the organization that is the focal point of scholarly work on the *new resource economics*. Most of the colleagues whose names appear with the chapters in this volume have been associated with PERC in one way or another. We also express appreciation to Clemson University where the editors were privileged to work and study together for eight years. We have taught many students and learned from them, and we have written many words about the environment.

How the Book Is Organized

The book contains ten previously unpublished papers that are organized into four units. Each section addresses topics that speak to the theme expressed in the book's title.

History, Tension, and Outcome

The book begins with an overview of the history and experience with major environmental legislation. This chapter, written by Robert Nelson, includes an assessment of benefit-cost studies of rules adopted to manage environmental use and provides a baseline for the chapters that follow.

Chapter 2, by Paul Heyne, examines the linkages between economics, ethics, and the environment. Versed in economics and philosophy, Heyne speaks to some of the concerns raised by Nelson in that ethical assumptions determine acceptable environmental outcomes.

The third chapter, by Richard Stroup and Jane Shaw, examines the government's stewardship record. Here we see how government policies (central planning), presumably designed to protect and enhance environmental quality, often produce perverse results. The chapter goes some distance in explaining why there is considerable disappointment regarding progress toward achieving environmental goals.

Taken as a unit, the first three chapters carry the reader from assessment of the overall record, to considerations of values that condition outcomes, to an examination of perverse effects that are environmentally destructive, are costly to many, and benefit only a few.

Policy Analysis of Major Legislation

The next three chapters focus on major pieces of environmental legislation. Roger Meiners and Bruce Yandle address the evolution of water pollution law, from the common law to the Clean Water Act, now pending reauthorization, and likely to be an expanded form of existing law. They offer short-run proposals they believe will improve the next legislative model. For the longer run, they propose a return to common law rules, which in their view will strengthen environmental protection, impose costs on polluters, and protect rights to clean water.

Chapter 5, by Brett Dalton, focuses on Superfund, which will be debated in Congress in the coming years. He gives a detailed report on the experience with Superfund in South Carolina. The history and status of more than 20 sites are provided, with particular attention given to the first Superfund site cleaned. It is clear that there is little relationship between the clean up costs and the benefits received. Dalton speculates as to how the affected communities might handle Superfund and other environmental problems if they had control of funding.

David Riggs' chapter on the acid rain provisions of the 1990 Clean Air Act traces the background of that legislation and offers an explanation as to why such costly action was taken in the face of congressionally funded studies that showed little scientific basis for acid rain controls. The discussion of special interest groups sheds considerable light on how the regulatory process can become far more important than environmental goals.

Property Rights and Risk Assessment

The book's third unit focuses on property rights, emerging markets, and how ordinary people assess environmental hazards. Taking a distinct institutional approach, Terry Anderson and Donald Leal make a case for assigning property rights to fish and explain how such a system would protect fish populations and improve economic well being. Ocean dwellers are considered among the species most difficult to protect—witness the near extinction of certain whales. Anderson and Leal provide evidence that the assignment of property rights can protect the stock of fish (and whales), thereby allowing rational harvesting, as we have long had for land animals. Their chapter illustrates an approach that, if taken, could resolve part of the environmental debate.

Chapter 8, by Bruce Yandle, turns to the agricultural sector and the problem of nonpoint source pollution, which can be thought of as runoff from fields, farms, and logging operations. Pending legislation will address this issue. Yandle describes specific actions that must be taken to develop permit markets that allow watershed communities to reduce the cost of improving water quality.

Daniel Benjamin offers a reinterpretation of work that examines how people assess the relative risks of environmental hazards. If environmental control is to be placed in the hands of communities, as suggested by Yandle, citizens will face problems now handled by government officials. Benjamin's argument and analysis of data suggest an optimistic outcome. His work indicates that when real decisions are being made, as opposed to hypothetical ones, ordinary people perform quite well.

Another Interpretation of the Saga

The book's last chapter, written by Robert Nelson, offers another explanation of the long environmental saga, that may help some readers to understand why the saga has been so long, so costly, and why feelings about the environment run so deep, and are often counter to logic and science. Nelson presents environmentalism as religion and shows many parallels to make his case.

We hope that those who read the book from cover to cover will find the intellectual journey to be stimulating. If in the next two decades we take the environment seriously, it will difficult to produce a set of papers like the ones in this collection. Reading the last chapter and contemplating the previous ones, readers will be left to decide if there is hope for economic, legal, and scientific rationality to be brought to the protection of our environment, or if it will be treated like sacred cows in India; worshiped, subject to official protection, but generally bedraggled.

Notes

1. Keith Schneider, "New View Calls Environmental Policy Misguided," *New York Times*, March 21, 1993, p. 1A.
2. The fact that there has been improvement in air quality appears to be denied by well-informed groups. The National Commission on the Environment, which consists of former EPA Administrators and leaders of large environmental organizations, stated, in 1993: "The *air* in U.S. cities threatens to deteriorate further...." *Choosing a Sustainable Future*, Washington. D.C., World Wildlife Fund: Island Press, p. XIII.
3. "Did DOE's Happer Fall into Ozone Hole?" *Science*, May 7, 1993, p. 743; Holman Jenkins Jr., "Al Gore Leads a Purge," *Wall Street Journal*, May 25, 1993, p. A14.

Chapter 1

How Much Is Enough? An Overview of the Benefits and Costs of Environmental Protection

Robert H. Nelson

Introduction

In his 1992 presidential campaign, Bill Clinton pledged to "renew America's commitment to leave our children a better nation—a nation whose air, water and land are unspoiled, whose natural beauty is undimmed." He promised major changes in environmental policy, including new steps toward "harnessing market forces" in order to provide strong encouragement for firms to integrate "environmental incentives into daily production decisions." In this and other ways, the "false choice" that some presented "between environmental protection and economic growth" would be avoided (Clinton and Gore 1992, 93-99).

Indeed, most Americans look to the economic system to provide both a high gross national product and a healthy, clean, and attractive environment. However, it is precisely in designing policies to serve both economic and environmental goals effectively that our past efforts have all too often failed. The nation has frequently made much greater expenditures than were necessary to attain the environmental goals sought, diverting scarce resources from other areas of pressing national need. The allocation of our environmental resources has often shown little relationship to the true severity of our environmental problems. Environmental policies often impose complex and time-consuming regulatory regimes, stifling the entrepreneurial energies on which the American market system depends. If we are serious about efforts to make the American economy more productive and efficient, improved policies for the environment must command one of the highest priorities.

The poor state of environmental policy today partly reflects our past unwillingness as a nation to make hard choices. To some degree, the problem has been a failure of political leadership, but politicians themselves always face many constraints. Perhaps the greater problem lies closer to home, in a resistance the American people have thus far shown to thinking about the environment in a realistic way.

Opposition to Considering Economic Factors

In a recent poll, fully 80 percent of the American public agreed with the proposition that "protecting the environment is so important that requirements and standards cannot be too high ... and continuing environmental improvements must be made regardless of cost."[1] Partly in response to such public attitudes, the Congress has on a number of occasions enacted legislation precluding the consideration of costs in environmental decision making. The Clean Water Act of 1972 set a goal to eliminate all water pollution by 1985, regardless of costs. The Endangered Species Act directs that an action of a government agency cannot put the survival of a species in doubt, no matter what the burdens imposed on government programs. The Clean Air Act of 1970 required the Environmental Protection Agency (EPA) to set air quality standards to avoid any adverse health effects, again without allowance for costs incurred. Does all this mean that the American public is prepared to devote all the resources of society to the environment? It hardly seems likely. Although they may not like to say so, the truth is that most people would at some point no doubt choose to make tradeoffs and to set priorities, requiring consideration of costs. EPA, moreover, recognizes that there is no choice but to balance costs against benefits, even when legally directed to do otherwise. As explained by one student of air pollution policy, "in actuality ... costs are considered [by EPA] whenever such [air quality] standards are set, although this practice is not openly acknowledged" (Portney 1990a, 77).

The "convenient fiction" that costs are not to be considered has partly reflected a desire on the part of the Congress to be able to enact legislation that pleases constituents by requiring the attainment of lofty goals of environmental purity (Melnick 1992). Someone else can then be left to do the dirty work of making the inevitable compromises with an unattainable ideal. Similarly, by asserting that the environment is "priceless," environmental advocates are free to propose every measure possible to protect the environment without having to address the less pleasant matter of the required sacrifices elsewhere. Many environmentalists contend that any loss of environmental quality represents a moral offense against nature—that polluting is a sin and therefore the goal must be that all sinning should stop. As the associate executive director of the Sierra Club, Carl Pope, recently remarked, "the environment is an ethical issue."[2]

For most economists, by contrast, the environment is a scarce resource and pollution merely one among the competing potential uses of this resource. An "optimal" pollution level should be attained, determined by the same economic considerations that apply to other inputs and outputs (Ruff 1970; Cropper and Oates 1992). There is no environmental morality here—probably one of the reasons why many environmentalists believe, as it was put by the editors of a journal of environmental opinion, that "economics, and economists, are traditional enemies of the environment" (Lindler 1988, 10). In the federal government, the Office of Management and Budget (OMB) has sought to assess the benefits from environmental regulations against competing ways in which the resources of society could be used. In response, environmental groups and prominent Congressmen have attempted to curtail or to eliminate the role of OMB economists in environmental decision making.

Escalating Environmental Costs

In these contentious circumstances, it has been difficult to assess the benefits and costs of government programs to protect the environment—indeed, for some program administrators it has been illegal to do so openly and explicitly. At the same time the costs of environmental protection have been shooting skyward. The EPA in December 1990 published figures on the total U.S. costs (public and private) for all pollution control activities (EPA 1990c). Total spending for pollution control equalled about $27 billion in 1972, rose to $58 billion in 1980, and then again to $100 billion in 1990 (1986 dollars). The great majority of this spending is by private industry and by others who are responding to EPA mandates, not by EPA directly, but the consequences for the total use of social resources are no less.

EPA also projected that in the year 2000 the total cost of pollution control will equal $160 billion. As a percent of GNP, pollution control will have risen from receiving less than 1 percent of GNP in 1972 to more than 2.5 percent in the year 2000. If current trends continue, EPA could soon end up commanding a larger share of the American economy than the Defense Department.

The burdens associated with environmental protection are growing rapidly in other areas as well. The full net costs of protecting the spotted owl in the Pacific Northwest, if current plans are maintained, are likely to be in the range of $10 to $20 billion over the long run.[3] The expected net economic cost to the nation —not the gross which is much larger—of keeping oil drilling out of the Arctic National Wildlife Refuge in northeast Alaska is likely to be about $15 to $30 billion. That comes to a one-time cost of about $200 to $400 for every family of four in the United States.

Environmental regulations not only mandate direct spending but have further sizeable indirect impacts on the economy. They reduce returns to labor and capital, thus diminishing the amounts of these factor inputs supplied and the growth of U.S. gross national product (GNP). A study by two Harvard economists, Dale Jorgenson and Peter Wilcoxen (1989), estimated that the effect of environmental regulations enacted since the 1970s has been to reduce the level of GNP by about 2.5 percent. Two researchers funded by EPA, Michael Hazilla and Raymond Kopp (1990), estimated that the effects of existing clean air and clean water regulations reduced GNP in 1990 by about 5.9 percent. Hazilla and Kopp further estimated that the inflationary impacts of air and water controls caused consumer prices to be about 6.3 percent higher than they would otherwise have been. Taking the full range of direct and indirect impacts on the economy into account, and allowing for the various possibilities for substituting among labor, capital, and leisure, their estimate of the full social cost in 1990 of air and water regulations exceeded the EPA estimate for direct compliance costs by a factor of more than 2.5.

Moreover, EPA figures for pollution control costs do not account for many types of environmental protection measures—such as changes in local land use patterns in order to protect the environment or environmentally mandated reductions in outputs from federally owned lands and minerals. Considering further EPA's projections of sharp increases in direct compliance costs by the year 2000, plus the rising percentage of GNP lost each year due to lower growth rates of the economy, it is possible that the total social burden for environmental protection measures will be approaching $500 billion per year by the year 2000.

Are the Benefits Large Enough?

As environmental protection commands a rapidly growing share of national resources, the time has come to take seriously the question of how much is enough—whether American society is receiving an adequate improvement in the environment to justify all this spending. It is also important to ask whether the existing level of spending is being utilized efficiently so as to achieve the maximum environmental benefits possible. Most authorities believe that, unfortunately, the answer is no on both counts. In a 1992 report, Robert Crandall (1992) of the Brookings Institution stated that "the inefficiencies in most federal environmental programs are well known as a result of decades of research.... We continue to spend far too much for the environmental results we obtain."

Past efforts by economists to put the benefits and costs of environmental protection in dollar terms have generated considerable controversy (Portney 1990a). In the environmental area, use of benefit-cost analysis often requires developing dollar figures for days of work that are not lost, for deaths that are avoided (or, more accurately, deferred), for aesthetic improvements, and for a number of other consequences of improved environmental quality. These impacts are often difficult to measure or to value with much precision. Nevertheless, economists have various techniques for estimating them in an approximate way (Freeman 1979). For example, estimates of the value of aesthetic improvements can sometimes be inferred from comparative studies of property values in more and less polluted areas.

Moreover, there is no getting around the fact that a benefit-cost assessment will eventually be done in one form or another; the only question is whether it will be explicit or implicit. A formal benefit-cost analysis thus should be seen as one useful tool, along with many other sources of information. An assessment of benefits and costs can also be done in a broader sense. Such an analysis asks in a general way what we are getting for our efforts to improve the environment and what we are giving up. Is there a reasonable relationship between the two? The goal need not be a final conclusion stated in dollar terms but simply a careful enumeration of the gains and losses in the most understandable terms possible.

Benefits and Costs of the Clean Air Act

The single most prominent area of environmental policy is probably air pollution control. The smog in Los Angeles may well have done as much as any other pollution problem to heighten environmental awareness in America. The efforts in this area illustrate many of the difficulties faced today throughout environmental policy.

Before the Clean Air Act of 1970, there was in fact already considerable effort being made to clean up the air—much of this activity initiated at the state level. According to EPA data, from 1960 to 1970 particulate levels fell by 22 percent at 95 sites around the United States. From 1966 to 1971, sulfur dioxide levels fell by 50 percent at 31 monitoring sites (Portney 1990a, 50). Significantly, these substantial improvements were made at a fairly low cost, especially compared with the costs of implementing few federal requirements in the 1970s and 1980s.

New Federal Legislation

In 1970 the enactment of the Clean Air Act imposed a whole new regulatory regime with much more federal control. The Act would be administered by the newly created Environmental Protection Agency (EPA). The level of spending on air pollution control began to rise sharply, going for the nation from $8 billion in 1972 to around $30 billion in 1990. Measured by changes in pollution levels, there were also some important gains. Particulate loads nationwide fell again by more than 50 percent from 1970 to 1990; levels of lead in the air have fallen by more than 95 percent since 1970. And there have been declines in measured levels of sulfur dioxides and carbon monoxides. Improvements in human health, atmospheric visibility, agricultural productivity, materials longevity, and other areas have all been felt.

The key question is whether these benefits have exceeded the costs. In the judgment of many respected analysts, the best available calculations of benefits from the Clean Air Act of 1970 were done by Myrick Freeman. Using 1978 as his benchmark year for examining benefits, Freeman developed a most likely estimate of around $37 billion in benefits in that year in 1984 dollars (Freeman 1982, 57). EPA estimates that air pollution control costs in 1978 were about $16 billion in 1986 dollars (EPA 1990c). So if Freeman's analysis is accepted, the benefits may even have been twice the costs.

To be sure, the costs were likely much higher than they needed to be. Many environmental analysts over the years have concluded that the same levels of air pollution reduction could have been achieved at much lower costs (Tietenberg 1985). But at least there are indications that in the late 1970s the benefits were enough to justify at a gross level the burdens imposed. Although important amendments to the Clean Air Act were made in 1977, air pollution policy in the 1980s was largely a continuation of policy directions in place by the mid 1970s.

The 1990 Amendments

Yet, as pollution levels decline, further improvements in environmental quality will become more difficult to achieve. The law of diminishing returns applies to the environment as well as to other areas of life. This possibility is important because the new Clean Air Act Amendments, passed in 1990, propose to undertake some heroic and very costly measures. The Act will eventually at least double the 1990 expenditures of around $30 billion per year for cleaner air. Estimates of the benefits and costs of this new spending have in fact been undertaken by a leading authority on air pollution policy, Paul Portney (1990). Portney is an economist and vice-president of Resources for the Future, a research organization created with strong support from the Ford Foundation in the 1950s, which has continued to do important studies of environmental and natural resource issues. His conclusions are somewhat disturbing.

The 1990 Act addresses three main areas: acid rain, urban air pollution controls designed to limit smog, and hazardous air pollutants. Portney takes into account that the impacts of acid rain on lakes and forests, as well as other damages originally feared, turned out to be much less severe than many people originally had thought. The National Acid Precipitation Assessment Program (NAPAP) reached this conclusion after many years of research and the expenditure of $500 million (U.S. National Acid Precipitation Assessment Program 1991). Nevertheless, it turns out that sulfate particles may have some adverse effects, mainly on human health. There may also be some aesthetic benefits in terms of visibility from reducing sulfur.

Portney takes a rough stab that the total benefits, mostly in possible health and visibility gains, will be in a range of $2 to $9 billion per year. The costs of the 10 million tons per year sulfur reduction mandated by the 1990 Act will be around $4 to $5 billion per year. So, even though the main benefits are not the original justification for an acid rain program, it is at least possible that this program will show some positive net gains—although it is also possible that the nation will be spending considerably more than the benefits received.

But that is the good news. For the smog control part of the new Act, Portney estimates benefits in the range of $4 to $12 billion per year. It is difficult to control smog, and the new program will certainly not eliminate the problem. Hence, the benefits in terms of further improvements on the margin may not be very great. Portney's estimates of costs, however, are in the range of $19 to $22 billion per year. Here costs could easily turn out to be twice as large as the benefits.

Portney reaches a similarly unfavorable conclusion for hazardous air pollutant controls. He considers that the benefits could be as low as zero. As will be discussed later, current knowledge concerning actual risks from hazardous substances is primitive. Portney suggests the upper bound of benefits is $4 billion per year. However, by comparison, he estimates costs of around $6 billion to $10 billion per year.

So if these estimates are accurate, the new Clean Air Act will require large expenditures to further clear up the air that are of very questionable overall benefit. Other well-informed people do not dispute the general thrust of Portney's conclusions. Robert Hahn, an economist at the American Enterprise Institute, has recently suggested that the total costs of the 1990 Clean Air Act Amendments will exceed the benefits by about $16 billion per year (Hahn 1992; Hahn 1991). These costs for the Clean Air Act do not include the inhibitions to business innovation, the procedural delays, the intensified bureaucratic oversight, and other burdens that may also be significant. The 1990 Act adds further layers of permitting requirements and extensive new requirements for reporting of business plans and activities to government regulators. It may generate a sharp increase in government micromanagement and second guessing of business decisions. In an attempt to ensure that EPA directives are closely followed, there are also new provisions for criminal prosecutions of business executives and for payment of bounties to those who turn in violators.

In summary, the national effort to improve air quality may have spent a lot more than was necessary, and some foolish things were no doubt done, but Americans did obtain some important and worthwhile benefits from the 1960s into the 1980s. However, regulation of air quality seems now to be getting into areas where the efforts are increasingly problematic and may indeed be highly wasteful.

The Clean Water Act of 1972

A second area of major importance in the battle for a cleaner environment has been water pollution control. Unfortunately, here matters look less favorable even at the beginning of the period of heavy federal involvement. The Federal Water Pollution Control Act of 1972 expanded the federal role significantly and required large new expenditures to clean up the waters of the nation. Many analysts regarded the legislation as gravely flawed from its inception. As was already being reported in 1972, "although there is growing disenchantment with federal water pollution policies, the recent legislative response has been more of the same.... If past experience is any guide, these efforts will at best be patch jobs on an already sieve-like structure" (Freeman and Waveman 1973, 130).

Again, Prof. Myrick Freeman has made some well-regarded estimates for the benefits of the Clean Water Act. These benefits include greater fishing, swimming, and other recreation; improved water supplies for drinking and other municipal and industrial purposes; aesthetic improvements in lakes and rivers; and so forth. For 1978, Freeman calculated benefits in that year of around $14 billion (1984 dollars) (Freeman 1990, 123). That same year the costs of the Clean Water Act, as estimated by EPA, were about $21 billion (1986 dollars). So there is considerable doubt about whether we were getting our money's worth even then.

Water Policy Failings

Why is this? What is the difference from the early air pollution control efforts? Several reasons appear important.

First, the benefits tend to be less. Swimmers, fishermen, and other recreationists can only make so much use of improved water bodies. Moreover, there are often many alternative forms of recreation available to them; partly for this reason, potential users may not value new recreational opportunities very highly, especially in comparison to the cost. And water pollution controls are very costly. EPA is now projecting costs of more than $60 billion per year in the year 2000.

To some extent the high costs reflect the prevailing philosophy to impose a uniform set of tight standards on communities and businesses all across the United States. Yet, many of the nation's waters were already in reasonable condition in 1972. According to the Conservation Foundation, 64 percent of stream miles and 84 percent of lakes and reservoirs were able to support all expected uses in that year (The Conservation Foundation 1984, 106-8). Very large amounts have been spent to clean up water bodies around the United States that were already quite clean.

ˌ

The difficulty of further enhancing the quality of these waters helps to explain why there has been a lackluster rate of overall improvement in water quality since 1972. According to an EPA study, "the broadest statistical analysis of water quality trends found no clear nationwide improvement over the period 1974 to 1981.... Far more [monitoring] stations showed no statistically significant change than showed an improving or worsening trend" (EPA 1990b, 82). Although there have been a few notoriously dirty rivers cleaned up and some other conspicuous exceptions, the decade of the 1980s on the whole does not seem to have been significantly different.

The water pollution strategy has been flawed in another basic way. Under the Clean Water Act, a large part of the control effort is directed at point sources such as factories, power plants, and municipal sewage plants. These sources are easy to identify and easy to regulate. They are also often big business, which makes them easy and inviting political targets. Unfortunately, they do not cause most of the water pollution. EPA estimates that only 9 percent of our impaired river miles are being affected by industrial plants. Even sewage treatment plants affect only 16 percent of impaired river miles. By contrast, agriculture affects 55 percent (EPA 1990b, 81).

Failure to Deal with Nonpoint Sources

The real water pollution problem today is a nonpoint source problem. As EPA's own analysts report, "relatively few river reaches nationwide are sufficiently affected by point sources to profit substantially from improved point source controls." However, the existing water pollution control strategy is still directed at point sources. Again, EPA is well aware of the problem: "Most types of nonpoint sources have proven far more difficult to control than point sources primarily because a command-and-control regulatory approach is difficult to implement for them. Nonpoint source dischargers are numerous and widespread, and are difficult to identify, monitor, establish control requirements for, and enforce against" (EPA 1990b, 82). They are also politically powerful. Instead the nation spends very large amounts to control point sources but does not obtain a great deal of improvement in water quality.

As of 1992, a leading student of environmental policy assessed the unsatisfactory state of affairs in the field of water pollution regulation as follows:

Legislation prior to the 1970s had little impact on the problem. Frustration then led to the enactment of a tough federal law that was so ambitious and unrealistic that little progress resulted.

[Current water pollution policy] has been hampered by delays, by problems in allocating funds, and by the fact that about half of the constructed plants are not performing satisfactorily. [Existing policy] has given rise to delays and to the need to define the standards in a series of court suits. In addition, effluent standards have assigned the control responsibility among point sources in a way that excessively raises cost. Nonpoint pollution sources have, until recently, been virtually ignored. Technological progress is inhibited rather than stimulated by the current approach. Benefit-cost analyses focusing on 1985 show the net benefit from the current approach to be negative. (Tietenberg 1992, 506)

To be sure, there may be what might be called symbolic benefits. A cynic might say that we feel better by trying harder, even if we don't succeed. Unfortunately, this mentality does seem to play a rather large role in many areas of current environmental policy.

A Flawed Basic Strategy

The problems of existing air and water pollution programs illustrate general problems in the way the nation goes about protecting the environment. As a result, the resources devoted to environmental programs are used inefficiently. Put another way, for the same level of total environmental expenditure being made, the environmental benefits to the nation could be much larger than they actually are.

The United States has generally gone about controlling pollution in a rigid command-and-control fashion. The same standards have tended to be applied all across the nation, the same technologies tended to be mandated for each firm in an industry. Under this approach, we have tried to force companies to reduce pollution levels by similar amounts, whether it would be very easy for a particular company or extremely difficult.

Economists often point out that, under market-based systems, the polluters who could reduce emissions at the least cost would do so (Kneese and Schultze 1975; Anderson 1977). Polluters for whom reductions were difficult and expensive would pay instead—under marketable permit systems they would pay those firms who would be making the larger cutbacks. It is less often remarked but also true that a command-and-control system could save large amounts by introducing a similar flexibility. For example, EPA could require that every polluter must reduce a type of emission as long as the reduction cost is less than so many dollars per ton. A company could then avoid reducing pollution further by demonstrating to EPA that this reduction would be too expensive and thus cost ineffective. If this level of effort did not result in enough overall pollution being curbed, EPA could simply raise the dollar figure per ton that would provide relief from further EPA mandates.

In any case, preferably by a system of market pricing of pollution, but alternatively by a new command-and-control approach, the potential for cost savings in greater flexibility is large. A survey of eleven case studies of air pollution controls found that in every case but one current policies were imposing costs at least 50 percent greater than necessary to achieve the same results as at present. In seven cases the costs actually being incurred were more than 400 percent greater than the least-cost solution (Tietenberg 1985). The 1989 annual report of the Council of Economic Advisors (CEA) concluded that "regardless of one's view of the value of environmental improvement, EPA's rigid regulatory strategy has clearly wasted a substantial portion of the Nation's investment aimed at improving air quality." The CEA reported that "the cost of air pollution control during the 1980s has averaged more than $30 billion annually, and economic studies indicate that more cost effective pollution control strategies could have achieved the same degree of environmental quality for billions less" (Council of Economic Advisors 1989, 216).

The Need to Decentralize

Another basic source of regulatory inefficiency is that EPA has typically tried to mandate uniform national solutions even where there are highly variable regional and local circumstances. The heroic efforts and high costs of reducing pollution in the most difficult areas are also imposed on places that may have much less of a problem and could devise cheaper solutions. One of the more infamous examples involved the new source performance standards for coal burning electric utilities, enacted under the Clean Air Act Amendments of 1977. In these Amendments Congress required that new power plants throughout the United States install control equipment (in practice one or another form of "scrubber") to remove sulfur dioxide from the coal they burned. However, many western, midwestern, and other utilities could have achieved the same (or lower) emission levels simply by purchasing and burning western coal that was already low in sulfur content. In *Clean Coal/Dirty Air*, Ackerman and Hassler describe how this congressional requirement drove "EPA to an extra-ordinary decision that will cost the public tens of billions of dollars to achieve environmental goals that could be reached more cheaply, more quickly, and more surely by other means. Indeed, the agency action is so inept that some of the nation's most populous areas will end up with a worse environment than would have resulted if the new policy had never been put into effect" (1981, 2).

Congress enacted this perverse requirement partly to protect coal companies and union workers in eastern and midwestern states. Coal in these areas tends to have much higher sulfur content, potentially exposing it to competition from the extensive deposits of low-sulfur coal found in Wyoming and other western states (to a large extent, it might be noted, coal owned by the federal government) (Nelson 1983). However, when Congress required that all coal be scrubbed for sulfur removal, the competitive advantage of western coal disappeared. Environmental groups allied themselves with eastern coal mining interests partly to buy off a potential strong opponent of tight controls and partly because they preferred a general strategy to impose uniform technology requirements across the United States. In the legislative process, such unholy alliances between environmental groups and special economic interests have occurred on a number of occasions. In a more recent example, midwestern agricultural interests succeeded in pressuring Congress to mandate greater use of ethanol (made from corn) in the 1990 Clean Air Act—despite the high cost and absence of clear environmental benefit (Adler 1992).

A Case Study: Urban Smog

The problems of existing pollution control strategies were highlighted recently in a study mandated by the 1990 Clean Air Act and undertaken by a committee of the National Academy of Sciences (NAS). The NAS study addressed the problem of smog or, more technically speaking, of ozone. The NAS reported that "despite the major regulatory and pollution-control programs of the past 20 years, efforts to attain the National Ambient Air Quality Standard for ozone largely have failed" (National Research Council 1991, 4). Our efforts have been at a huge cost, including most recently further costs of at least $10 billion per year under the provisions of the 1990 Clean Air Act. Some people also question the validity of the standard itself, and whether it is an adequate way of representing the nation's real air quality objectives.

The control strategy has emphasized reducing what are called volatile organic compounds, or in trade jargon, "VOCs." As NAS observed, there has recently been a much greater appreciation that VOCs are also generated in substantial magnitudes by natural vegetation. The NAS study found that naturally occurring sources of VOC, in combination with man-created nitric oxide and nitrogen dioxide, could cause significant violations of existing smog standards. As a result, the nation could spend billions to reduce further emissions of VOCs from cars and factories, but in some areas the existing standards could never be met.

Operating under regulatory strategies, however, there has not been as much concern with nitrogen oxides. In fact, the situation is apparently quite complicated. The NAS study states that the appropriate control strategy can depend significantly on what is called the VOC/nitrogen oxide ratio. For ratios in one range reductions in nitrogen oxides are needed; in another range more nitrogen oxides might actually be needed to curb smog. And this ratio is variable from one place to another in the United States. Hence, a uniform national approach to reducing smog will not only impose unnecessary burdens in some areas but could be counterproductive in other areas in terms of causing smog levels to increase. The problems of smog control further emphasize the importance of flexibility to tailor control strategies to local atmospheric, geographic, population, traffic, and other circumstances.

The NAS study revealed some other bothersome matters. First, existing measures of actual ozone trends within metropolitan areas are unreliable. Often, EPA does not know what is really happening in the atmosphere of urban areas. Second, existing predictive computer models for ozone levels do not work well; yet, strategies for controlling ozone are based in significant degree on these models. Third, existing control strategies even for "anthropogenic" (human created) VOCs have failed to deliver the VOC levels promised. Apparently, they have been based on unrealistic assumptions. Larger actual VOC emissions from mobile sources than had been factored into calculations have been a major problem.

In sum, existing knowledge of ozone levels and atmospheric conditions is apparently inadequate to design an efficient and effective strategy to reduce smog. And this, of course, is more than 20 years after the EPA was created and the first major national Clean Air Act passed. It suggests still another major problem, that often there is not enough basic information collected and science done before jumping to conclusions. And EPA has done a poor job in getting organized to identify and make up the major scientific deficiencies.

Hazardous Substances and Waste Disposal

The third major area of pollution control includes a broad range of regulatory activities involving waste disposal and the regulation of chemicals, pesticides, and other potentially hazardous substances. For total U.S. public and private pollution control costs in 1990, the three major areas of activity break out about as follows. Air pollution received almost 30 percent of the approximately $100 billion spent directly throughout the United States. Water pollution received about 40 percent. And the various hazardous substance and waste disposal programs received about 30 percent. These are the big three.

Poor Science

The problems in this third area stir the greatest public fears because they raise the specter of threats to human health. Many public anxieties are associated with that most fearsome threat of all, the possibility of getting cancer. It is also in this area that there have been some of the most questionable scientific practices. With poor science combined with public hysteria, the results have sometimes made the regulation of air quality and of water quality seem by comparison to be models of sober minded practicality and rationality.

The scientific problems of testing for cancer causing agents have become well known by now, at least among those who pay close attention to these matters. For a while there were many adherents to what Edith Efron called the Garden of Eden theory of cancer (Efron 1989; Efron 1984). It was difficult for many people to believe that nature in its original—and presumable innocent—state could have yielded something as terrible as cancer. A more appealing view was that it had been fallen men with their penchant for greed and the rise of industrial civilization that had brought cancer into the world. And, as mankind is committed to eradicate sin, it must be committed to eliminating every possible chemical, waste, or other agent that could cause cancer. Such attitudes helped to lead to actions like the 1958 Delaney amendment, whereby Congress said that any food additive causing cancer in any test must be banned by FDA. Moreover, a main way to tell if a chemical causes cancer would be to subject animals to massive doses and then to determine whether cancer rates among these animals rose above normal levels. Professor Bruce Ames of Berkeley was one of those who originally was a developer of these kinds of tests. For many years he has been one of the leading scientists in the world in this field. But somewhere in the 1980s he decided that the basic research design was radically in error. Ames now states that: "The attempt to prevent cancer by regulating low levels of synthetic chemicals by using worst-case, one-in-a-million risk scenarios is not scientifically justified. Testing chemicals for carcinogenicity at near-toxic doses in rodents is misleading, enormously costly, and counter productive. It diverts resources from much more important tasks.... Perversely, it decreases consumption of foods that help to prevent cancer" (Ames 1991, 4).

As indicated by Ames, one of the potential costs of pesticide regulation, if it drives up the price of certain food items, is that some people might eat a less healthy diet. In this way they could even raise their overall risk of cancer, the risks of the poorer diet exceeding any risks associated with the pesticide itself. Ames further comments that "plants produce toxins to protect themselves against fungi, insects and animal predators.... We estimate that Americans eat about 1.5 grams of natural pesticides per person per day, which is about 10,000 times more than they eat of synthetic pesticide residues" (Ames 1991, 4). Apparently the risk of cancer—to the degree that a real risk exists—is far greater from natural pesticide sources than from man-made sources.

It thus seems that the existing knowledge of what causes cancer is much like the existing knowledge of what causes smog. It is evolving rapidly, previous leading theories have recently been cast aside, and it is on the whole shockingly incomplete in light of the regulatory burdens that are being placed on it. American society is in fact going to heroic lengths to eliminate supposed cancer causing agents that could well be harmless.

Ignoring Relative Levels of Risk

To compound matters, even if current test results are accepted, and it is assumed that some cancer really is being caused, the expenditures being made in some areas are wholly disproportionate to the risk. For example, recent EPA and OMB calculations show that new landfill regulations will avoid one cancer case for the expenditure of around $20 billion (Scarlet 1992, 55). There are many places around the world (say America's inner cities, or Africa) where the expenditure of this amount of money would not only save many more lives, but there could be widespread additional benefits as well. (Consider the savings in lives from spending $20 billion to provide improved medical care for the people of poor nations in Africa.)

In its 1992 Annual Report, the Council of Economic Advisors indicated that prior to 1985 there had been only two regulations for which the cost per death averted exceeded $100 million (Council of Economic Advisors 1992, 189). Eight such regulations have been issued since then. In one instance an EPA rule for wood-preserving chemicals is estimated to avoid only one case of cancer every 2.9 million years at a cost of more than $5 trillion dollars per death avoided. Of course, regulations such as this one can not be applied very widely. If they were, it would mean the spending of almost one full year's worth of GNP to save one life.

It is true that this case qualifies as an extreme even in this area of extremes. However, a broader view still suggests severe problems. Roger Dower, then with the Congressional Research Service, wrote in 1989 that for hazardous waste regulation "the fragmentary evidence to date suggests that with respect to health, at least, the risks are not great. The hazardous waste management program is not the first environmental protection strategy that may involve serious economic inefficiencies, but it may eventually go farther in that direction than any other" (Dower 1990, 183).

By now, it is widely agreed on all sides that one of the major failures of environmental policy has been the "Superfund" program to clean up old toxic dump sites. EPA's staff found that "the health problems caused by and risks attributable to these sites are very difficult to quantify" (EPA 1990b, 95). Only about 100 sites have been cleaned up, while the number of sites needing attention is in the thousands. Where cleanup has been completed, large amounts have been spent to try to return the site virtually to an immaculate condition. Some estimates have suggested that full compliance with the precise letter of the law could eventually push total compliance expenditures above even $500 billion (Litan 1992). A recent analysis concludes that "Superfund has produced an enormous legal morass that constitutes a substantial drain on public and private resources; yet it has yielded very little in the way of environmental improvement." The actual output of Superfund has been "spending more and more money at a small number of sites so as to reduce what have already become small risks to ever more infinitesimal levels" (Landry and Hague 1992, 71).

The 1992 annual report of the Council on Environmental Quality included figures showing for a wide range of government regulations the "cost per premature death averted." For 10 of the regulations the cost was less than $500 thousand, while for 21 other regulations the cost exceeded $10 million per death averted (Council on Environmental Quality 1992, 234-35). These figures illustrated how, by concentrating regulatory efforts and spending in those areas where the relative costs are lower, the total number of lives saved in American society could be significantly increased. But such attention to cost-effectiveness and economic rationality is seldom found in environmental policymaking. As suggested above, perhaps the explanation is that Americans are more interested in environmental policy as a collective form of doing penance, relieving feelings of guilt about the material abundance of modern civilization. In that case, of course, the more you waste, the greater the benefits.

Spreading Public Hysteria

In the hazardous chemicals and substances area, there have been some well publicized cases in the last few years where initial reports caused wide public hysteria but then it turned out later that the risks had been greatly exaggerated. In the meantime, however, Congress and the executive branch, facing a fearful public, had already introduced new programs with huge costs. Heroic efforts ended up producing very little benefit. In an editorial in *Science* magazine, the deputy editor for engineering and applied sciences wrote that "stringent regulations and attendant frightening publicity have led to public anxiety and chemophobia. If current ill-based regulatory levels continue to be imposed, the cost of cleaning up phantom hazards will be in the hundreds of billions of dollars with minimal benefit to human health" (Abelson 1990, 1357).

One of these situations involved asbestos. A fearful public was stirred to tear up schools and other buildings across the United States in order to remove old asbestos. By some estimates as much as $3 billion a year has been spent on asbestos abatement, much of it on removals. Further review, however, led researchers to conclude that asbestos in place typically involved little risk. In fact, removing it creates much more risk, both for the workers and because of particle residues that remain in the air. Hence, in 1990, after at least tacitly encouraging billions of dollars in asbestos removal, the government issued a new manual explaining that "removal [of asbestos] is often not a building owner's best course of action to reduce asbestos exposure. In fact, improper removal can create a dangerous situation where none previously existed" (EPA 1990a, viii).

In another example, shortly after the Exxon Valdez oil spill in Alaska occurred, one judge involved in the case stated publicly that it was the most destructive thing to have been done by mankind since Hiroshima. Exxon reacted to this kind of hysteria by attempting literally to clean the oil off the rocks and beaches with steam and other crude methods. Exxon did at least stimulate the Alaskan economy to the extent of several billion dollars. But when the panic had subsided, the verdict was that it had probably all been a big mistake environmentally. After a visit to Alaska, Democratic Representative Wayne Owens of

Utah—a strong supporter of environmental causes—wrote that "I concluded that the value of the massive spill-cleanup effort lies primarily in public relations, not just for Exxon but also for Alaskan and federal officials and for Congress" (Owens 1989).

The "60 Minutes" CBS television report on Alar and the resulting unjustified public fears—orchestrated by the Natural Resources Defense Council—is yet another of these cases. And the whole panic over dioxin is one more. The citizens of Times Beach in Missouri vacated their whole town, but today it appears that there was no real danger. At least in the case of dioxin, it seems to have been an instance of well-intentioned scientists making premature judgments and then only later realizing they were probably off the mark.

Similar problems have been experienced in trying to deal with all the solid wastes—some hazardous but many not—that American society will certainly continue to produce. To sum it up, the whole area of waste and hazardous substance policy has been beset by emotionalism and ineffective policy development.

Conclusion

As this chapter has been examining, there are many serious problems with the way environmental policy is made in the United States. Yet, it is also important to keep in mind that, on the whole, the American environment is much cleaner than many other places around the world. In comparison with eastern Europe and the former Soviet Union, the quality of the environment is far superior here. The United States is also much better off compared with Mexico and most of the undeveloped nations of the world.

The point is often made that the superior quality of the American environment is one of the signs that capitalism and the American democratic system work better than other systems. It is in fact American political institutions that gave the American public ample opportunity to express a strong preference for greater environmental amenities. The American market system created the substantial wealth to be able to respond and to have cleaner air and water, more parks, more protection of rare species, and so forth.

However, these successes have been obtained at a high cost. It is fortunate that the United States is a wealthy nation, because that is the only way these costs have been bearable. Moreover, the burdens of environmental protection have been rising rapidly, while the American economy has been performing less successfully.

It is time, therefore, to learn from our mistakes. Our resources devoted to the environment are too large and too valuable to continue to squander as we have in the past. If the nation is truly interested in strong protections for the environment, while contributing to maintaining a healthy and growing national economy, our environmental policies must be changed. New policies must take economic considerations and relative real risks to the American public explicitly into account. They must reflect the common sense that has been missing thus far in the environmental field but which Americans have so amply demonstrated in many other areas in the past.

Environmental policymaking has a number of similarities to the development of health care policies. In fact, the two areas often overlap, as when they both address ways of reducing the risks of cancer. Each involves troublesome ethical questions such as the willingness of society to spend to save human lives. Claims are made in both areas that there exist well-defined "rights" that must be satisfied no matter what the cost. The confluence of these and other circumstances has yielded an exploding cost burden for American society in the environmental and health fields. It is clear in both areas that past rates of increase can not be sustained.

Abandon the Moral Crusade

The problem of setting some environmental priorities and finding a way to contain the currently escalating costs is complicated by the tendency of many people to see the issue solely in moral terms—as a battle between good and evil in which to implement further environmental protection must always mean the triumph of the good. For some people the point of environmental policy seems to have little to do with whether we have cleaner air, less cancer, etc. It seems instead to be more a matter of the desire to make a commitment to doing something good in the world. Twenty-five years ago such idealism was directed to helping the poor; today it is more often directed to the environment. Children used to collect money at Halloween for UNICEF; now they collect for whales. Environmental policymaking thus has become something that often seems to be more about saving our individual and our collective national souls than it has to do with the practicalities and technical details of the environment. There is a deeply religious element underlying it all (Nelson 1990; Nelson 1993).

Then, given this public mood, the media and the environmental organizations play on it. It is a good way to sell newspapers or boost TV ratings. For environmental groups, it raises money and gives them political clout, helping to sustain what have now become environmental bureaucracies. The desire to do good is also manipulated by various special interests—including business corporations that may be happy to exclude competitors, that may be producers of environmental equipment, or that may gain in other ways through greater regulation. Our environmental moral crusade results both in poor policies and in creating a shield behind which all kinds of special interests hide—in fact an old story, also once seen, for example, with respect to the actions of the Baptists and the bootleggers in an earlier moral crusade, the prohibition movement (Yandle 1983).

There are obviously no sure answers to these problems. But certainly public education and a more enlightened public opinion are a critical part of the answer. In this regard, much of the burden will probably have to fall on the scientific community itself. Currently, it does not do enough to refute its sensationalists who feed public emotionalism. It is important that a wider range of scientists step forth from their laboratories to speak in language comprehensible to laymen. Unfortunately, at present the limited number of scientists likely to get involved tend to be those who have already enlisted in the moral crusade.

Future Directions

As far as future changes in environmental policies, a few overall directions can be suggested:

1. Spend more on science, data gathering, and collecting basic information (EPA 1992).

2. Abandon much of the centralization and allow for much greater state and local flexibility—in other words, decentralize both policy and administration in a major way. Maybe this will even mean eliminating current EPA authority to have the last say at the state and local level.

3. Let EPA play more of a scientific, technical assistance, informational, and coordinating role, rather than issuing coercive mandates.

4. Make more use of markets and especially of tradeable emission permit systems. The recent proposed introduction of a trading system for achieving air quality goals in Los Angeles is a significant development in environmental policy that should be watched closely.

5. Repeal existing laws that prohibit EPA and other agencies from considering benefits and costs in making environmental decisions. Instead, require that estimates of benefits and costs—calculated in the manner most illuminating—be fully incorporated into environmental impact assessments and other parts of the official record on which agency administrators will base their decisions.

6. In general, set priorities in the allocation of environmental resources that reflect closely the true risks to the American public and the actual gains for a healthy, clean, and attractive American environment.

Environmental policymaking shows in an exaggerated form some of the problems that generally seem to afflict American government today. There is the prominence of the mass media, often poorly informed but extremely powerful, especially in setting the agenda for public attention. Government tends to become an exercise in theater, putting on performances for the media, generating entertainment for the American public, rather than rationally devising administrative and policy solutions. Decision making in American government has also become more and more politicized in all areas, not only the environment. There has been a decline of public confidence in the expertise of professional groups. Environmental problems illustrate how policy issues today seem increasingly to raise basic conflicts over social values, making it all that much more difficult to find agreement and precluding their resolution on technical grounds alone.

So progress in the environmental area may depend on progress in coming to terms with a general set of problems that afflict American government today. Of course, it is a circular process. One of the main tests for American government will be its ability to find better ways to satisfy what is undoubtedly a top priority of the American public—to maintain strong and effective protections for the environment.

Notes

1. This poll was conducted by the Wirthin Group. The results were summarized by Hugh L. Carey, Executive Vice President, W. R. Grace Company, in a speech delivered to the Rotary Club of Los Angeles, June 12, 1992.
2. Remarks quoted in *USA Weekend*.
3. See Mead et al. The forgone timber values estimated in this report are somewhat overstated, since projected timber harvest declines in the report exceed current expectations of decline.

References

Abelson, Philip H. 1990. Testing for Carcinogens with Rodents. *Science* (September 21): 1357.

Ackerman, Bruce A., and William T. Hassler. 1981. *Clean Coal/Dirty Air, Or How the Clean Air Act Became a Multibillion Dollar Bailout to High-Sulfur Coal Producers and What Should Be Done About It.* New Haven: Yale University Press.

Adler, Jonathan H. 1992. *Clean Fuels, Dirty Air.* In *Environmental Politics: Public Costs, Private Rewards,* ed. by Michael S. Greve and Fred L. Smith Jr., New York: Praeger.

Ames, Bruce N. 1991. Pesticides, Pollution, and Cancer. In *Free Perspectives* (Fall/Winter): 4.

Anderson, Frederick, et al. 1977. *Environmental Improvement Through Economic Incentives,* Baltimore, MD: Johns Hopkins Press for Resources for the Future.

Carey, Hugh L. 1992. *Vital Speeches of the Day* (August 1).

Clinton, Governor Bill, and Senator Al Gore. 1992. *Putting People First: How We Can All Change America.* New York: Times Books.

Conservation Foundation. 1984. *State of the Environment: An Assessment at Mid-Decade.* Washington, DC: The Conservation Foundation.

Council of Economic Advisors. 1989. *Annual Report* (January).

_____. 1992. *Annual Report* (February).

Council on Environmental Quality. 1992. *22nd Annual Report* (March).

Crandall, Robert. 1992. *Why Is the Cost of Environmental Regulation So High?* Washington University: Center for the Study of American Business, Policy Study #110 (February).

Cropper, Maureen L., and Wallace E. Oates. 1992. Environmental Economics: A Survey. *Journal of Economic Literature* (June) 30: 675-740.

Dower, Roger C. 1990. Hazardous Wastes. In *Public Policies for Environmental Protection,* ed. by Paul R. Portney. Washington, DC: Resources for the Future.

Efron, Edith. 1989. The Big Cancer Lie. *The American Spectator.* March.

_____. 1984. *The Apocalyptics: Politics, Science and the Big Cancer Lie.* New York: Simon and Schuster.

Freeman, A. Myrick III. 1979. *The Benefits of Environmental Improvement.* Baltimore, MD: Johns Hopkins University Press for Resources for the Future.

_____. 1982. *Air and Water Pollution Control: A Benefit-Cost Assessment.* New York: Wiley.

_____. 1990. Water Pollution Policy. In *Public Policies for Environmental Protection,* ed. by Paul R. Portney. Washington, DC: Resources for the Future.

Freeman, A. Myrick III, and Robert Haveman. 1973. Clean Rhetoric and Dirty Water. In *Pollution, Resources and the Environment,* ed. by Alain C. Enthoven and A. Myrick Freeman III. New York: Norton.

Hahn, Robert W. 1992. No More Blank Checks for Regulators. *Wall Street Journal.* (August 2): op ed page.

_____. 1991. *U.S. Environmental Policy: Past, Present and Future.* Paper presented at the American Enterprise Institute Annual Policy Conference, December 3-4, Washington, DC.

Hazilla, Michael and Raymond J. Kopp. 1990. Social Cost of Environmental Quality Regulations: A General Equilibrium Analysis. *Journal of Political Economy* 98: 853-73.

Jorgenson, Dale W., and Peter J. Wilcoxen. 1989. *Environmental Regulation and U.S. Economic Growth.* Discussion Paper #11458 from the Harvard Institute of Economic Growth (October).

Kneese, Allen V., and Charles L. Schultze. 1975. *Pollution, Prices and Public Policy.* Washington, DC: Brookings Institution.

Landry, Mark K., and Mary Hague. 1992. The Coalition for Waste: Private Interests and Superfund. In *Environmental Politics: Public Costs, Private Rewards,* ed. by Michael S. Greve and Fred L. Smith Jr. New York: Praeger.

Lindler, Bert. 1988. Making Economics Less Dismal. *High Country News* (October 10): 10.

Litan, Robert E. 1992. *Superfund: Assessing the Program and Options for Reform.* Paper presented at the Conference on Enhancing Environmental Quality through Economic Growth, Washington, DC (September 30).

Mead, Walter, Dennis D. Murooka, Mark Schniepp, and Richard Watson. 1991. *The Economic Consequences of Preserving Old Growth Timber for Spotted Owls in Oregon and Washington.* Santa Barbara: University of California at Santa Barbara, Community and Organization Research Institute (May).

Melnick, R. Shep. 1992. Pollution Deadlines and the Coalition for Failure. In *Environmental Politics: Public Costs, Private Rewards,* ed. by Michael S. Greve and Fred L. Smith Jr. New York: Praeger.

National Research Council. 1991. *Rethinking the Ozone Problem in Urban and Regional Air Pollution.* Washington, DC: National Academy Press.

Nelson, Robert H. 1983. *The Making of Federal Coal Policy.* Durham, NC: Duke University Press.

_____. 1990. Unoriginal Sin: The Judeo-Christian Roots of Ecotheology. *Policy Review:* 53-59.

Owens, Wayne. 1988. Turn the Valdez Cleanup Over to Mother Nature. *Wall Street Journal* (July 27): 1.

Portney, Paul R. 1990a. Ed., *Public Policies for Environmental Protection.* Washington, DC: Resources for the Future.

_____. 1990b. Policy Watch: Economics and the Clean Air Act, *Journal of Economic Perspectives* (Fall) 4: 173-81.

Ruff, Larry E. 1970. The Economic Common Sense of Pollution. *The Public Interest* (Spring) 19: 69-85.

Scarlet, Lynn. 1992. Environmental Myths and Realities. In *Seeing Another Shade of Green: New Perspectives on Economics and Ecology,* ed. by John Baden. Seattle: Foundation for Research on Economics and the Environment.

Tietenberg, T. H. 1985. *Emissions Trading: An Exercise in Reforming Pollution Policy.* Washington, DC: Resources for the Future.

_____. 1992. *Environmental and Natural Resource Economics.* 3rd ed. New York: HarperCollins.

U.S. Environmental Protection Agency. 1990a. *Managing Asbestos in Place: A Building Owner's Guide to Operations and Maintenance Programs for Asbestos-Containing Material.* Washington, DC (July).

U.S. Environmental Protection Agency, Office of Policy, Planning and Evaluation. 1990b. *Environmental Investments: The Cost of a Clean Environment: A Summary.* Washington, DC (December).

U.S. Environmental Protection Agency, Science Advisory Board. 1990c. *Reducing Risk, The Report of the Strategic Options Subcommittee-Appendix C.* Washington, DC (September).

U.S. Environmental Protection Agency, Expert Panel on the Role of Science at EPA to William K. Reilly, Administrator. 1992. *Safeguarding the Future: Credible Science, Credible Decisions.* Washington, DC (March).

U.S. National Acid Precipitation Assessment Program. Summary Report. 1991. *Acidic Deposition: State of Science and Technology.* Washington, DC (September).

USA Weekend. 1992. What on Earth Will They Do? (April 17-19): 6.

Yandle, Bruce. 1983. Bootleggers and Baptists: The Education of a Regulatory Economist. *Regulation.* May/June: 12-16.

Chapter 2

Economics, Ethics, and Ecology

Paul Heyne

How much is enough? Are the costs too high to justify the benefits? As Chapter 1 points out, we cannot ignore these questions if we want to be responsible guardians of the environment. They are ethical as well as economic questions.

During most of this century, economists who chose to write or talk publicly about ethics risked the contempt of their colleagues. The standard objection to mixing economics and ethics contained two arguments. One was that ethics should not be brought into economics classrooms, textbooks, or journals because economics is a science. As such it is in principle independent of any ethical or value judgments, and the progress and well-being of the science require that it be kept clean and clear of all corrupting admixtures. The objective truths of economic science would be contaminated if they were linked in any way to the arbitrary pronouncements of ethics.

Ethics, according to the orthodox dogma, was entirely arbitrary, a matter of subjective personal preference. That was the second argument. Ethical assertions rest upon value judgments, which, unlike factual judgments, cannot be true or false. Since there is no way to test ethical assertions, economic scientists should not touch them in the course of their professional work.

Do Economics and Ethics Mix?

This position would appear to be mistaken on both counts. Taking the latter argument first, we do not in practice behave as if our ethical judgments were nothing but subjective preferences that cannot be tested. What we actually do in almost all cases of ethical disagreement, at least when the disagreement is important enough to bother about, is discuss it. We give reasons, predict consequences, suggest principles, point to experience, argue for logical connections, compare alternatives. Economic science can be useful in such a process, especially when our ethical disagreements have to do with the operation of economic systems.

Of course, there is no *ultimate* foundation for ethical or value judgments that everyone is compelled to accept. But there is no ultimate foundation that everyone must accept for any other kind of proposition, either, including the propositions put forward in the name of science. That is the fatal flaw in the other half of economists' traditional argument against mixing economics and ethics. Economic research always employs presuppositions, and some of these presuppositions will almost inevitably have ethical implications. Those who claim to be engaging in value-free economic analysis are simply unaware of all the subtle ways in which values influence economic inquiry.

The result of all this is that economists can now discuss ecology and ethics in public without losing their licenses. A good place to begin is with the concept of *efficiency*, a concept dear to the heart of most economists and usually central to any policy analyses they construct.

The Subjective Nature of Efficiency

The crucial fact about efficiency, although one widely ignored by economists, is that at its core it is fundamentally and inescapably an *evaluative* concept. There is no such thing as *technical* efficiency, an efficiency that is independent of subjective valuations. Efficiency refers to the relationship between ends and means. One process is more efficient than another when it achieves a given end with less means, or uses given means to achieve more ends, or does some of both. From a purely technical point of view, however, every process is exactly as efficient as every other process. The ratio of output or ends to input or means is necessarily unity from a technical point of view, if physics is correct in its claim that matter-energy can neither be created or destroyed. Even when we do not realize that we are doing it, we always attach value to the ends and the means when we are trying to assess the efficiency of alternative procedures. The engineer who says that one engine is more efficient than another because it does more work with a given amount of fuel really means that it does more *useful* work, work that some party values.

Since the variables in any calculation of efficiency are valuations, not physical quantities, the question immediately arises of *whose valuations are to count.* I like to present my students with a multiple choice question before introducing them to the concept of efficiency: "Which is the most efficient way for a suburbanite to commute to work in the downtown area?" I give them a wide range of options: single-occupant passenger vehicle, car pool, bus, bicycle, on foot, hitchhiking. One option I always include is "In solemn procession, carrying candles and chanting psalms," and another is "Whatever way the commuter chooses." The point I want to dramatize is that, if the values to be served are the values of the individual commuter, the most efficient way to commute has to be the way that each commuter chooses. The commuter assigns values to all the inputs and outputs, including the values that decide whether a variable such as physical effort is an input (pain) or an output (exhilaration), weights them all according to a subjective calculus (which may well contain substantial amounts of concern for other persons), places the result in context ("Is it raining?" "Will I have a chance to jog when I get home tonight?" "Do I have a cold?" "What are the most pressing demands upon my time at the moment?"), and then chooses, almost surely while recognizing that it is not efficient to spend too much time worrying about how to maximize efficiency.

It follows that someone who tells suburbanites they are behaving inefficiently when they commute to work all alone in their cars is mistaken. If it were inefficient, they would not do it. The fact that they choose to do it is irrefutable evidence that, for them, it is efficient. What such critics may mean (assuming they aren't just saying that their own values are different from those of the commuters) is that the suburbanites are paying insufficient attention to the costs that their decisions impose on one another and on noncommuters. Alternatively, the critics might mean that they can imagine a differently organized world in which people would not choose to commute to work each day in single-occupant passenger vehicles. Whatever the critic means, efficiency does not seem to be the relevant concept.

Why Does Efficiency Matter?

According to the conventional understanding of the concept among economists, efficiency is maximized when net value is maximized, which means when the difference between the value of benefits and the value of costs is at a maximum. Inputs or means are the costs; outputs or ends are the benefits. Efficiency so defined is an appropriate goal for social policy because it expands the range of possibilities. It enables us to obtain more of what we want without having to give up anything else that we also want. The opposite of efficiency is *waste*, and our moral intuitions tell us that waste is inherently reprehensible. It deprives us of resources that we could otherwise use for worthy purposes and represents a kind of ingratitude for what we have received. That is why everyone will agree that the first step in balancing the budget—*any* budget, but especially the government budget—is the elimination of waste.

The problem is that when we begin to talk about efficiency from the standpoint of society, we have no common denominator in terms of which we can compare the costs and benefits of different people. If we want to insist that individuals maximize—as many economists insist—then the single individual could be said to maximize utility. When we are talking about more than one person, however, utility fails to provide a workable common denominator, because we have no way to compare one person's utility gain with the utility loss of another.

Economists usually dodge this difficulty by using the *monetary* values of costs and benefits. Thus most economists would say that protective tariffs are almost always inefficient because the increase in monetary wealth they create for those who benefit from the tariffs is characteristically less than the decrease in the monetary wealth of those who lose from the tariffs. Monetary value, or what people are willing to pay, provides a common denominator that allows us to aggregate and compare the benefits and the costs of different people. Sometimes this is expressed by saying that a change is efficient if the benefits to those who gain are sufficient for the gainers to purchase the consent of those who lose and still have something left over for themselves.

All of this depends, however, on the conditions from which we begin. The set of outcomes that is "most efficient" in one social context might be grossly inefficient under a different system of laws, customs, and property rights. The upshot of the matter is that the concept of efficiency is of very limited use when we want to resolve disagreements about the proper use of resources—including disagreements over environmental policy—because such disagreements are typically disagreements over *what the rules of the game ought to be.*

What Are We Arguing About?

The situation is further complicated by the fact that the contending parties often cannot even agree on what the rules are about which they are disagreeing. Consider, for example, recent controversies over the trading of rights to emit harmful substances into the air. Imagine the following dialogue between an efficiency-loving economist and a "typical" environmentalist:

"I understand that you want to reduce electrical utilities' emissions of sulfur dioxide," the economist says to the environmentalist. "What's your goal?"

"Cut those emissions in half," the environmentalist replies.

"All right," says the economist. "Here's what you do. First, assign each utility the legal right to emit, after whatever target date you choose, only 50 percent of the amount of sulfur dioxide being emitted currently. Then allow those rights to be traded. You will thereby achieve your goal at the lowest possible cost. Net value—taking your target as a given—will be maximized. We shall have achieved your environmental goal in the most efficient way."

The economist is predicting in this case that the lowest-cost emissions reducers, the ones with a comparative advantage in emissions reduction, will specialize in producing cleaner air. This will occur because the utilities able to reduce their emissions at very low costs will find it profitable to reduce them by more than 50 percent in order to sell their unused rights to those utilities whose costs of reducing emissions are higher and that will therefore want to purchase rights to continue their higher levels of emissions. Economists proudly refer to such arrangements as "using the market to serve the environment." They are somewhat hurt, as well as puzzled, when environmentalists spurn their offers of assistance and refer contemptuously to tradable emissions rights as "licenses to pollute."

Costs and Moral Wrongs

Economists think of sulfur dioxide (or any other) emissions as costs, costs of achieving the much-desired benefit of usable electricity. The economist sees nothing immoral about the generation of costs in the pursuit of socially desirable goods.

Many environmentalists see it quite differently. They view sulfur dioxide emissions as *wrongs*. In an imperfect world, they will concede, wrongs can never be *completely* eliminated. *But wrongs should never be condoned.* These environmentalists might compare sulfur dioxide emissions to muggings. We could reduce the number of muggings that occur on our city streets to almost any number we chose if we were willing to pay for a sufficient quantity of police officers, but we accept some muggings, because "we can't afford more police officers." (The economist would prefer to say that, at the margin, we have more valuable uses for the police officers; but this is a quibble.) When we decide not to hire more police officers and thereby implicitly to "accept" a certain number of muggings, we do not thereby condone any single mugging! We do not "license" the muggers whose crimes we are in effect unwilling to prevent because the cost of doing so would be too high.

Similarly, we may decide to let electrical utilities put some sulfur dioxide into the air because it would cost too much to stop them completely. But we do not want to *approve* those emissions. We certainly do not want to grant the utilities a *right* to emit sulfur dioxide. If any utility finds itself able to reduce its emissions below the target level, it should do so. It should most emphatically not then be allowed to authorize some other utility to emit the sulfur dioxide that it has stopped emitting by selling a "right to pollute."

The issue we must decide, therefore, is whether the emission of sulfur dioxide by electrical utilities is an immoral or only a costly activity. Let's look at the matter more closely.

Can There Be a Right to Pollute?

One trouble with the argument just given is that the principle behind it cannot be consistently applied. If every action that contributes to what we call air pollution is morally wrong, then it is wrong to breathe, because the everyday act of breathing emits carbon dioxide and so contributes to global warming. I don't know of anyone who thinks that exhaling is a wrongful act.

We can push this argument further. All of us want certain goods whose provision will necessarily entail the burning of fossil fuels and other acts that lower air quality. Is it not mere self-deception or hypocrisy to will the end and refuse to concede that we are willing the means? Is it not better to be clear and explicit about what we are doing? Do we really want to say that it is legally and morally acceptable to turn on your home furnace on a cold day but wrong to contribute to global warming through the burning of fossil fuels?

The fact is that we do concede rights to emit undesirable substances into the atmosphere. My favorite example is the emissions test form I must submit if I want to renew the license on my automobile. It states explicitly that I am legally and, I presume, morally, authorized to emit specific quantities of hydrocarbons and carbon monoxide when driving. While I am not allowed to sell my unused emission rights, I have without question been granted a "right to pollute." I doubt that many motorists think of themselves as engaged in wrongful acts when they exercise such rights.

Open and authorized emission of sulfur dioxide is a *costly* act. Mugging, by contrast, is a *criminal* act. They are not the same. The person who emerges from jail and says, "I have paid for my crime," is employing a misleading metaphor. You are not authorized to commit a crime if you are willing to go to jail for it or to pay the fine established by law. Someone who treats a fine as if it were a mere fee is likely to discover that the "fee" increases exponentially with consumption. On the other hand, if the generation of electricity in the midwestern United States is a socially desirable activity, as it surely is, then sulfur dioxide emissions should be viewed as costs, not as crimes. The owners or managers of a utility should indeed be able to say, "We have a right to emit these quantities of sulfur dioxide."

Incommensurable Goods

This does not settle the issue of tradable emission rights, however. Steven Kelman has made the important point that a law which grants explicit rights to pollute—and the trading of rights will not occur in the absence of explicit, well-defined rights—interferes with consciousness-raising efforts (Kelman 1981, 106-23). Some environmentalists will argue that the advantages of a system for trading emission rights are more than offset by the negative political consequences of granting that anything less than zero emissions is acceptable.

The economist has no conclusive rejoinder to such an argument, because it exposes a conflict between incommensurable goods. The economist wants to achieve *given* environmental targets at the lowest cost in other goods forgone. "At least every one favors greater efficiency," says the economist who is looking for a neutral vantage point from which to begin. "Whatever our goals, we all want to achieve them at the lowest cost." Economists are completely baffled by environmentalists who refuse to specify any goals, because their objective is *cleaner* air without any relaxation of the pressure to do *still better*. Efficiency is for them a mixed good insofar as it pushes air pollution issues lower down on the political agenda.

Exclusive concentration on issues of efficiency does not, as it turns out, enable economists to deal constructively with environmental issues while avoiding all normative questions. One might even ask whether the concept of efficiency does any useful work at all. Nobody is actually opposed to efficiency. Moreover, the issue in dispute never turns out to be, "What is efficient?" but rather, "Whose valuations should enter our benefit-cost calculations?" Is there any point at all in asking whether it is more "efficient" to leave a section of national forest standing or to turn it into lumber? We cannot determine which alternative would have the largest net value without first deciding whose valuations we are going to count. That is a decision about who should have which property rights and about the processes through which we are going to arrive at decisions affecting the evolution of the natural environment. It is not a question about efficiency.

My doubts about the usefulness of the efficiency concept are not doubts about the usefulness of economic analysis. They are doubts about the usefulness of a certain kind of economic analysis, one that tries to aggregate different people's benefits and costs in order to compare the totals. The type of economic analysis that I find useful in the examination of environmental issues and other problems of public policy is one that pays at least as much attention to processes as to outcomes, and that tries to predict or explain the consequences of alternative laws and institutions, without ever attempting the kind of quantitative measurement and summing-up required by the economist's standard judgments of efficiency.

Recycling and Dumping: A Case Study

The current debate in our society about recycling as an alternative to solid-waste disposal nicely illustrates both the usefulness and the limitations of economic analysis in disputes over environmental policy. The rising cost of solid-waste disposal in the 1980s prompted many cities to promote recycling programs that would reduce the volume of solid waste. The programs made eminent sense, at least at the outset. Why should city governments pay large sums to bury old newspapers that, if properly collected, could be sold for a profit? Using a mixture of financial incentives, ecological appeals, and threats, a growing number of cities have in the past few years induced their residents to recycle large proportions of the solid waste that formerly had to be trucked to landfills for burial.

When recycling saves money, everyone is happy, from the environmentally insensitive boor who sees no further than his checking account to the environmental activist who with Wordsworth's "high Heaven" totally "rejects the lore of nicely calculated less and more." It is now becoming clear, however, that the rising cost of solid-waste disposal in the 1980s was due to a lack of political imagination. There are plenty of places in the United States to bury, at quite tolerable costs, the solid waste that Americans regularly generate. Clark Wiseman, a visiting fellow at Resources for the Future, has calculated that all the municipal solid waste generated over the course of the next 1,000 years would fit in a square hole 44 miles wide on each side and 120 feet deep. That may seem like a big hole to people living in the eastern United States; but it would scarcely be noticed in many of the western states. The problem is not a scarcity of land for fills but a scarcity of people willing to have landfills in their neighborhood.

To an economist the solution is obvious: pay the surrounding community to accept solid waste, just as we pay people in other areas of life to accept costs for the benefit of others. That is now beginning to be done. Early efforts are already demonstrating that the cost of constructing safe and environmentally sound landfills, of transporting waste to these sites, and of fully compensating people who are adversely affected by the landfill is far less than the cost of many of the recycling programs that federal, state, and local governments have either already instituted or are contemplating.

Many of the initiatives that advocates of recycling are pushing will have very large hidden costs. For example, have those who are eager to ban disposable diapers, because they use up space in landfills, thought about all the costs of the alternative? The effects on our water supply of laundering cloth diapers? The impact on urban air quality of all the diaper trucks that would return to circulation? The discomfort and diaper rash of the babies who are kept so much drier overnight by disposable diapers? The infections that would spread more readily through child-care centers? If the people who want to use disposable diapers are willing to pay the full cost of dumping them in landfills—through, for example, a disposal charge included in the price—why should they be prohibited from exercising their preference for disposable over cloth diapers?

The economist conceives of social problems as the product of systems in which, for some reason, people are either not compelled to bear the full cost of the burdens they impose on others or are unable to collect adequate compensation for the benefits to others that their activities will generate. The economist's first move is therefore to see whether some low cost way can be found to assign the costs and the benefits to those who are responsible for them. If people who want to generate solid waste are not imposing burdens on anyone but themselves and others whom they are compensating appropriately, *there is no problem.*

Most environmentalists don't see matters quite in that way, and some don't see it that way at all. They think of recycling more as a moral duty than as an effort to minimize costs. The process of searching for products sold without elaborate wrapping; of separating junk mail, facial tissues, and newspapers; of sorting cans, bottles, and plastic containers; of putting all these things out at the curb in neat piles each week—this is a ritual of dedication through which we ought to go willingly. It is an educational, consciousness-raising process, that gradually changes the "tastes and preferences" beyond which economists refuse to go, even when those tastes and preferences are increasingly generating environmental problems. Recycling may cost more than it saves in the short run; but in the long run, when values have been transformed, it could well prove to be efficient from even the economist's narrow perspective. In some ways the application of benefit-cost analysis to a household's recycling efforts is akin to using time-and-motion studies to appraise the act of lovemaking.

Pursuing Justice Rather than Efficiency

What would happen if economists abandoned their preoccupation with efficiency and talked openly about *justice?* Since judgments about efficiency presuppose judgments as to who shall have which rights, economists who employ efficiency criteria are implicitly making use of a theory of rights. Does economics have anything useful to say about the rights that people *ought to have?*

One thing economists can say with some confidence is that clear and stable rights promote more effective cooperation than rights which are vague and subject to unpredictable alteration. Given that voluntary exchange increases the value of resources and that clear and stable property rights (and other "rules of the game") facilitate voluntary exchange, economists can construct a strong argument in favor of clear and stable property rights. In doing so, they are also supporting a particular conception of justice, one associated with what has come to be known as "the rule of law."[1]

"Unconstitutional by reason of vagueness" is a sound judicial principle for assessing legislation, because vague laws grant arbitrary power to enforcement authorities. The liberty of the citizen disappears in the presence of arbitrary governmental power. Unclear laws constitute a fundamental violation of the principles of justice for anyone who believes that arbitrary government is the essence of political injustice. It follows that the government is violating the rules of justice when it obscures people's rights and makes it difficult, if not impossible, for people to know what they may and may not legally do.

It is also violating the rules of justice when it arbitrarily decrees that an activity which had previously been lawful and protected is now illegal. The emphasis here is again on the *arbitrary* nature of the govenment's actions. An arbitrary action is one dependent solely on the will of the actor, rather than one that is determined or at least constrained by principles laid down and known *in advance*. While *ex post facto* legislation cannot in practice be avoided completely (an absolute prohibition of rules changes that penalize actions already taken would bar *all* new legislation), the avoidance of such legislation is a fundamental tenet in the American legal and political tradition.

A regime of clear and stable property rights, as it turns out, will be supportive of both efficiency and justice. If we pursue justice by establishing the rule of law, efficiency will largely take care of itself. This is, of course, a limited conception of justice: clear and stable property rights and other rules of the game. But it is not nearly so limited as one might at first suppose. It is a conception of justice deeply rooted in the American political tradition and one with extensive and important implications for environmental policy. I want to develop, apply, and defend it briefly. Those three activities—development, application, and defense—are interrelated. Showing the applicability of a theory defends it, and the process of defending the theory against criticism results in its development.

How Do We Begin Talking about Justice?

It may help the reader to realize at the outset how unsympathetic the writer is to all forms of foundationalism. A synonym for foundationalism is fundamentalism, a word familiar to most of us in another context. Religious fundamentalists have historically maintained that there are a few fundamental doctrines upon which all other doctrines can be constructed. If these fundamental doctrines are not affirmed, they maintain, the system collapses.

The same kind of fundamentalism can often be found in the sciences. Scientific fundamentalists also insist upon the acceptance of certain basic dogmas, such as "*the* scientific method," the nature of causation, the nonexistence of particular entities, or—to take a dogma from economics—the consistency of preferences. While I have the highest respect for heuristic postulates, I acknowledge no fundamental dogmas. I shall therefore not take the approach of beginning with the foundations. I have never found it to be true in political or moral discourse that we proceed most effectively if we begin with solid foundations. The best place to begin is with the questions that seem most interesting or important, or the ones on which progress seems most likely, or the ones that we need to settle to take the next step. And when we have finished, the whole will often be more than the sum of its parts.

The Importance of Property Rights

I have already suggested that disagreements about environmental policy can usefully be viewed as disagreements about property rights. They are disagreements about the property rights of human beings, it must be added, even if we should finally decide to grant legal rights to natural objects. As Christopher Stone observed in his seminal law review article "Should Trees Have Standing?" (Stone 1974), any legal rights assigned to natural objects would have to be asserted, so far as we can presently ascertain, by human beings acting as "guardians." Moreover, any dispute about the rights of trees, streams, or mountains becomes at some point a dispute about the rights and obligations of human beings. So I think we beg no important question by saying that environmental disagreements are disagreements about the property rights of human beings.

It has long been complained by Marxists and other radical critics of orthodox economics that economists, or at least bourgeois economists, "take property rights for granted." In one sense this is no longer true. The critics have not been keeping up. Bourgeois economists have in fact been diligently examining the origins and evolution of property rights systems and inquiring about the prerequisites and consequences of alternative systems for the past 30 years or so. There is a better response to the radicals' complaint: "Of course! What else should we do? We take existing property rights for granted almost all the time."

You do not upon leaving a restaurant ask whether the cashier is authorized by the owner to collect payment for the meal. You do not then inquire to find out whether the owner's title is in order. Nor do you refuse to pay until you have been assured that the system which validates the owner's legal title is itself valid against the claims of Native Americans. In some situations these might be legitimate questions to ask. But for the most part we simply take generally accepted property rights for granted. In part we do so to avoid wasting our time. But we also take for granted generally accepted property rights because *it would be unfair not to do so.*

We all make decisions, committing ourselves through our actions, on the basis of the rights we *think* we hold. Our opinions about our rights are continually monitored and confirmed for us by the ongoing actions of others in society, who acknowledge through their transactions with us that we do indeed own the resources that we are regularly controlling, allocating, transforming, or distributing. It is unfair for those who have encouraged us in our commitments by going along with our claims to declare suddenly and arbitrarily that we are not entitled to the rights we have long been exercising.

Recognizing Injustices

The key concept is *un*fair or *un*just. I want to direct your attention not to justice but to *in*justice. When I ask, "What's fair?" you can almost hear the skeptical tone and see the cynical shrug: "Who's to say?" But we are much more ready to give definite answers when we are asked, "What's *un*fair?" There are some very important differences between "striving for justice" and "striving to correct injustices." The former is presumptuous and dangerous, at least insofar as it means anything more than trying to correct injustices. The only defensible way to pursue justice in the political realm, I submit, is to work at eliminating recognized injustices.

Although we cannot begin to say what justice would require for each person in our nation, Americans agree substantially and extensively about what's unfair or unjust. Stated most simply, it is *violating the rules.*

I am here making an empirical claim, one that you should test against your own experience. My claim is that Americans overwhelmingly agree that injustice is done whenever persons are not treated in accordance with the rules that are supposed to apply in the situation. I test this proposition regularly, for example, when students come to me asking for some kind of special treatment. (I teach a lot of very large classes.) I always begin by pointing to the rules: the course syllabus, the university regulations, the other known and accepted rules of the game. And I ask them whether the exception for which they are asking would be within those rules. It would be unfair to grant an exception that violates the rules by, for example, giving this particular student an advantage that cannot be granted to everyone else who is similarly situated. And my students agree. I have regularly found that students arrive at the same conclusion I reach when they are asked to decide whether the granting of their request would be unfair to others.

An interesting book appeared about a decade ago, written by a professor of politics named Jennifer Hochschild, who wondered why the poor in the United States did not give effective political support to the downward redistribution of wealth. The book, titled *What's Fair? American Beliefs about Distributive Justice,* was based on in-depth, open-ended interviews with 28 working adults who had been carefully chosen to represent both high- and low-income white residents of New Haven, Connecticut. Hochschild concluded from her study that Americans fail to support downward redistribution because they are confused, a state in which they are encouraged to remain by corporations and other components of "the hegemonic process." But I was more impressed by the actual reports of her interviews than by her conclusions, which seemed to me to fly frequently in the face of what her respondents had actually said.[2] For the most part they were saying that inequality, even enormous inequality, in the distribution of income was not in itself unfair. It was unfair only if it had been gained by *cheating.* By breaking the rules, in other words.

Does Agreement Make It So?

One could still ask about the significance of the fact (assuming it is a fact) that Americans generally agree on what violates the principle of fairness. Does mere agreement establish the truth of the matter? Was our treatment of women "not unfair" during all those years when almost everyone agreed that a woman's place was in the home? Is the treatment of women in Iran today "not unfair" if almost no one in Iran considers it unfair? Was racial slavery "not unfair" in the United States at the time when the Constitution was approved?

My response is that I don't know how we can talk sensibly and usefully about justice and fairness independently of specific cultural contexts. As what I have called "the rules of the game" evolve over time, so do our generally accepted notions of what is unfair or unjust. We can look back and claim that we have made progress with respect to justice, but we always do so from the perspective of our current values, institutions, and practices. We can also compare our culture with other contemporary cultures and make comparative judgments, but we ought always to recognize that we do so within the limitations of our knowledge and experience, and that injustice cannot be eliminated from any society until the institutions that permit it are in place. (I have long found the propensity to condemn other cultures and our own ancestors a pointless exercise at best, and at its worst a technique for justifying self-righteous obtuseness.)

The question about the relativity of standards is an important one, however, because many environmentalists are now objecting precisely to the reigning "rules of the game." Just as we once enslaved Africans and even more recently denied women their basic rights, and did so with a good conscience, so we are now with a good conscience trampling on the rights of nonhuman nature. We cannot appeal to any American consensus, the environmentalists say, to find out whether our treatment of nonhuman nature is unfair, because there is no consensus, and because the closest thing we have to a consensus is woefully inappropriate.

These objections deserve thoughtful attention. But I want to postpone any attempt at discussing them until we have dealt more adequately with the issue of justice and injustice in our dealings with one another.

Promises, Rights, and Injustices

A crucial element in our concept of *social* ethics—our obligations to one another as human beings—is *promise*. Consider what it is we are objecting to when we complain about "unethical behavior" and what we are taking for granted. We are objecting because others have not done what they promised to do, either implicitly or explicitly. They have violated the agreed-upon rules. And that is simply *not fair*. If that is not the foundation of all social ethics in our society, it is certainly the dominant principle. The implications for environmental legislation are extensive.

To begin with, the principle calls into question the command-and-control approach to protecting the environment. The *Annual Report of the Council of Economic Advisors* for 1990 defined command-and-control regulation as "a system of administrative or statutory rules that requires the use of specific control devices on classes of selected pollution sources or applies admission standards to narrowly defined pollution sources" (Economic Report of the President, 1990, 189-91). At first glance there would seem to be no ethical objection to such a system. In practice, however, the command-and-control approach will almost inevitably substitute arbitrary decisions for the rule of law. Fairness requires that the rules of the game be laid down in advance and that the rules treat those who are similarly situated in similar ways. This ideal is unlikely to be realized when the regulatory authorities are allowed or even commanded to operate on a case-by-case basis. Command-and-control systems provide no incentive to design a set of generally applicable rules.

Trying to protect the environment by requiring environmental impact statements is another approach that is ethically hard to defend for the same kind of reason. The law mandating the filing of environmental impact statements (EIS) arbitrarily and, therefore, unfairly reduces the property rights of the party that wants to act. It does so by allowing projects to be challenged on the grounds that the EIS is incomplete when, as everyone knows, *all* environmental impact statements are necessarily incomplete. In practice the EIS requirement enables determined parties to hold up projects indefinitely until the project developers agree to pay ransom or decide to abandon their project. It should be added that members of Congress were evading their ethical obligations when they mandated environmental impact statements as a way of satisfying the environmentalist lobby without offending any other specific interests. Bad laws often originate in this way.

Environmental regulations that impose politically intolerable costs are also ethically indefensible because they will not be uniformly enforced. It is unfair to impose costly requirements and then, after some have made substantial investments to meet the requirements, to suspend them for everyone else because it turns out to cost too much. Not only does that create incentives not to cooperate; it also discriminates against those who have been the most cooperative.

Allowing environmental regulations to be shaped by a political process that is dominated by special interests is another ethically indefensible procedure. While this is, of course, the only political process we have, we can at least recognize that environmentalists who object to the political influence of special interests are themselves often special interests, sometimes with no strong regard for the principles of fair play. The Natural Resources Defense Council, "60 Minutes" Ed Bradley, and the others who orchestrated the national hysteria over

Alar showed no concern for the apple growers who had to bear the cost of their publicity-seeking. This was inexcusably unfair behavior that was undertaken to promote the institutional interests of the NRDC and the CBS network.

Finally, there exists a strong ethical case for reviving and applying once again the constitutional prohibitions against uncompensated takings. When we discover that concern for the environment requires a change in property rights, the necessity of paying compensation acts both to avoid injustice and to assure that this really is a public interest requirement, not a special interest action. Rezoning, for example, is an unfair way to "preserve public amenities." If the public interest requires that a particular urban hillside be left as a greenbelt, rather than be developed, the public should not be allowed to secure its amenity at the expense of those who own the land by rezoning the land to prohibit development. Fundamental fairness requires that the public purchase the development rights from the owner.[3]

Observations on Conservatism

It cannot have escaped the notice of even the most sympathetic reader that all these implications of the fairness principle are profoundly conservative, and that my conception of social ethics privileges the status quo. I am not bothered by that. If social justice requires above all else that we honor our promises, then social justice is itself profoundly conservative. Promise-keeping is conservative in that it binds the future to the past. And that is of enormous human importance. When we honor our promises, we help one another to realize in the future the expectations that we have formed on the basis of our past transactions. Promise-keeping facilitates planning, including the formation of those life projects that constitute our individual identity. There is an important sense in which the opposite of *conservative* is *capricious*.

As Edmund Burke observed, a society without the means of some change is without the means of its conservation. What was tolerable yesterday and therefore allowed may become intolerable with the passage of time. This would seem to be especially likely in the case of actions that damage the environment.

It must be noted first of all, therefore, that the principle of fairness does permit extensive revisions in the rules of the game. The constraint it imposes is the constraint of compensation for those who thereby become the victims of broken promises. Those who have incurred substantial unrecoverable costs by investing in good faith reliance on the laws of the land should not be made to bear a heavily disproportionate share of the costs of changes designed to benefit everyone.

"But polluters don't *deserve* compensation," someone responds indignantly, "anymore than slave owners deserved compensation after the Civil War."

I would ask in response whether the offer of compensation (prior to 1860, of course) might not have been a better route than civil war toward the abolition of slavery. Be that as it may, it is not at all clear that pollution, when explicitly tolerated by law and custom, is a morally reprehensible act. Moreover, when we reflect on the social changes that have produced the environmental movement and the demand for changes in the rules of the game, the case for compensation grows stronger.

One change has been rising private incomes and a consequent increase in the relative value of such public goods as clean air. When we were much poorer, we placed a positive value on discharges from factory smokestacks because they were signs of prosperity. Insofar as rising incomes have increased the demand for a cleaner environment, increased ability to pay for those improvements accompanies the increased demand for them. So we have the ability to pay the compensation that fairness calls for. We cannot plead poverty.

Another factor lending interest and strength to the environmental movement has been dramatic increases in the impact of human activities on the environment—due partly to rising income levels and consequent increases in consumption, partly to new technology, partly to population increases. The implications here for our obligation to provide compensation are less clear. New technology and increased consumption are associated with greater wealth and hence enhanced ability to pay, but population increases present more ambiguous implications. In general, though, there seems to be a strong case for purchasing the environmental improvements we want by compensating the losers. The temptation, of course, is for the most politically adept and influential—who are frequently also the most wealthy—simply to extort the changes they want from their victims.[4] The necessity of providing compensation helps to counter this temptation.

Duties and Aspirations

The most interesting and challenging stream nurturing the environmental movement in recent years is the one that has been fed by changes in our moral conceptions. We have begun to develop new perceptions of our moral obligations and of the kinds of entities that are deserving of moral consideration. These changes are raising fundamental questions about the adequacy of our inherited moral traditions. How can we address these questions?

We might begin with a useful distinction made by the legal philosopher Lon L. Fuller between the *morality of aspiration* and the *morality of duty* (Fuller 1969, 3-32). The morality of aspiration has to do with the desire for excellence. It is an open-ended pursuit, one whose goals are never fully achieved. A person in the service of the morality of aspiration is always striving for more. The driving force is the desire to realize every potential excellence or virtue. Satisfaction with what one has achieved is in itself an offense against the morality of aspiration.

The morality of duty imposes much more limited demands. Its goals are clear and attainable. Its prescriptions are predominantly negative: *"Thou shalt not."* The morality of duty is basic. It may not be particularly inspiring, but it is essential to social order, fundamental to all social relations. Its importance is demonstrated by the fact that it is regularly supported by legal sanctions to secure compliance with its demands.

The justice I have been talking about largely expresses the morality of duty. But the environmental movement is fueled by the morality of aspiration. Direct evidence may be seen in the phenomenon referred to earlier: the unwillingness of environmentalists to become specific about the goals that will satisfy them. They want *less* pollution, *cleaner* air, *more* recycling, *less* consumption. Environmentalists' talk about the rights of nature is further evidence that they are serving a morality of aspiration. If nature has rights, where do those rights begin and end? If whales have rights, do other mammals have them, too? Do all animals have rights? And what about other living things, such as plants? What about such nonliving entities as rivers and mountains? It is not my intention to criticize the claim that human beings have duties to the nonhuman world, a claim which I shall subsequently defend. I am only trying to characterize the morality of aspiration and to make the case that the environmental movement is nurtured and informed by a morality of aspiration.

Aspirations and the Morality of Duty

Any good society will contain both a morality (or moralities) of aspiration and a morality of duty. But one component of any defensible morality of aspiration must be commitment to the morality of duty, or what we might call "a passion for justice." Moral aspirations that ignore duty are a proper object of severe criticism. The man who aspires to help all of humanity, for example, but neglects his duties toward his wife and children is not an admirable figure. Does not the environmental movement sometimes slight the morality of duty?

Environmentalists want us all to live more responsibly, to be more attentive and respectful toward nature, toward that which is given to us independently of our own actions. This aspiration is certainly a part of my own morality. But we do not want to forget that the polis, the human community in which we live, has also been given to us independently of our own actions. Responsible persons are not free to improvise without regard for what has been given—including the legitimate expectations of their fellow citizens. In our efforts to express respect for nonhuman nature and to nurture that respect in others, we may not display contempt for the rights of those human beings among whom we live.

Many features of contemporary political conflicts over environmental issues can be usefully viewed as aspects of a struggle between the morality of aspiration and the morality of duty, in which our duties, including our legislated duties, are being raised over time by our aspirations. Two simple examples of how aspirations generate duties and of aspirations that cannot easily become duties may clarify the argument.

Nondiscrimination on the basis of race in hiring or promoting was an aspiration of many before it became a legal obligation for all. The duty was sufficiently clear (notice its negative character) to make it suitable for legal imposition. The contrast with "affirmative action" is instructive. As the controversy over "quotas" and "rigid goals" has shown, we cannot state the goals of affirmative action programs with sufficient clarity and precision to make affirmative action a duty. Significantly, the duty cannot be stated as a prohibition.

Child abuse provides another example. The moral aspiration to assure a safe haven for children has led to a spate of laws and ordinances that have not worked out as well as we had hoped. For one thing, it turns out that what we want from parents is considerably more than not beating their children. We want something positive. We want parental love and concern. But these are more a matter of aspiration than of duty. Moreover, our attempts to marshal the larger community against child abuse has produced laws imposing positive duties on doctors, ministers, social workers, and child-care providers whose effects have been quite mixed. Protecting someone else's children against parental abuse cannot be made a clear, definable duty (and therefore a duty that may appropriately be imposed by law) unless we are willing to deny parents *any* special authority over their children.

Moral aspirations are important! But the moral aspiration to transform moral aspirations into legal duties must be examined with judicious skepticism before we act upon it. To what are we aspiring when we proclaim ourselves dedicated environmentalists?

When an environmental "extremist" says that human beings are not "superior" to animals, or to plants, or to natural objects, I have no immediate argument. Human beings, so far as I can tell, are in fact inferior to elephants, Douglas fir trees, and mountains. I am judging superior and inferior here by the criterion of height. I do so not to be perverse, but to make the point that in much of the debate over these matters the parties are talking past each other. What precisely is the criterion of superiority or inferiority that we have in mind? Is a newborn baby superior to its mother? Not by most of the criteria we could think of. But that does not prevent the child from presenting moral claims upon the mother that overwhelm, in the mother's own judgment, any moral obligations the child might have toward the mother. If we want to bridge the gulf that is widening between many environmentalists and their opponents, we must think more carefully about what exactly we do and do not want to claim.

Forms of Tyranny

Some of the more extravagant statements of environmentalists ought to be seen first of all as responses to the attitude expressed in a sentence such as this: "A tree in the forest that few or no people can see may still exist in the philosophical sense, but a bloody lot of good it does for anyone." Or this:

> By fulfilling our nature and responsibilities as human beings, we *bring* meaning and value into the world.... [U]nseen and unappreciated, the environment is meaningless. It is but an empty frame, in which we and our works are the picture. From that perspective, environmentalism means sacrificing the picture to spare the frame. (Emphasis added.)

The authors of those statements, whose anonymity I shall protect, are saying explicitly what is implicit in the way many of us have learned to behave: There is no meaning or value in the universe except the meaning or value that human beings experience. *But how can we possibly know this?* It is sheer dogmatic assertion. What's worse, it is self-serving dogmatic assertion, and it smacks of tyranny. It is a license to do as we please.

Statements of this sort remind me of Bishop George Berkeley, the eighteenth-century British philosopher who was able to deny the existence of a material world by pointing out that all we really know are our own perceptions. And I wonder why the authors of statements such as the two above don't go all the way and insist that it is only their own private seeing and appreciating that allows the world to have meaning and value. I think I know the answer to that question. It's because other human beings would protest such solipsism, and no one is indifferent to the opinions of other human beings. Why is that? Why do we care so much what other human beings think or say about us and our opinions? What gives their opinions so much weight in our calculations when all the rest of nature has no moral significance for us at all?

Jeremy Bentham, no one's candidate for fuzzy-minded idealist of the year, inserted a disturbing footnote into Chapter XVII of his *Introduction to the Principles of Morals and Legislation* (Bentham 1948, 310-11):

> Under the Gentoo and Mahometan religions, the interests of the rest of the animal creation seem to have met with some attention. Why have they not, universally, with as much as those of human creatures, allowance made for the difference in point of sensibility? Because the laws that are have been the work of mutual fear; a sentiment which the less rational animals have not had the same means as man has of turning to account.... The day has been, I grieve to say in many places it is not yet past, in which the greater part of the species, under the denomination of slaves, have been treated by the law exactly upon the same footing as, in England for example, the inferior races of animals are still.

Bentham suggests that we show respect only to what we have learned to fear. That may put the matter too harshly. It would be more accurate to say that we generally learn to show respect only for that which *commands our respect*. The key fact is that respect cannot be "given." It has to be "earned" or it is not respect; it is only condescension.

This does not imply that we have no obligations in the matter. Our obligation is to *be attentive*. No person can earn the respect of another person who is not paying attention. Inattentiveness, of course, is commonly rooted in a lack of respect, which creates a circular bind. Think of the way we "turn off" someone whom we take to be merely babbling. Adults are often inattentive to children because they assume that the child has nothing important to say. Teachers are inattentive to the questions of students whom they do not take seriously. Members of groups with social power often block out the distinctive characteristics of "inferiors" with whom they interact by assuming that "they" are "all the same," and that this "sameness" does not include the rich inner life that we are aware of in ourselves.

Nature will hardly be able to command the respect of anyone for whom it is an unchallengeable dogma that we human beings bring into the world all value. I have no cure for the disease of inattentiveness, especially since inattentiveness *per se* is not a disease at all but a condition for any sort of effective action and perhaps for sanity itself. How do we learn to ignore that which deserves no attention while remaining alert to everything that merits our attention? A short excerpt from Aldo Leopold's *Sand County Almanac* presents the dilemma (1966, 19-20):

> A cardinal, whistling spring to a thaw but later finding himself mistaken, can retrieve his error by resuming his winter silence. A chipmunk, emerging for a sunbath but finding a blizzard, has only to go back to bed. But a migrating goose, staking two hundred miles of black night on the chance of finding a hole in the lake, has no easy chance for retreat. His arrival carries the conviction of a prophet who has burned his bridges.

> A March morning is only as drab as he who walks in it without a glance skyward, ear cocked for geese. I once knew an educated lady, banded by Phi Beta Kappa, who told me that she had never heard or seen the geese that twice a year proclaim the revolving seasons to her well-insulated roof. Is education possibly a process of trading awareness for things of lesser worth? The goose who trades his is soon a pile of feathers.

Rights and Duties

I am not now going to argue that nature or even nonhuman animals should have "rights." Those who argue on behalf of rights for whales and trees risk losing everything by claiming too much. They fail to make an effective case for the duties upon which they really want to insist because they have pinned everything on a weak case for rights. They overlook the fact that, while rights entail duties, duties do not entail rights. For example, I acknowledge a moral duty to make charitable contributions of various kinds; but my acceptance of this obligation creates no rights for any potential beneficiary.

Laws that prohibit cruelty to animals are grounded in the belief that human beings owe certain duties to animals, duties to at least do no needless harm and to minimize suffering. I do not know of any one who wants to remove all such laws from the books, although I know of many people who would vehemently deny that animals have legal rights. Here is a clear case where duties, even legally enforceable duties, exist and flourish in the absence of anything analogous to human rights. Our enforcement of laws against cruelty to animals reflect our widespread belief that animals suffer in a manner with which we can identify. There is no implication of moral equality in the assertion of a duty toward animals.

Do plants suffer? Most of us don't seem to think so, at least not in any way that interferes with our pruning them. Does this imply that we have no duties toward plants? Not necessarily; the ability to suffer is not the only characteristic of nonhuman entities that is capable of generating duties toward them. We might have duties toward nonhuman entities that require allowing them to behave in accordance with what we perceive as their nature. We might have a duty not to dam a free-flowing stream, for example, or a duty to remove an obstruction that was causing a plant to grow in a distorted manner, or a duty to keep a wilderness area uncontaminated by machinery.

But are these *moral* duties? Are they duties *toward the nonhuman entities*? Or are they mere *aesthetic preferences*?

Duties, Preferences, and Other Distinctions

I might have a better notion of how to reply if I were more sure of the difference between the moral and the aesthetic, if I knew the grounds of duty, and if I could always distinguish duties from preferences. (Why do I so dislike the word *mere*?) This is not to say that there are no differences, or that one can be reduced to the other. It is rather a recognition that moral and aesthetic claims often overlap and reinforce one another, perhaps because they have a common ground in the way things fit together, and that we can have strong preferences (aspirations?) toward the fulfillment of our duties. Our duties do not necessarily conflict with our interests, and they will very rarely conflict for those with a strong interest in maintaining their self respect.

I would particularly want to emphasize the way things fit together, or what we might call *appropriateness*. In *The Theory of Moral Sentiments*, Adam Smith pays a great deal of attention to *propriety,* or appropriateness (Smith 1982). All of Part I, one-sixth of the entire book, is devoted to that topic. We recognize that conduct can be appropriate or inappropriate. By what criteria? I suspect that we often recognize the propriety or impropriety of conduct more easily than we can identify the criteria by which we made the judgment. The concept seems to be closely connected with a sense of *creatureliness.* I am not the creator of all this; I am not even my own creator. While I do have creative capabilities, they are the capabilities of one who is himself a creature. The world is not mine to do with as I please. I may do much of what I please to do; but what I please to do will not be good—not true and right and lovely—if it is not appropriate to the world that has been given to me.

All this may strike the reader as bordering dangerously on the religious. Yet one need not be at all religiously inclined to agree that none of us has created the world in which we live. The implications of this fact will no doubt be perceived differently by religious people, but the underlying claim is quite similar to the one insisted upon by Richard Rorty, a thoroughly nonreligious philosopher, in his emphasis upon the importance of contingency for the understanding of oneself and one's world (Rorty 1989, 5):

> To say that the world is out there, that it is not our creation, is to say, with common sense, that most things in space and time are the effects of causes which do not include human mental states.

In Conclusion

It seems to me that some of the more extreme claims of environmentalists have at least this virtue, that they call our attention to possibilities foreclosed by our attachment to modes of thought that are proving increasingly inadequate. Even their intolerance will have served us well if it reveals to us our own intolerance. "The duty of tolerance," Alfred North Whitehead once said, "is our finite homage to the abundance of inexhaustible novelty which is awaiting the future, and to the complexity of accomplished fact which exceeds our stretch of insight" (Whitehead 1933, 52).

The comprehensive eloquence of that simple and powerful statement summarizes most of what I want to say in conclusion. The morality of aspiration is both essential to a free society and dangerous to it. It is essential insofar as it generates respect for the rights of others; and I do not see how a democratic society can remain free unless such respect deeply informs the great majority of its members. The morality of aspiration is dangerous, however, when it tempts us to employ coercive measures to establish a Kingdom of Righteousness.

We can recognize injustices; but we can never really know what justice requires. Central economic planning was perhaps the most momentous product of the godlike aspiration in this century. A godlike aspiration—the desire to establish a human regime that would be omniscient, omnipotent, and universally benevolent—was the source of the zeal with which Marxist governments pursued the conceit of a centrally planned economy long after its futility should have been obvious. This aspiration was also the source and justification of all the cruelties perpetrated in the course of that long and tragic pursuit. Ardent environmentalists need to discover and acknowledge that the same limitations which made central economic planning impossible will make it impossible to establish a comprehensive system of central environmental planning.

Some of the intransigence of conservatives in the environmental area stems from the fear that environmentalists are eager to legislate all their aspirations, with utter disregard for the costs that this will impose on others. The morality of aspiration will inevitably run ahead of—and *ought to* run ahead of—the morality of duty. It is legitimate to entertain, nurture, and advocate aspirations for which society is not yet ready, aspirations that cannot be considered duties and should not be legislated because the institutional preconditions for their implementation have not yet evolved. But our aspirations should not induce us to neglect or violate our duties. When we take the *whole* environment seriously, we will acknowledge that our primary moral obligations are to respect the persons, the liberties, and the rights of those among whom we live. After all, these are the people upon whose cooperation we must ultimately rely, whether it is to "make a living," to "save the earth," or to see the realization of any other of our larger aspirations.

Notes

1. A clear exposition of this conception of justice may be found in Leoni, especially Chapter 4.
2. Hochschild summarizes her conclusions on pp. 278-83. The "ambivalences" she finds among her interviewees seemed to me largely their refusals to accept her interpretations of social reality.
3. In some cases where government legislates controls on development, the incentive to develop was originally created by questionable government actions, such as bridges built from the mainland to barrier islands or implicit promises of disaster relief to those who then built in flood plains. To what extent is the government obligated to *continue* a promised subsidy? The ethical problem in removing an unjustified subsidy arises from what lawyers call *detrimental reliance*.
4. In July 1991 San Francisco passed a law prohibiting owners of service stations from converting the land to other uses if they had earned a "fair return" over the past two years. The newspaper headline reprinting this story from the *San Francisco Chronicle* proclaimed: "Urban Ecology: New San Francisco law protects gas stations." (Rights for gas stations?)

The ideas presented in this essay were originally a part of three lectures delivered in June of 1991 at a conference sponsored by the Foundation for Research on Economics and the Environment (Seattle, Washington) and supported by a grant from The Liberty Fund of Indianapolis, Indiana.

References

Bentham, Jeremy. 1948. *An Introduction to the Principles of Morals and Legislation*. New York: Hafner Publishing Company.
Economic Report of the President. 1990. *Annual Report of the Council of Economic Advisors*. Washington, DC: U.S. Government Printing Office.
Fuller, Lon L. 1969. *The Morality of Law*. New Haven: Yale University Press.
Hochschild, Jennifer L. 1981. *What's Fair? American Beliefs about Distributive Justice*. Cambridge, MA: Harvard University Press.
Kelman, Steven. 1981. Economists and the Environmental Muddle. *The Public Interest* 64 (Summer): 106-123.
Leoni, Bruno. 1991. *Freedom and the Law*. Indianapolis: Liberty Press.
Leopold, Aldo. 1966. *A Sand County Almanac with Essays on Conservation from Round River*. New York: Ballantine Books, Inc.

Rorty, Richard. 1989. *Contingency, Irony, and Solidarity.* Cambridge: Cambridge University Press.
Smith, Adam. 1982. *The Theory of Moral Sentiments.* Indianapolis: Liberty Classics.
Stone, Christopher D. 1974. *Should Trees Have Standing? Towards Legal Rights for Natural Objects.* Los Altos: William Kaufman.
Whitehead, Alfred North. 1933. *Adventures of Ideas.* New York: The Macmillian Company.

Chapter 3

Environmental Harms from Federal Government Policy

Richard L. Stroup and Jane S. Shaw

Introduction

Again and again, authoritative polls show that the American people are serious about maintaining and improving environmental quality. Many Americans also believe that centralized control by government is the best way to protect the environment. Ironically, however, many environmental problems in the United States have been caused by governmental ownership and control. Long before the Congress gave the federal government a big role in regulating pollution and cleaning up the environment, the government had developed an unfortunate environmental track record. Plentiful evidence supports the view that when resources are controlled by centralized government agencies, rather than by individual owners whose personal wealth is tied up in the value of those resources, the standard of care is not as high. Other political goals are more likely to overcome the wealth-preserving desire to conserve.

Environmental consciousness has been rising in the United States, along with incomes, for several decades. Even as environmental awareness led to large increases in political action around 1970, the environmentally destructive programs of the federal government were already in place. Most continue, though many with some refinements. The U.S. Forest Service was clear-cutting trees in fragile areas where trees are difficult to grow. The Army Corps of Engineers was helping to drain wetlands at a rapid rate. The Bureau of Reclamation was building dams that inundated canyons and free-flowing streams. The Department of Agriculture was encouraging drainage of wetlands, overuse of marginal agricultural land, and excessive use of pesticides. The Bureau of Land Management was subsidizing the destruction of pinion-juniper "elfin forests" in parts of the Southwest and letting wild horses and burros destroy the rangeland in other parts. The Armed Services were developing hundreds of hazardous waste dumps that may haunt us for decades to come.

Government management is plagued with difficulties because government managers lack the incentives that private managers have to nurture and protect resources. Government officials are not owners but managers. The owners—the people—are rarely able to effectively monitor and control the actions of public officials.

Recently we have learned about the environment in the Eastern European countries, including the Soviet Union. The Soviet economy was under the control of a strong central government dedicated, according to its constitution, to bettering the lives of its people and to protecting the environment. Yet the environmental results are catastrophic.

Air pollution is severe and sewage treatment virtually nonexistent in many Eastern European countries, and natural resources have been treated with negligence at best. Perhaps the most spectacular disaster caused by governmental control of land and other resources is the shrinking of the Aral Sea, a body of water on the border between Kazakhstan and Uzbekistan, near the center of the former Soviet Union. The Aral Sea was once larger than any of the Great Lakes except Lake Superior. According to an article in *Science* (Micklin 1988, 1170-76), diversion of irrigation water from the rivers that feed into the Aral has reduced the area of the sea by 40 percent since 1960 and the volume of water by 66 percent. Most of the fish have disappeared.

Lake Baikal, the largest and deepest fresh water lake on earth, now has a zone of pollution 23 miles wide. It was caused by the Soviets' decision to locate paper mills on the shores of the lake. They allowed the effluent from the pulp mill to be discharged directly into the lake.

It is clear that the environmental problems in the Soviet Union and Eastern Europe are enormous in scope. So much for the claims that private business and industry are always the culprits in environmental issues: The Soviet Union had little or no private industry.

In the United States, where we have a democracy and a tradition of restraint on government, the environment never was treated as badly as in the Soviet Union. But the tendency in our current political system to turn more responsibility and authority over to government is likely to make matters worse than they are today. As many of the chapters in this book indicate, we are already seeing serious problems in the attempts by government to improve environmental conditions.

This chapter will illustrate how the U.S. government has historically failed to protect the environment and to explain how this history reflects characteristics inherent in government, even in a democracy. Politicians and bureaucratic decision makers are not incompetent or evil; in general, quite the opposite is true. But political and bureaucratic pressures inevitably develop and lead to unplanned consequences. Some of these are bad for the environment.

In this chapter we will show how various forces put pressure on government officials to act in an environmentally irresponsible manner. We will look at government policies that encourage loss of wetlands and see how farm programs, especially subsidies, spur farmers to use more pesticides and wipe out habitat for wildlife. We will learn how the construction of dams and the diversion of water by the Bureau of Reclamation has shrunk lakes and led to the buildup of harmful minerals in soil; how coastal beaches have been made fragile, thanks to government subsidies; and how Forest Service policies encourage excessive logging.

We will then discuss the factors that push government officials in the direction of such policies. Usually, these factors are the narrow professional interests of bureaucrats, combined with the support of special interests and the politicians' need for campaign support. Sometimes, however, populist pressures direct government officials toward unwise decisions, and we will look at some examples of environmentally destructive policies that result.

We will conclude that there are few good reasons for placing more control of the environment in the hands of the federal government.

Environmental Destruction by the Government

Destruction of Wetlands

Wetlands are lands that often have standing water (either saltwater or fresh) and have vegetation typical of wet soil. They soak up floodwaters, cleanse groundwater and surface water, and reduce erosion from coastal tides and storms. They provide habitat for fish and migratory waterfowl, as well as mammals. Until recently, they were usually called swamps, marshes, or bogs. The change in terminology, along with changing attitudes toward wetlands, reflects the growing recognition of their ecological importance.

Drainage to convert wetlands to dry land that can be used for crops, or to build cities on, is often feasible. And it's not necessarily bad, since some of the land uses are extremely valuable. Much of Washington, DC, and Boston are built on drained wetlands. According to the Interior Department, about half the nation's original wetlands had been drained by the 1970s (Dahl 1990).

Nevertheless, draining wetlands can have undesirable environmental effects, and these have gradually received more public attention. In Florida, for example, by the 1970s it became noticeable that wildlife populations were decreasing, fisheries were declining, and the numbers of famous wading birds such as herons and egrets were precipitously falling. Water quality in Lake Okeechobee and other rivers and lakes was also deteriorating. One reason was the drainage of Florida's wetlands. Clearly, there are benefits to preserving wetlands, though some are much more valuable than others, and disaster would not result if further, relatively small amounts of wetlands were drained.

In 1988, presidential candidate George Bush recognized the benefits of wetlands preservation, but ignored three facts: a) some wetlands are far more important than others, b) not all wetlands are crucial to the survival of the ecosystems in which they are a part, and c) certain existing wetlands could be converted to much more valuable property with little or no environmental penalty. Bush promised that under his administration there would be a policy of "no net loss" of wetlands. Thus the policy shifted from what most people would consider excessive draining of wetlands to a policy intended to virtually halt draining. To carry out this policy, the Bush administration used the permit procedures under the Clean Water Act to prevent private individuals and companies from draining wetlands. But "no net loss" is impractical, because wetlands are constantly changing, often day by day. And no one knows precisely how much wetlands we have in a given year.

Largely ignored in the debate over wetlands is the fact that federal policies have encouraged wetlands drainage, even where it cannot be justified by the benefits generated. Wetlands drainage is costly, and private parties will expend their own resources only when the benefits outweigh the costs to them. The same calculus does not hold in the world of politics. Years of flood control by the Army Corps of Engineers and subsidies to development, along with agricultural policies that keep farm prices up and encourage the farming of marginal lands, have fostered conversion of wetlands.

In 1990, two Harvard economists attempted to identify the reasons why so much of the lower Mississippi alluvial plain, the largest remaining wetlands area in the country, had been turned to cropland (Stavins and Jaffe 1990, 337-52). They estimate that the wetlands initially covered 26 million acres; by 1983 they extended over some 12 million acres; since then, another 6.5 million acres have been cleared. This area consists largely of hardwood forests that grow in wet soil, often with water covering much of the trees' roots, and sometimes the lower trunks. While some of these trees can be logged with the land undrained, it is sometimes profitable to drain the land, cut down the trees completely, and convert it to use for crops. But if it is profitable only with the subsidy, then wetlands are being unnecessarily lost.

Stavins and Jaffe found that by controlling flooding and by draining federal lands, the Army Corps of Engineers made this area more attractive for conversion to cropland. Their econometric study concluded that since 1934, federal flood-control or drainage projects were responsible for nearly one-third of the conversion in the Mississippi alluvial plain.

Another study of the conversion of these "bottomland forests" identifies additional government incentives to convert wetlands (Shabman 1980, 402-12). Among these are the below-market interest rates of the Farmers' Home Administration; direct payments to farmers who drain wet soils by the Agricultural Stabilization and Conservation Service; and the technical assistance program of the Soil Conservation Service. Another is government-provided disaster assistance for natural hazards such as flooding, which shifts the costs of flood damages from owners of developments on flood-prone land to the taxpayer.

But of all government programs, farm price supports may be the most important in encouraging excessive conversion of wetlands. According to the U.S. Fish and Wildlife Service, 87 percent of wetland losses between the mid-1950s and 1974 were due to agricultural development. Losses between 1974 and 1982 were even greater because of growing farm subsidies (Tiner 1984, 58-59).

Farm subsidies amount to roughly $25 billion per year (Bovard 1989, 1). These subsidies have encouraged farmers to plant "fence row to fence row," even when the land is not especially suitable for cropland. Farmers qualify for federal subsidies in part according to the number of acres of each subsidized crop they planted in previous years. Thus, the policies encourage farmers to maximize their acreage, in some cases through drainage of wetlands, so they will have a more extensive "crop history" on which to base federal subsidies (Bovard 1989, 214).

Since subsidies have led to over production and surpluses, some federal programs pay farmers not to grow crops. But even these policies give farmers an economic incentive to drain the land in the first place. If they have drained it and planted on it for a few years, they can enter a program that pays them several hundred dollars per acre not to grow anything more. Of course, it is the marginal or nearly worthless land that is best suited, from the farmer's perspective, for such a program. It has the least value for other purposes.

Environmental Impacts of Farm Programs

Farm subsidies have other bad environmental effects, as well. In their book *Free Market Environmentalism*, Anderson and Leal point out that farmers' incentives to expand acreage have meant the virtual disappearance on farms of small game animals such as ring-necked pheasants, ducks, cottontail rabbits, and bobwhite quail (1991, 57). These birds and mammals once thrived on farms with shelter-belts, in shrubs along fence rows, and in the thick growths of cattails along streams and marshes. Now, however, as farmers drain wetlands, grow the same crop year after year, convert bushes to row crops and rely heavily on pesticides and herbicides, such animals may disappear. "The result is a bland, repetitious countryside that offers minimal habitat for wildlife."

According to some analyses, the support of the U.S. Department of Agriculture programs over the years has encouraged heavier use of pesticides and herbicides than would have otherwise occurred. Runoff from excessive use of these chemicals pollutes streams, and percolation pollutes groundwater. Bosso argues, in *Pesticides and Politics*, (1987, 29) that the government's restrictions on acreage, coupled with generous price supports, encouraged farmers to increase yields on their remaining acres by using fertilizers and pesticides at levels that would have been noneconomic without the government programs. Acreage restrictions thus had less impact than planned in reducing the surpluses brought on by the artificially high prices. In addition, says Bosso, the combination of such programs "may have forced farmers onto an endless pesticides treadmill."

Harms from the Bureau of Reclamation

Many other environmental problems in this country stem from the actions of government agencies. The Bureau of Reclamation, which built hundreds of dams around the country over the past 90 years, has had enormous impact on the environment, especially in the West. Created in 1902, this agency had a mission to "make the desert bloom"—an idea that may have some merit, but which was accepted with moralistic fervor by many who paid little attention to the cost of doing so. After all, the bulk of the costs was spread widely among taxpayers nationally. The Bureau of Reclamation is still in business, even though it has run out of economically promising dam sites. The desert has bloomed, but too often it has created less value than the resources it used up and has wreaked environmental havoc in the bargain.

Dams and the canals carrying water from them drastically change the shape of river basins and often fill up spectacular canyons such as Glen Canyon in Utah. The impact on canyons spurred environmental activism in the past few decades (especially when the Bureau talked about damming the Grand Canyon).

In addition, the Bureau's irrigation programs had long-term consequences that have only been fully recognized in recent years. The most important are probably the increased salinity of the soil, which is often caused by continual feeding of farmland with diverted water, and the buildup of sometimes dangerous minerals and chemicals for the same reason.

Drainage water from California's San Joaquin Valley, for example, led to a highly visible environmental problem in the early 1980s—the deformation and deaths of birds in the Kesterson Wildlife Refuge. High levels of selenium, carried to the Refuge by irrigation water that had passed through the fields, were causing bass, catfish, and carp to die and newly hatched waterbirds to have severe deformities.

The flow of drainage water into the Kesterson Wildlife Refuge had a long history. In order to irrigate lands in the San Luis Unit/Westlands Water District of the San Joaquin Valley, the water had to be drained. The soil simply could not absorb all the water applied; without drainage, the water table would rise so high that it would invade the root zones of the crops, hurting crop productivity. So a system of drainage canals was established and begun in the 1960s. However, of the planned 188 miles of canals, only the first 85 miles were completed. So, instead of flowing into the ocean, the water has been flowing into the Kesterson Reservoir, part of the Kesterson National Wildlife Refuge (Wahl 1989, 202).

In its course as irrigation water, the water picked up a lot of selenium, a natural substance that is useful to animals in small quantities, but harmful in the large doses that resulted when water reached the Refuge and evaporated, concentrating the selenium. Birds and fish ingested the selenium, leading to the deformities that came to public attention. Reacting to a good deal of political heat, the Interior Department cut off the flow of drainage water into the Kesterson. The department is still trying to figure out what is to be done in its place; and whatever the solution will be, it seems likely to cost millions of dollars.

Kesterson is a particularly visible example of irrigation-induced harm, but there are many others. For example, back in 1905, the Bureau of Reclamation dammed the Truckee River, which flowed from the California side of Lake Tahoe to lakes in Nevada. The Bureau diverted half the Truckee's water into the area around Fallon, Nevada, for agricultural use. This diversion had severe impacts on the two Nevada lakes that had previously received most of the Truckee's water. Gradually, one dried up completely; the other lost so much water that one fish species, the Lahontan cutthroat, became extinct and, by the early 1980s, the cui-ui fish was placed on the endangered species list.

This led to a lawsuit, and in 1984 a federal court ruled that the project violated the Endangered Species Act, and told the Bureau of Reclamation to reduce diversions from the Truckee. This decision had ironic consequences: the Stillwater Wildlife Refuge near Fallon, which consisted of marshland fed by much of the diverted water, began to shrink. By 1988 it was less than 300 acres, down from 14,000. The water became increasingly saline and polluted with heavy metals and in 1988, avian botulism spread by poor water quality killed 21,000 birds (Chase 1989; Mitchell 1991, 88-90).

The problems of Kesterson, Stillwater, and other preserves stem in large part from the fact that federal water delivered to farmers is heavily subsidized. Farmers pay about 15 percent of the capital cost, and none of the operating cost, on the federal water they get. (That does not mean that all the current farm owners enjoy a windfall: many of them bought the privilege of "cheap" water by paying the full capitalized value of this privilege from the previous landowner. The point is that the cost of using the water, rather than conserving it, is artificially low.)

These subsidies mean that water is used to grow crops in areas where growing them would not be economically feasible if the users paid the full costs of the water. Had the large federal subsidies been absent, so that farmers would have been paying the full cost of water supplied to the lands around San Luis, fewer acres would have been cultivated and less drainage water would have contaminated the Kesterson Refuge. When decision makers are allowed to reap the benefits of their decisions without paying the full cost, the wasteful use of resources is to be expected.

Besides input subsidies, another way to encourage the wasteful use of resources is to subsidize outputs. While plenty of agriculture would exist if water were not subsidized, some of the land would be growing different crops using less water, and other acres might not be cultivated at all without federal subsidies to the sale of farm outputs. It's interesting that rice and cotton farmers use over six million acre-feet of water in California each year (an acre-foot is enough water to cover an acre of land with a foot of water, or 326,000 gallons) (Reisner and Bates 1990, 33). This is enough water each year to put the entire state of Connecticut under two feet of water. But rice is a monsoon crop, and cotton is traditionally grown on moist Mississippi delta land; neither crop is usually grown on dry desert land. And the market suggests they should not be: even with cheap water, rice farmers depend on crop price subsidies as well. They have been paid up to three times the market price for their product and cotton farmers 1.5 times the market price, thanks to government price supports (Luttrell 1989, 143). Meanwhile, water rationing is common in California cities, where city governments also refuse to allow the market pricing of water.

Additional Distortions from Subsidies

Agriculture is only one of many areas in which the government manipulates prices and user costs with results detrimental to the environment. Another example is the case of federal subsidies to construction and development on coastal barrier beaches. These sandy beaches, invariably described by environmentalists as fragile, serve as barriers to tide waters, protecting the mainland beaches from damaging tides and windblown floodwaters during storms. They are unstable, shifting over time as water slowly but continually moves the sand under them. Building on them is costly and perilous because of their instability and their extremely exposed coastal location. Structures that storms do not destroy are often undermined over time or left without beaches as the sands continue to shift with the relentless tides. Human lives, as well as capital assets, are at risk when people live on coastal barriers.

The federal government provides hundreds of millions of dollars in subsidies to those who do build on coastal barriers, and who rebuild again and again after destructive storms, which frequently recur. Roads, bridges, sewers, water lines, housing, and flood insurance are all federally subsidized on such developments. Environmentalists object to construction on barrier beaches because it so often involves attempts, frequently futile, to change the natural forces moving the sands, and because development usually brings pollution from storm and sanitary sewage as well. Yet the federal subsidies have made development financially attractive.

Fiscal conservatives object to such subsidies on the grounds that anyone wealthy enough (and, some would say, foolish enough) to build in beachfront locations should do so without taxpayer assistance. Environmental activists and fiscal conservatives joined forces in 1982 to persuade Congress to pass the Coastal Barrier Resources Act. This act made some undeveloped barrier beach areas ineligible for federal development and flood insurance subsidies. Development is not forbidden by the Act, but those who build and live there will be much more on their own financially. (Many forms of disaster relief, however, would presumably be available.)

However, many coastal barriers remain outside this system and still retain their eligibility for all forms of subsidies. A report jointly sponsored by the National Wildlife Federation and the National Taxpayers Union (Miller 1989) recommended that another 423 miles of shoreline on the Atlantic and Gulf coasts, 120 miles along the Pacific coast, and 164 miles of Great Lakes shoreline be added to the system. To do so, according to the report, would save the federal government between $1.9 billion and $10.8 billion (1988 dollars) over the following 20 years in subsidy expenditures (discounted to present value). (The larger estimate assumes a high level of development on the affected coastal barriers in the future; the lower estimate assumes a low level of development.) Since these recommendations did not become law, these figures represent estimates of the existing level of subsidies over a 20-year period.

Forest Service Policies That Promote Logging

Some U.S. Forest Service practices are also often harmful to the environment. The Forest Service is almost as old as the Bureau of Reclamation. It was one of the very first embodiments of "scientific management," a key tenet of the Progressive movement before the turn of the century. Late in the nineteenth century, partly because of fear that private industry would cut down all the trees in the country, and partly because of a growing Progressive mentality that the public sector could handle natural resources better than private industry, the government slowed, and in fact almost halted, its policy of turning territory over to private individuals and enterprises. Among other things, it created the Forest Service to carry out the Progressives' idea of public "scientific" management.

The Forest Service was intended to be guided by this doctrine, with its heavy emphasis on keeping out political pressures. "Politics should not become involved; rather scientific knowledge is to be applied by the experts in the field," writes Robert Nelson (1985, 32). "Such a vision underlay not only the development of the Forest Service, but much of the growth of government under the progressive banner during the first two decades of this century."

But the move to scientific management hasn't turned out to be as benign as expected. The singular emphasis on growing and logging trees led the Forest Service to pay little attention to the environmental consequences of its choices of logging practices. Today for example, the Forest Service is under heavy criticism from environmentalists for excessive logging in parts of the arid Rocky Mountains. There the climate and elevation assure that trees grow slowly, and steep terrain and unstable soil often mean that heavy logging will encourage erosion. Slow reforestation together with the wrong choice of logging methods sometimes means that wildlife populations are disturbed. And when timber is harvested, environmentalists say, little emphasis has been given to the visual effects of clear-cutting.

Private firms such as International Paper have shown that logging and the protection of wildlife can go together. International Paper found in its southeastern forestlands that if it took care in maintaining an attractive environment, it could charge people for hunting, fishing, and family camping on its lands. It leases more than a million acres for recreation. And the company also found that it could protect endangered species, such as the red-cockaded woodpecker, even while logging (Anderson and Leal 1991, 68, 71-72). Other owners of timberland, seeking added current and future revenues from the new land management techniques, are doing the same thing. But until public pressure became extreme in the 1980s, the Forest Service kept its emphasis on logging and did little to combine logging and recreational use. Forest managers had no way to capture added revenues and thus capitalize on the new demand for natural recreation areas. Recreation fees, after all, went to the U.S. Treasury. Portions of the logging revenues, however, could be kept by the forest in which they originated, to finance added replanting activities.

Ironically, this environmental harm is occurring without producing very much in the way of economic benefits. Forest Service data indicate that the seven national forests surrounding Yellowstone National Park (in Wyoming and Montana) lost $7.15 million on their timber sales in fiscal 1988 (Anderson and Leal 1991, 53). The Forest Service, to be fair, faces a great many cost-increasing regulatory constraints that private firms do not. But these figures still suggest that much of the logging in this area might not be done, or would be done so as to reduce the damage to future forest services and land values, if the land were in private hands.

Similar concerns have been raised about the Tongass National Forest in Alaska. This is the largest forest in the system. Most of the trees are giant Sitka spruce and hemlock, some as old as 800 years. Whether or not these areas should be logged or preserved is a subject of debate, but the losses on the sales of these trees are enormous. The Forest Service recoups less from selling these trees than it pays for preparing the trees for sale; in fact, in some cases, it gets back as little as two cents for every dollar it spends. These figures suggest that the Forest Service is logging unnecessarily, at taxpayer expense (Anderson and Leal 1991, 53).

A Major Source of Problems:
Narrow Interests and Special Interests

The environmental problems outlined so far reflect the tendency of government agencies to pursue narrow goals to the exclusion of what we call "the public interest." Their narrow goals are bolstered by special interests outside government who benefit directly from their actions, and who lobby intensively to maintain the narrow goals of agency programs. Agencies such as the Forest Service or Bureau of Reclamation have developed "clients" or supporters that benefit directly from the actions of the agency. Unfortunately, the clients are not accountable for the environmental or external effects of the results of public policies.

Were the officials in the Department of Agriculture, say, or the Army Corps of Engineers antagonistic to environmental protection? Probably not. They were simply pursuing their own goals, such as the encouragement of farm productivity and the reduction of natural flooding. Until public pressure began to be exerted through Congress, they probably never gave a serious thought to the possible implications of their policies on wildlife habitat or recreational amenities. They were not necessarily selfish, but like most humans most of the time, their view was a narrow one. Each saw his or her own goals as so important that careful consideration of other goals—preservation of wetlands, say—was viewed as secondary at best. Specialists in their fields, they felt that what they were doing was good for society. But their goals were simply not broad enough to encompass what is often called the "public interest."

Narrow professional interest is a factor throughout society in both private and public sectors. Individual decision makers are inherently limited to a narrow view. Each lacks the knowledge, and usually the inclination, to seek out an understanding detailed enough to allow him or her to weigh the effects—the sacrifices and the benefits—that others will experience as a result of the decision maker's choice. In the private sector, however, the cost of an action is normally paid from private funds or by a reduction in the capital value of an owned resource. The private decision maker may not understand why an action is costly; but facing the cost, and the need to pay it privately, the private decision maker will weigh the effects on others as reflected in the costs. (These costs include any legal liability for damage unintentionally done to others.)

Government officials face a different concept of the cost of a project. Few of the costs are paid personally or reflected in stock prices, as they would be for private sector decisions. Whatever constraints are in place, such as budget restrictions, are often viewed as obstacles erected by stingy politicians and "the green eyeshade types" who, the official may reason, simply do not understand the power, the beauty, and the importance of the official's mission.

The heads of bureaus and agencies are generally career individuals drawn to government service because of a sense of mission. To them, expansion of the agency is a good thing both for society and perhaps for their own professional advancement as well. Furthermore, expansion can help leaders to be effective. Since civil service regulations make it nearly impossible to get rid of incompetent or nonperforming people in the bureaucracy, a growing agency can make it possible for agency heads to shunt employees to the side if they do not show the requisite degree of enthusiasm for the mission as the leader sees it, replacing them with others more likely to perform well. The theory that agency behavior can best be predicted by assuming that they will attempt to maximize their budgets has been argued by Niskanen in *Bureaucracy and Representative Government* (1971). He agrees with skeptics that such a notion is oversimplified and not strictly true. Yet it captures some of the flavor of a narrow vision held by those most in control of any government program.

Randal O'Toole has detailed the ways in which, in the case of the Forest Service, timber sales are heavily supported by congressional appropriations, and Forest Service offices are able to keep large portions of the receipts from timber sales. According to O'Toole, Congress gives the Forest Service close to $500 million per year to arrange sales and design and build roads for carrying the harvested timber out of the forests. In addition, from the timber receipts, the Forest Service is allowed to spend about $300 million for such purposes as reforestation, erosion control, and wildlife protection. The Congress appropriates an additional $250 million or so to cover recreation, wildlife, and other goals (O'Toole 1988). Thus, the appropriation for and receipts from timber sales swamp the budget devoted to other purposes.

Even though backpackers, hikers, and campers use the forests (after all, they consist of 190 million acres) for recreation, it is illegal to collect fees from anyone other than campers in certain situations, outfitters, and resort developers. Most of the recreation in the forests is exempt from fees. And even the fees that do come from recreation go mostly to the Treasury. Thus, a Forest Service official gets little benefit for the agency by increasing the value of the forests to people who simply want to enjoy them. Under the rules that have prevailed, the agency prospers when it emphasizes logging, even if such an emphasis is unwise from a broader perspective.

O'Toole says, writing in his *Citizens' Guide to Reforming the Forest Service*: "Most national forest managers are sincerely interested in doing what is best for the land. But not everyone agrees about what is 'best.' Through a process that resembles natural selection, those people who sincerely believe in activities that happen to increase the agency's budget are more likely to be promoted" (1988, 24).

The "Iron Triangle"

The narrow interest of agency professionals is not, of course, the full explanation of environmental destruction by the government. These agencies have great support from special interests and politicians. Together, in fact, these three groups—bureaucrats, politicians, and special interests—form what political scientists call the "iron triangle."

To expand their programs, bureaucratic officials must have help from politicians—especially at budget time. Politicians, in turn, obtain campaign support from the special interest organizations that are clients of the agencies and work closely with them. In essence, politicians broker the interests of organized special interest groups and government officials, using the taxing and regulatory powers of the public sector as a means to reward (and thus to gain the support of) both.

Congress can raise tax revenues without seeking taxpayers' support for any specific government activity. At election time, congressional representatives go before the voters, but specific government expenditures are rarely the subject of political debate. The lack of accountability to American taxpayers for the costs of specific expenditures allows bureaucrats to develop expensive programs with high environmental costs. No private corporation has such an expansive funding mechanism.

The entanglement with special interests also prevents agencies from moving in more productive directions. Clearly, the intense relationship between the Forest Service and logging companies makes it difficult for the Forest Service to further emphasize recreation if it means less logging. Over time, the Forest Service is hiring more people whose interest and clientele are focused on recreation. But decisions dominated by those people are likely to be equally narrow. Decisions will be tilted in the opposite direction, at the expense of even the better logging projects. Without market signals, it is difficult to know when the best balance has been achieved, much less to actually make each decision in the best way.

The Bureau of Reclamation has resisted many efforts to raise the price of water since that would cause hardship on some of its important clients. And the fact that a relatively few landowners gain enormously from Bureau projects, despite the history of attempted legal restrictions on the concentration of such benefits, illustrates that the "iron triangle" works to support the interests of the few who are well organized, normally at the expense of the many.

The history of the 1902 Reclamation Act illustrates the way that political pressure operates. As Richard Wahl outlines in his book on Western water (1989, 69-106), the Act was supposed to limit the size of land-holdings entitled to receive federally supplied water. But from the beginning enormous efforts were made to obtain water at the subsidized price, not just for the legally allowed amount (160 acres or 320 acres for a husband and wife) but for larger amounts of land. Such efforts included multiple ownerships within one family, deeding to children land that was still being farmed by the parents, and the creation of farming operations that had multiple owners. The Bureau of Reclamation helped this process along; in 1926, the Bureau decided that it was all right for families to exceed the limit as long as they had "recordable contracts" to sell the acreage within 10 years—a concession to practice, apparently. Wahl summarizes the history of the acreage limitation issue: "During these eight decades, the affected water users have been successful in securing administrative, legislative, and judicial actions that in one way or another either exempt some categories of project lands from the application of acreage limitation or expand the acreage entitlement, thereby protecting the property and financial interests of larger farming operations" (1989, 105).

Another effect of the "iron triangle" is to limit the flexibility and innovation of an agency. Even though environmental groups are far more powerful than in the past, in many cases even their political clout cannot budge the entrenched goals and interests of agencies and their clients. For example, environmental groups such as the Environmental Defense Fund have promoted water marketing for some years, but the Bureau of Reclamation has continually put obstacles in the way of this innovation.

As we saw, farmers often use irrigation water wastefully because it is cheap. Yet Western cities are willing to pay far more for some of this wasted water than it is worth in agriculture. Also, traditional law requires that irrigators lose their right to divert water if they leave it in the stream. Yet this means that streams dry up, killing fish and reducing vegetation. If irrigators could sell or lease a portion of their water to environmental groups, who would leave it in the stream, such fish kills might disappear. The environment would be better protected, and no farmer or rancher would lose by being deprived of water involuntarily.

The Bureau of Reclamation has resisted such trading, even though it has sometimes (under political pressure) paid lip service to the idea of water marketing. So far, little trading outside agriculture has been allowed, reflecting the Bureau's "professional" commitment to dams, canals, and agriculture, rather than to the larger "public interest."

The Rational Ignorance of the Voter

Previously, we noted that narrow professional interests exist throughout society. In government, however, they are particularly strong because they are bolstered by the power of special interests and the goals of politicians. But why doesn't the electorate do something about it? Voters, after all, decide who runs the government.

A primary problem with governmental activity, from which many other problems flow, is that the average citizen is unable to monitor government, with its wide-ranging activities, very effectively. Most people are largely ignorant of the major issues in most agencies and certainly are unaware of the details.

Most Americans, for example, are probably unaware of what the Army Corps of Engineers does to control floods (and they may not be aware that the Army Corps has any such responsibility). They are especially unlikely to know the environmental consequences of its actions. Similarly, few Americans are probably aware that the Department of Agriculture, far from "saving the family farm," is engaged in multibillion dollar handouts, the majority to farmers with far more wealth than the average taxpayer.

The costs of these programs, while enormous in both dollar amounts and negative environmental impact, are spread too thinly for the average voter—or even those concerned about the environment—to be aware of them. Indeed, polls consistently show that the average American of voting age does not know the name of his or her congressman. It's unrealistic to expect such people to have detailed knowledge of the environmental impact of many government programs.

This lack of knowledge has been called by some academic scholars "rational ignorance." These scholars emphasize that voters are not stupid; they are just acting rationally. The reason is that the individual voter does not really decide an election; the voter is one of many people who ultimately choose a representative. Even if a voter takes the time and trouble to investigate all of the important issues, that effort will almost surely be wasted at election time because the individual voter is extremely unlikely to decide who is actually elected.

Furthermore, a citizen votes for a congressional representative only once every two years; the candidate he or she selects will make decisions on literally thousands of issues. The citizen faces a "bundled purchase" problem; the voter can't select one candidate for his views on agricultural policy and another for his views on defense; the voter must choose a single candidate, and often the voter will focus on one overriding issue.

The upshot is that the vast majority of problems that government agencies deal with occur without informed, detailed monitoring by those who have to pay the bills—the taxpaying voters. Officials at agencies such as the Bureau of Reclamation and the U.S. Forest Service pursue their goals and work out their deals quietly, largely outside the public spotlight. If their work does hit the headlines for a few days or weeks, it may stir up some congressmen and lead to some hearings. By and large, however, the situation is ultimately settled not by the public but by the bureaucrats, politicians, and special interests who created the situation in the first place.

The Role of Populism

So far, we have focused on environmental problems caused by the "iron triangle," in which an agency's narrow professional interests combine with the support of special interests and the politicians' need for campaign support to perpetuate narrow goals that benefit a few. But there is another problem in environmental decision making that occurs even when narrow professional concerns and special interests have a much smaller role.

Sometimes "the people" are emotionally aroused to a sufficient degree that even without being well organized they write letters and speak out to intervene and influence agency decisions. Such public or populist pressure can force agencies to act in ways that are environmentally unsound. Most environmental problems are quite complex. A seemingly simple environmental problem such as excessive silt in a stream can be caused by a variety of factors—overgrazing, cattle near the stream, erosion caused by fire or excessive timber cutting, etc. Technical information is needed by anyone trying to sort out these causes. Such technical information is frequently not understood by the public, most of whom do not take the time and effort needed to become well informed. As a result, many letter writers do not have the information needed to separate well-intended but disastrous policy options from those that will achieve better results. Yet individual citizens, stirred by pictures or stories from a particular perspective may feel quite strongly about such things. Elsewhere in this volume, the difficulties of EPA professionals in ordering their priorities and writing regulations are discussed. Other agencies face similar problems. Consider our national parks.

Problems of the Parks

Most people think that the nation's national parks, managed by the National Park Service, are in good hands. To a large extent, that is because the Park Service does many things well, emphasizes good public relations, and works hard to prevent critics from being treated seriously. But there is substantial evidence that all is not well within our large national parks. Some of the most serious problems are environmental in nature.

For many years, Park Service officials worried that there were too many elk in Yellowstone National Park, the 2.2-million acre tract of land with unusual geological features that straddles northern Wyoming and southern Montana. Historically, before the advent of heavy human development and population in the areas around the park, it appears that elk didn't even congregate in the park because so much of it is cold and dry. Furthermore, at one time the elk had more predators, such as wolves, that kept their numbers down. But in the mid-twentieth century, much land that previously had been elk habitat became farmland, and the numbers of elk in the park began to climb; they began to overgraze the area where most were located, the park's Northern Range. The elk were not just eating grass; they were eating up small sprouts of aspen and willow, gradually reducing the number of aspen and willow trees. This left beavers with little to use for their dams, which formerly created ponds and stream pools that reduced the rapid runoff of rain in the springtime and slowed stream siltation.

Beginning in 1961, Park Service officials started killing elk to reduce their numbers, partly to prevent a "crash" of elk populations if they ran out of food, and partly to keep the range healthy with vegetation (Chase, 1986, 31-37). But their culling of the elk herds did not last long. Newspaper photos of park rangers —people who were hired to *protect* wildlife—actually killing elk caused a public outcry. Public alarm and distaste were high, understandably so, since most people did not understand the need for the policy. But the Park Service couldn't stand the political heat. The population control measures were stopped. Unfortunately, the environmental results, according to a number of knowledgeable critics, have been severe.

The Park Service adopted a "natural regulation" policy, which means that it will keep "hands off" nature where possible. Environmental groups endorsed the natural regulation policy, possibly without fully understanding its implications, and they generally support it today. Nevertheless, the Park Service probably wouldn't have adopted it without the uninformed but powerful populist pressure against the other chief option, culling elk herds.

The results of "natural regulation" have been hotly debated since 1986, when Alston Chase wrote a devastating critique of the approach in *Playing God in Yellowstone*. Experts say that the problems of the park, especially the Northern Range, are worsening. By the late 1980s, the elk herds were much larger, reaching about 20,000 on the Northern Range, and the traditional vegetation of the range had completely changed. Then the devastating fires came in 1988. Seventy-five percent of Yellowstone suffered some level of burning, and much of the vegetation on which the elk depended disappeared. According to press reports, about one-fourth to one-third of the elk in Yellowstone died of starvation the following winter.

The problem of too many elk in Yellowstone is similar to other problems in national parks. Rocky Mountain National Park is also experiencing degradation of its vegetation because of too many elk. But populist pressure against population control by the killing of the excess animals stymies a policy that could correct a problem—overgrazing and excessive browsing—that is generally decried by environmental groups.

Wild Horses and Burros

Such problems in government management are not limited to parks. The vast rangelands supervised by the Bureau of Land Management have for many years faced a problem of overgrazing by wild horses and burros. But the Bureau is virtually paralyzed.

Wild horses and burros are not native to the American Southwest. Introduced by the Spanish conquistadors, some escaped and became wild (or feral). According to the National Audubon Society (National Audubon Society 1985,

376-80), the number of these animals fell from several million in the early 1800s to as low as 25,000 in the early 1970s. However, capturing these animals—sometimes for saddle animals, sometimes to be killed for pet food—was deeply disturbing to some people, who viewed them as part of Western heritage. Congress came under enormous political pressure, especially through a national publicity campaign run by Velma B. Johnston, an advocate of protecting these horses who became known as "Wild Horse Annie" (Dobra and Uhimchuk 1982). The campaign reportedly[1] included the placement of articles in *My Weekly Reader*, used in classrooms across the nation, and, as a result, numerous letters were sent to Congress from school children. In 1959, Congress passed a law making it a crime to hunt wild horses or burros on public lands with aircraft or motor vehicles. In 1971, the Bureau of Land Management adopted a policy explicitly protecting the horses.

The number of horses began to increase. By 1974, the population was up to 57,000, a number that caused environmentalists alarm because they felt that these animals had the potential for causing serious resource damage. The BLM responded with an effort to get people to adopt these horses for a fee, but the program languished when the fees rose to $200 for a horse and $75 for a burro.

Just how serious this damage may be has been debated. A 1982 study by the National Academy of Sciences expressed doubt that the horses were causing much damage. But 1991 testimony by an official of the General Accounting Office called the problems with the wild horse program "among the most difficult that BLM faces. Satisfying the dual legislative mandate of protecting wild horse populations while at the same time protecting the rangelands they roam from deterioration is not an easy task."[2] Whatever the ultimate impact, the Bureau has virtually no choice. It is prevented from seriously culling the herds because of the populist outcry against killing horses and burros.

Populism and Prices

Populist pressure on the governmental control of pricing and production in the realm of natural resources also has environmental ramifications. Consider, for example, the pressure to keep down the rates of electricity generated by government-subsidized hydropower projects. Earlier we spoke of the many dams built by the Bureau of Reclamation to divert river water for irrigation. In many cases, the cascading water of these rivers also provides a natural source of electrical energy, and many dams were built to harness this power and divert water as well. In fact, the power was so cheap that revenues from it subsidized the diversion of irrigation water. Yet the power, priced according to out-of-pocket costs rather than according to its replacement value in the power system, is used wastefully because it is relatively cheap. As a result, other means of generating power—the burning of coal, for example—must be overused to supply the power demands brought on by the artificially low power price. The result, of course, is needless environmental harm.

The Bonneville Power Administration, which markets the power from dams along the Columbia River, illustrates the problem. It is one of the many cases nationally in which users are not charged the full value of the power they receive. Because they pay less than the true value of the power, users of BPA power have little incentive to conserve power by buying more efficient appliances or insulating their homes. Thus, demand is greater and grows faster than it would be if power prices fully reflected the higher value of power (as it would if private companies were in charge of pricing). This poses a serious problem because, while hydropower is relatively cheap, additional power is far more costly.

This situation has led to the construction of additional power plants, coal-fired and nuclear, before they would otherwise be needed. This has added to the total cost of power and led to undesirable environmental effects. Meanwhile, users without access to federally marketed hydropower are paying more and would even be happy to buy some of the BPA power from current users at an intermediate price. Such purchases, by slowing demand for additional power, would lead to a cleaner environment.[3] But such transactions are forbidden by the government, since they would provide a profit for the sellers. After all, the avoidance of profit was an important justification for the federal production and distribution of power in the first place.[4] It is an unfortunate fact that avoiding the possibility of profit has also foreclosed enormous opportunities for resource and environmental conservation.

Conclusion

We have not exhausted the examples of governmentally induced environmental harms, such as the history of "chaining" on Forest Service and Bureau of Land Management lands (Stroup and Baden 1983, 48-49) and the accumulation of hazardous waste on federal property. According to the *New York Times*,[5] there are between 5,000 and 10,000 federal sites with an estimated cost of cleanup of between $75 and $250 billion. This compares with the *Times'* estimate of 4,000 potential nonfederal Superfund abandoned sites, which would cost between $80 and $120 billion to clean up. And, of course, far less land is owned by the federal government than by private owners.

Nevertheless, this chapter has given an overview of the kinds of environmental problems that come from government management and control. None of these problems can be blamed on simple incompetence or malfeasance of government employees. Rather, each illustrates some of the reasons that government, at least government beyond the local scale where citizens have the ability to easily monitor performance, is simply incapable of representing the diverse interests of a large public.

The draining of huge areas of wetlands by the Army Corps of Engineers and by programs of the U.S. Department of Agriculture, the reduction of wildlife and the induced pollution from excessive use of pesticides and chemicals brought on by agricultural price subsidies, the damming of rivers and diversion of their water to uneconomic uses, and subsidies to construction and development on coastal barriers, along with environmentally destructive and economically inefficient logging practices in the national forests, can all be explained in large part by the power of special interest organizations, together with the striving for honorable but excessively narrow goals by professional agency decision makers.

An often opposing but sometimes equally destructive force, populist politics, largely explains other problems. These include overgrazing and excessive populations of some animals in national parks and on lands of the Bureau of Land Management, along with electric power rates that are wastefully low, leading to excessive power production, with the environmental impacts typical of power plants.

These cases occur because citizens are rationally ignorant of complex matters of ecology and economics. Each individual citizen, being rational and knowing that his or her vote will not be decisive at election time, has little incentive, and thus little inclination, to gain the detailed knowledge needed to cast a well-informed vote. And with the exception of initiatives and referenda, the individual has only one vote (usually for one of two candidates) by which to register a preference on thousands of issues.

Today, as a society we are becoming more concerned about protecting our environment. But the track record of our federal government does not engender confidence. And once we understand the reasons for such a track record, we are even more wary about placing additional responsibility on the shoulders of government officials. The evidence that we have compiled here should make us recognize that if we are serious about environmental quality, we should avoid relying heavily on government to provide it.

Notes

1. Based on conversations with Interior Department officials.
2. Testimony by James Duffus II before the U.S. Senate Subcommittee on Interior and Related Agencies of the Committee on Appropriations, June 20, 1991, p. 1.
3. This suggestion has often been made. See Kleit and Stroup.
4. See Metcalf and Reinemer for a version of the populist view on why public, rather than privately supplied, power was deemed to be better.
5. September 1, 1991.

References

Anderson, Terry L. and Donald R. Leal. 1991. *Free Market Environmentalism*. San Francisco: Pacific Institute for Public Policy Research, Boulder, CO: Westview Press.

Bosso, Christopher J. 1987. *Pesticides and Politics*. Pittsburgh: University of Pittsburgh Press.

Bovard, James. 1989. *The Farm Fiasco*. San Francisco: Institute for Contemporary Studies.

Chase, Alston. 1986. *Playing God in Yellowstone: The Destruction of America's First National Park*. Boston: Atlantic Monthly Press.

_____. 1989. Buying Water Rights to Save Wildlife. *Bozeman (MT) Daily Chronicle* (May 17).

Dahl, T. E. 1990. *Wetlands Losses in the United States 1780's to 1980's*. Washington, DC: U.S. Department of the Interior, Fish and Wildlife Service.

Dobra, John L., and George A. Uhimchuk. 1982. *The Wild Horse Controversy: An Irony of the Commons* (typescript), July.

Kleit, Andrew N., and Richard L. Stroup. 1987. Blackout at Bonneville Power. *Regulation* 2: 30.

Luttrell, Clifton B. 1989. *The High Cost of Farm Welfare*. Washington, DC: Cato Institute.

Metcalf, Lee, and Vic Reinemer. 1967. *Power to the People*. New York: David McKay Co., Inc.

Micklin, Philip P. 1988. Desiccation of the Aral Sea: A Water Management Disaster in the Soviet Union. *Science* (September 2): 1170-76.

Miller, H. Crane. 1989. *Turning the Tide on Wasted Tax Dollars*. Washington, DC: National Wildlife Federation and National Taxpayers Union (mimeo), April.

Mitchell, John G. 1991. Stillwater: An Embattled Refuge for All Seasons, and Reasons. *Wildlife Conservation*. (March/April): 88-90.

National Audubon Society. 1985. *Audubon Wildlife Report 1985*. New York: The National Audubon Society.

Nelson, Robert H. 1985. Mythology Instead of Analysis. In *Forestlands: Public and Private*, edited by Robert T. Deacon and M. Bruce Johnson. San Francisco: Pacific Institute for Public Policy Research.

Niskanen, William A. 1971. *Bureaucracy and Representative Government*. Chicago: Aldine.

O'Toole, Randal. 1988. *The Citizen's Guide to Reforming the Forest Service*. Eugene, OR: Cascade Holistic Consultants.

Reisner, Marc, and Sarah Bates. 1990. *Overtapped Oasis*. Washington, DC: Island Press.

Shabman, Leonard. 1980. Economic Incentives for Bottomland Conversion: The Role of Public Policy and Programs. *Transactions of the 45th North American Wildlife and Natural Resources Conference,* edited by Ken Sabol. Washington, DC: Wildlife Management Institute.

Stavins, Robert N., and Adam B. Jaffe. 1990. Unintended Impacts of Public Investments on Private Decisions: The Depletion of Forested Wetlands. *American Economic Review* 80 (June): 337-52.

Stroup, Richard L., and John A. Baden. 1983. *Natural Resources: Bureaucratic Myths and Environmental Management.* San Francisco: Pacific Institute for Public Policy Research.

Tiner, R. 1984. *Wetlands of the United States: Current Status and Recent Trends.* Washington, DC: U.S. Department of the Interior, Fish and Wildlife Service.

Wahl, Richard W. 1989. *Markets for Federal Water: Subsidies, Property Rights, and the Bureau of Reclamation.* Washington, DC: Resources for the Future.

Chapter 4

Clean Water Legislation: Reauthorize or Repeal?

Roger E. Meiners and Bruce Yandle

Introduction

For more than twenty years, the United States has struggled to build one national blueprint for achieving uniform water quality goals. The effort has been fraught with frustration and disappointment. Many who encounter the complex rules governing how plants are built and operated are frustrated. For them, the U.S. Environmental Protection Agency (EPA) and related state agencies form a regulatory maze that denies flexibility, creates uncertainty, and increases costs, sometimes, it seems, for little reduction in pollution.

Those who believed that federal regulation could deliver an improved environment quickly are disappointed. The 1970s legislation promised that pollution would end in little more than a decade. By the 1980s, all the nation's rivers and streams were to be fishable and swimmable. Cities would no longer pump raw sewage into lakes, rivers, and oceans. Drinking water was to be made free of impurities. Landowners downstream from industrial plants would no longer have to sue to gain improvements. The new statutes would do the job.

There was no way to attach accurate price tags to the water quality improvement programs. The task was simply too gigantic to allow for that. But somehow that did not matter very much. At the beginning of the federal environmental saga, in 1970, it seemed the nation could afford to disregard costs. We felt wealthy, and for good reason. Real family incomes were at all time high. The nation was on an economic roll. Protection at any cost seemed to be the underlying slogan of the time. Now, considerably poorer than we were then, we have received the bill, but the environmental quality has not been not delivered.[1]

A Time to Reappraise

We are a bit more pragmatic than we were in the early 1970s. Some who called for purity then are looking for practical ways to protect and enhance the environment now. Discussions about economics, once considered to be irrelevant, if not irreverent, have become commonplace. Many now see the environmental problem in terms of scarce resources on "spaceship earth" and the inescapable requirement to ration use among competing interests.[2] Even EPA, which has strong incentive to stay with the command-and-control approach, indicates interest in making a break with its past way of doing business.[3]

The debate associated with the next version of the Clean Water Act involves issues like those faced by world auto producers in the wake of the first OPEC embargo. Something had to be done to make future autos fit a world with more costly energy. Industry had two choices. It could downsize existing models, using old design and engineering concepts, or it could redesign from scratch, building on innovations that accounted for higher priced energy. In a pragmatic way, the industry did both. Tinkering at the margin was a short-run strategy that bought time for development of a new generation of fuel efficient automobiles.

The situation confronting environmental policymakers is more serious because it involves every facet of life. Global competition now pits regulators against regulators, just as auto producers in one country face off against producers from other countries. If environmental rules in Europe are less burdensome, yet more effective, than those in the United States, European producers may expand their share of the world market. The way a country regulates is an element of the complex calculations that create comparative advantage in world trade.

Getting the greatest bang for the buck, while widening the field for competition and innovation, is just one part of the problem faced by policy-makers. They must also find ways to "make the environment count" in the calculations of economic decision makers.[4] Taking the environment seriously requires us to rethink the legal incentives we give ourselves to protect the environment.

How This Chapter Is Organized

The discussion that follows examines water quality regulation and suggests distinct short-run and long-run paths that could lead to more environmental improvement at lower cost. The chapter is divided into two distinct parts.

The first part of the chapter gives a short-run analysis. That analysis follows the model of water quality regulation as it has evolved at this point. Recognizing the flaws in the basic structure of the still-evolving Clean Water Act, the analysis attempts to polish some of the rougher places.

While convinced that current regulatory institutions do not bode well for American producers in a competitive world, we accept the current administrative framework for the short-run. If implemented, the marginal, but important, changes proposed can improve cost effectiveness and make it easier to achieve the statute's goals. In some cases, short-run marginal changes require major modifications in the way Congress instructs EPA to approach its duties. In other instances, the proposed changes involve reordering some basic priorities in the management of water quality. We offer a summary of short-run recommendations at the end of the first part.

Ultimately, we argue, much more is needed than just tinkering at the margin of the regulatory blueprint followed for so long. Instead of tinkering and updating statutes, Congress needs to go back to the drawing boards and examine a path not taken two decades ago when federal water pollution regulation was first formulated. We examine that path—the common law—in the second part of the chapter.

The review of common law treatment of pollution includes discussions of cases that involve private and public parties. The common law rules applied just before passage of federal statutes are tougher on polluters than the statutes that displaced them. The rule of law rests on clearly defined property rights that are protected from the invasion of pollution, but which can be alienated through mutually beneficial contracts. Common law rules also contain strict legal standards that force public managers and private managers to control pollution effectively.

The Short-Run Analysis: Reforming the Statute

The Evolving Clean Water Act

The Clean Water Act (CWA) is a composite body of law dating to 1972 when the first major federal law was written.[5] The 1972 law focused on improving the quality of navigable waters. However, the law did not and still does not address water quality directly. It does so indirectly. The 1972 law dealt with discharge into rivers, streams, and lakes in three ways:

1. Permits. The law required the development of an industrial pollution discharge permit system that would lead to management and control of point source (such as city sewer systems and manufacturing operations) pollution.
2. Industrial pollution control. Legislation and the resulting regulation imposed technology-based effluent limitations that would lead to zero

discharge of all pollution by 1985. (Of course, that did not, could not, and cannot happen.)

3. Municipal waste treatment. Appropriations provided massive federal aid for construction of publicly owned sewage treatment works (POTWs). Technology-based treatment standards were set for the POTWs.

The CWA did not establish a system of national water quality standards, as was established by the Clean Air Act for air quality. The CWA adopted a vague goal concerning fishable and swimmable water quality. The CWA did not address nonpoint source pollution, such as run-offs from farms, construction activity, and mining operations, which now contribute over half the known waste received in our waters.[6] The basic statute provides for each state to designate ambient water quality standards, which are the expected normal conditions to be maintained in their lakes and streams. However, effluent limitation standards set by EPA still must be met by all point source dischargers.

The 1972 law seems to reflect a belief that enough industrial and municipal waste can be controlled to offset completely the wastes that flow from urban streets, agricultural, forest and mining lands, and construction sites. Indeed, so little attention has been paid to nonpoint source pollution that data on the amount and effects of that major pollution source have not been gathered systematically.

The Zero Discharge Goal

In 1972, there was no reliable water quality data base that focused on specific rivers, lakes, and coastal waters. That is, no one knew the magnitude of the gap between the existing quality of water and the goals to be accomplished. The absence of data and lack of attention to defining and maintaining a baseline for tracing progress partly reflected the "ending all discharge of pollutants" bias of the law.[7] If the goal is zero, why worry about current conditions?

The controversial and unattainable zero discharge element of the 1972 law was sponsored by Senator Edmund Muskie (D, Maine), who aspired to be president.[8] The House version of the bill took a softer approach on zero discharge and called for the National Academy of Sciences to gather data on its implications before the law was implemented. The Senate version with zero discharge and no data requirement, which was far more popular at the time, was passed over President Nixon's veto.

Taken seriously, zero discharge implies that some natural level of water quality will result. But there is no way of knowing what that is. In effect, there is no quality constraint, since no one knows what the natural parameters will be until they are achieved. No one can really define the meaning of "natural." What might be natural can be unfit for human use. Even the adjectives "fishable" and "swimmable" used to define the nation's water quality goal are vague and subjective to widely varying interpretations. Since there are no measurable goals and no baseline, it is impossible for EPA to provide a meaningful report card on progress, other than reductions in discharge. Growth of the total number of dischargers, even with each discharging less, can leave the nation in worse shape than it was before embarking on the federal program.

How the Goal Was Translated

A zero discharge standard is at odds with concerns about cost-effective control, which implies that measured pollution reduction will be accomplished at least cost. Instead, the CWA focuses on technology-based standards without regard to minimizing cost. The law instructs EPA to develop effluent limitation guidelines for industrial processes, by industry and subgroups within industries. The guidelines are applied regardless of the quality of receiving waters. Water capable of receiving some level of wastes that have no known environmental consequence are treated the same as water that suffers severe damage from the same level of wastes. The regulations spawned by the 1972 CWA are based on technology, not on environmental quality. There are no ambient water quality standards.

The 1977 amendments to the CWA added pretreatment requirements for industrial firms that discharge wastes into publicly owned treatment works (POTWs), and tightened treatment requirements for POTWs. Expansion of POTWs by tens of billions of dollars in federal grants provided opportunities for industrial dischargers to avoid some treatment costs by discharging to expanded (subsidized) municipal facilities. The 1977 law recognizes resource costs and mandates that operators of POTWs impose fees on industry dischargers to recover the full cost of treatment.

The 1977 amendments added requirements for handling toxic wastes and ordered states to develop management plans for nonpoint source pollution. Despite these changes, the 1977 CWA is still a technology-based statute that focuses on industrial and municipal waste treatment. The burden of the law is met by industrial firms that absorb costs or pass them on to consumers. The federal grants program provides funding to ease the costs placed on municipal treatment works.

Benefits and Costs

It was only after the command-and-control approach taken by the CWA took hold that the compliance costs could be estimated and compared with estimates of benefits provided by various federal agencies. Freeman's comparison of benefits and costs, estimated for 1985, showed the annual benefits of federal water pollution control ranged from $5.7 to $27.7 billion.[9] The values here do not take into account actions by state and municipalities that would have continued had there been no federal action. In that sense, the effects are "total," not marginal.

The "most likely point estimate" of annual benefits calculated by Freeman was set at $14 billion. The categories of benefits in the estimate included recreation, aesthetic and property values, commercial fishing, and benefits that result from reducing the cost of treating wastes and producing drinking water. Freeman's cost estimates are for 1979 through 1988. They include private and public sector direct capital and operating costs, but do not account for changes induced by implementation of the statute. The narrowly construed direct costs of pollution control form a lower bound estimate of total annualized cost that rose from $17.4 in 1979 to $33.4 billion in 1988. Annual average costs for the decade were estimated to be $23.2 billion. Weighed against the $14 billion estimate of benefits, the benefit-cost ratio is found wanting.

The benefit-cost analysis is discouraging for two reasons. First, as Freeman points out, one must take the high estimate of benefits and the low estimate of costs to conclude that the CWA is cost beneficial. In addition, remember that the cost estimate is a lower bound. Research that accounts for direct compliance costs and indirect costs that have been induced across all sectors of the economy suggests that cost estimates like Freeman's should be doubled (Hazilla and Kopp 1990).

There is one more discouraging note. Discussing the effects of the CWA on water quality, Freeman offered a guarded assessment:

> There has been some improvement in water quality since 1972. In terms of aggregate measures or national averages, it has not been dramatic. But there are local success stories of substantial cleanup in what had been seriously polluted water bodies. (1990, 120)

His summary is much like that found in another report that indicates the most serious charge to be leveled against the CWA is that hardly any real progress has been made since 1972 (Ingram and Mann, 1984).

The Proposed Amendments

The next major water quality legislation, which began to be debated in 1991, will form the third major chapter in a regulatory story that continues to emphasize technology instead of water quality. The major provisions of the proposed law are:

- Continue the use of effluent limitations but require that new and old point sources face the same standards.
- Add additional effluent pretreatment requirements for users of POTWs.
- Maintain a POTW construction program that places more of the funding burden on states.

The proposed elements expand the domain of regulation by including non-point source pollution and wetlands, which have not been regulated systematically in the past. Finally, the proposed legislation contains new water quality management activities that:

- Speak to the water quality data problem by requiring the development of consistent monitor-based data to be regularly reported to the public.
- Address the control of storm and other wet weather water flows that overload sewage treatment facilities in urban areas.
- Allow for innovative water quality management approaches, such as the use of effluent fees and other economic incentives, to be used by states.
- Impose fees on industries to cover the cost of developing state regulatory plans.

How the Basic Law Should Be Reformed

Zero Discharge Is Not a Practical Basis for Pollution Control

The CWA mandated in 1972 that there be zero discharge of pollutants into the nation's waters by 1985. Passing the deadline has simply postponed an impossible mandate. Now is the time to forget about zero discharge. While political rhetoric is important and a goal of pollution prevention may reflect the content of environmental dreams, taking the environment seriously requires that we regain contact with reality. Ordinary people with common sense do not want to contaminate the water they consume, but they know that certain concentrations of many pollutants can be assimilated naturally. Control resources should be allocated where they provide the largest environmental benefits.

Inevitable encounters with increasing control costs come when approaching the point where pollution vanishes. Scientific evidence about the consequences of pollution tells us that we can stop short of zero discharge for many pollutants but that we should strive for zero for certain toxic materials. The old fixation on zero pollution is a barrier to effective, lower cost control. If ambient quality standards are set for receiving waters, or the amounts of pollutants that may be discharged are established, decision makers can solve the resulting problem. They know where they are headed; they must then find the most effective way of getting there.

Make the Regulators Honest

In practice, EPA effluent limitations allow some pollution, which awkwardly establishes a goal for cost effectiveness. Unlike Congress, which wrote the "zero discharge" law, EPA regulators work in the real world and set standards that allow human life to continue in America. EPA's effluent guidelines are based on known technologies applied to "model" plants and carry a specified technology bias. Ordering firms to use specific technology to control pollution is a command-and-control approach.

This should be contrasted to a major canon of regulation that tells us that strict performance standards induce cost-effective behavior in for-profit firms whereas technology-based standards do not. The logic is based on the notion that managers of industrial plants are better equipped to discover and implement controls than are EPA technicians and consultants. The notion does not reflect relative adequacies of information and intelligence but draws on the assumption that incentives matter greatly.

Competition forces cost minimization, rewards successful firms, and punishes those with higher costs. There is no public sector competitive spur that might cause the most dedicated EPA employee to lie awake at night searching for new solutions to pollution control problems.

Performance standards that simply set a mandatory proportion of wastes to be reduced, or an absolute amount of waste to be allowed, place a different and perhaps a heavier burden on regulators than do technology-based standards. Performance standards require regulators to monitor output, not inputs. Simply determining that specific pollution control machinery is in place and operating, or exists and could be installed, does not get the best job done. Discharge or the environment itself has to be monitored. Regulatory safeguards involve random inspections, the installation of systematic monitors, and reliance on citizen actions to assure that permit requirements are met.

The narrow cost-effective elements of performance standards involve comparisons of how an industrial polluter might control wastes if given complete flexibility relative to the costs of following prescribed treatment methods. The apparent gains may be large, but they will be weighed against the value of certainty that comes to managers who simply do as they are told. While individual managers may like simplicity when dealing with regulators, society benefits from the cost reductions induced from competition.

Performance Standards and Pollution Permit Trading

The logic of performance standards extends readily to plant and river basin operations that allow operators collectively to meet regulatory goals. Instead of specifying point-source controls on a process-by-process basis within plants, the emphasis shifts to performance by all pollution sources within a plant. Attention then focuses on rivers, streams, and lakes that receive wastes from multiple plants.

Plant performance standards reduce costs when treatment costs for the same pollutant are different at different points within a plant. While piping wastes in some plants accomplishes the same cost-effectiveness goal, plant performance standards allow plant managers to tighten control where costs are lower in order to offset relaxation of control of higher cost sources. Furthermore, the incentive for firms to innovate continually on internal pollution controls is stronger under performance standards than under technology standards, where regulators determine the technology firms must use.

There is good evidence that cost savings can be obtained from implementing performance standards in plant and river basin controls. One study analyzed a raft of EPA background documents related to effluent limitations for the control of biological oxygen demand (BOD), a basic measure of pollution, for a large sample of industry and subindustry groups (Magat et al. 1986).

The analysts identified the added cost of removing a unit of BOD across many sources and found the cost varied from 10 cents per kilogram to $3.15, more than a thirtyfold difference in cost (Magat et al. 1986, 136-37). A survey of capital costs for the same sample of industries found the incremental annual cost of capital for removing a unit of BOD varied from one cent to $59.09 per kilogram. Think of the potential cost savings implied here. By spending one penny to remove a unit of BOD at one location, $59.09 can be saved at another location.

Most likely, the possible gains from attempts to bring a national program of cost-effective control would not be this dramatic. Other surveys that estimate the ratio of the cost of command-and-control technology standards to the cost of performance standards find the largest ratio to be 2.6 (Tietenberg 1988, 346-48). But whatever the potential, these gains simply cannot be obtained in a system of technology standards.

Nothing is gained by announcing that industrial plants on the same river can collectively reduce BOD levels by adjusting their discharges, but then instructing each plant to use specified technology limitations at each source. Similarly, nothing is gained by instructing plant operators to minimize control costs across multiple sources, but then advising them that they must use specific controls that reduce set amounts of pollution at every source.

Breaking the Regulator's Habits

A break with command-and-control technology regulation means placing more attention on monitoring and management, and less attention on further designations of discharge limitations. Industry has been the primary pollution control focus for 20 years. During that time, industrial discharge has been reduced 71 percent (Council on Environmental Quality 1989, 32-35). The resulting high level of compliance to date means that the cost of further reductions in industrial point source pollution will be higher than it will be for uncontrolled nonpoint source pollution and poorly operated POTWs, which since 1972 have reduced discharge by just 46 percent.[10]

To minimize the total cost of reducing particular pollutants, an authority must either have the uncommon knowledge, ability, and incentive to tighten and relax controls across all sources until all incremental costs are identical, or admit the impossibility of the task and assist the birth of a market for reductions that spontaneously achieves the same end. If BOD reductions can be obtained at a lower unit cost at a POTW than for a neighboring paper mill, then the POTW should be instructed to reduce pollution. The same logic applies to nonpoint sources.

The possible gains from cost-effective control are far easier to see now than when EPA effluent limitations were first announced. EPA developed its regulations one industry at a time. Before having much data, it was impossible for even a super regulator to compare costs across industries. Accumulated knowledge and experience would enable an all-knowing regulator to make comparisons and adjust control levels across sources. But it has long been recognized that neither regulators nor any one else can obtain and assimilate the requisite information to achieve efficient outcomes across an entire economy. At the same time, it is widely appreciated that decentralized markets effectively and efficiently deal with the complexities of resource allocation. However, recent efforts to bring artificial markets to bear on environmental regulation have not been all that successful.

Elaborate schemes for developing marketlike systems that allow dischargers of pollutants to buy and sell pollution rights, within the confines of some overall limit, have been discussed for years.[11] One can imagine a paper mill manager approaching a broker of pollution discharge rights to ask about the going price of pollution reductions. Along a river basin, plants having lower control costs would sell treatment to plants with higher treatment costs. On learning the price of discharge rights, the manager could decide whether to expand treatment facilities or purchase discharge rights from the broker. In the process, total treatment costs across all sources would be minimized. A given level of pollution would be achieved at the lowest cost as market forces were used to enhance environmental quality.

Systems of this sort have been tried in Wisconsin, and the 1990 Clean Air Amendments allow electric utilities to trade sulfur dioxide reduction rights to meet new restrictions.[12] But the bureaucratic restrictions accompanying the schemes are deadly to markets.[13] Markets and heavy government intervention do not flourish together.

Regulators brought up under the CWA lack the incentive to bother with the messy business of allowing pollution sources to trade permits. The regulators gain nothing in the process. Indeed, life is made more complicated for them. Just a small amount of regulatory indifference to innovative approaches for reducing combined treatment costs can be enough to chill the process completely. Firms will not invest in helping to devise a market for pollution permits unless there is substantial certainty that regulation will not gut the process. Command-and-control will win the day.

Accordingly, a sharply revised CWA must give states the authority to manage river basins on the basis of performance standards. The law should require regulators to review past actions, search out opportunities to reduce combined treatment costs, and justify actions that disregard efforts to minimize costs. Permit trading and other such approaches should be the standard approach. Forced command-and-control should be the default position.

In sum, the time is ripe for implementing performance standards for industrial dischargers and for extending the system to embrace plants and river basins or sectors of water courses. Emphasis should be on monitoring and managing, as opposed to setting higher technical standards for the equipment that controls conventional pollutants. The reauthorized CWA can accomplish this by giving states the full responsibility for managing water quality, while refocusing EPA's activities to the provision of consulting expertise and research about the consequences of pollution.

States are already responsible for classifying rivers and streams on the basis of EPA-determined water quality criteria, which establishes rough ambient standards. The move to performance standards logically follows the definition of minimum ambient standards. As national consultants, EPA can encourage performance standards, but each state will be free to implement its own regulatory approach. Competition among states for citizen support and industrial development will yield variety and the discovery of cost-effective control.

Command-and-Control Is Logical for Public Sector Polluters

Recent episodes of pollution on public beaches and careless disposal of hazardous waste by public hospitals, military bases, federal agencies, and universities speak to incentives and how they differ across organizations. Public units cannot and will not comply with rules in the same fashion as private organizations. In many cases, public agencies are immune to suits brought by unhappy or damaged recipients of pollution, or they are subject to less liability for polluting their neighborhood than are private parties. There is no monitoring by owners who fear the costs of litigation that might arise due to negligent handling of pollutants. Since there is no identifiable financial interest at stake in public operations, incentives to minimize cost are weak. The logic for performance standards is not compelling for public sector sources of pollution.

The fundamental differences between public and private sector organizations should be recognized in the law. Technology-based standards should be kept for public sector organizations. Indeed, they should be reinforced. However, since public and private organizations often discharge the same pollutants and use the same waterways, opportunities for cooperation and combined cost minimization are to be embraced. State regulators should be instructed to encourage taking a shared approach to an overall pollution control plan based on measurable goals and performance standards that will apply to private sector organizations.

The resulting mixed system will allow for marketable pollution permits and their exchange across public and private sector polluters. However, public entities will have less flexibility than private ones.

Cutting the Remaining Linkage for Construction Grants

The 1987 CWA Amendments recognize the fact that the federal gravy train has run out of fuel. Having redistributed about $60 billion in construction grants from taxpayers nationwide to specific municipalities since 1972, Congress put in place a program that will phase out federal grants by 1995. The new revolving fund program gives states the responsibility to raise funds and the authority to manage redistribution within their borders. What was a federal pork barrel has been turned over to state politicians, but not completely. Congress still writes the rules of conduct.

It is logical that states and municipalities should plan and pay for their own water treatment programs. Most benefits accrue to local citizens. Since the federal purse cannot be squeezed for more, there is no choice but to return local programs to local citizens. At the same time, federal rules affecting the quality of interstate waters and ocean discharge can still be imposed, but there is no efficiency reason for Congress to dictate how states organize and manage the distribution of construction funds. There are, of course, political reasons for Congress to hold on to the power to influence which groups receive funds. However, political accountability should be fixed with state and local officials who tax and spend.

Returning Water Quality Management to the States

Reauthorization of the CWA provides the opportunity to give to states and local governments what is logically theirs. This should be done, in spite of the understandable cry for federal dollars that comes from state and local governments that have become accustomed to federal grants.[14] It is estimated that $83.5 billion will be needed by the year 2008 to improve and expand wastewater treatment facilities across the nation.[15] But these survey results are based on the old way of doing business.

Freed of federal rules and control, state and local governments will become fertile ground for improving the management of water treatment resources.[16] The brick and mortar bias associated with construction grants will be gone. Local taxpayers will know that they alone will bear the cost of building and operating water treatment facilities. No one will have to testify before Congress to inform people of common sense that water and sewage treatment fees should recover the cost of facilities. Local tax revenues will be the only other alternative. Responsible for their destiny, local authorities will move more quickly to meter water use, set appropriate charges, require technically efficient plumbing and piping, and reduce leakages in their distribution systems.

The gains from taking such action are large, but the availability of federal funds blunts the incentive to take action. Evidence that water conservation can be obtained from pricing an important resource like water is provided by the National Wildlife Federation (Osann 1991; Pacella 1991). According to the Federation, moves taken to meter and charge for drinking water in Boulder, Colorado, led to a 36 percent reduction in residential use. Other studies cited by the Federation tell us the demand curve for water is indeed downward sloping. Metered systems can reduce consumption by as much as 42 to 63 percent. Simple steps like testing for and correcting leaking pipes in municipal water distribution systems will come quickly when local citizens and their elected officials know that they will bear the cost of not taking action.

Dealing with Nonpoint Source Pollution Control

From the outset, the national effort to reduce the flow of pollution to rivers, streams, and lakes has focused on industrial and municipal waste treatment. Regulatory approaches to reduce point source pollution could be designed more readily, and compliance with the law is easier to enforce.

Requiring states to implement plans to reduce nonpoint source pollution will cause them to focus on runoffs from agricultural, mining, forestry, and construction. Controlling these sectors moves regulators to new areas of concern and provides an opportunity to apply some of the learning accumulated from 20 years' effort to control industrial and municipal wastes. Again, the logic of performance standards applies here. Instead of being required to focus on inputs and operating methods, farmers, loggers, contractors, and mining operators should be given pollution reduction goals that focus on desired results.

Nonpoint sources by their nature tend to defy the development of federally favored technology-based standards. Because of this, regulators should devote their energies to the development of data bases on practices that achieve run-off reductions and research on the poorly understood problems of pollution from nonpoint sources. Among others, Land Grant universities can be logical partners in the effort. Traditionally involved in transferring knowledge to agriculture, they are now extending their focus to include the modern problems of the environment of agriculture, forestry, and mining.

Regional efforts to reduce run-off pollution will often involve the same pollutants now controlled by industrial and municipal sources. At the outset, nonpoint source polluters will encounter relatively low costs in controlling pollution, since little has been done to date. In contrast, complying industrial and municipal polluters are now incurring relatively high incremental costs per unit of treatment since they have been required to achieve ever increasing levels of reduction. One can visualize the family of cost schedules confronted by the polluters.

Differences in incremental pollution control costs for point versus nonpoint source pollution provide opportunities to reduce the combined cost of pollution control. Once allowable levels of discharge are defined for nonpoint sources, sources of industrial waste can find it to their advantage to trade reductions with the operators of nonpoint sources. The CWA should do more than allow such flexibility. When developing compliance plans, state authorities should be required to consider cost minimizing strategies that include all sources of the same pollutants and to justify plans that fail to allow trading.

Providing Baseline Data on Results

Considering the immense importance of clean water and the massive resource commitment to control water pollution, it is ironic that greater attention has not been devoted to the systematic assembling of national data on water pollution.[17] In the first place, it is illogical to allocate effort to high priority locations without an environmental basis for ordering priorities. Lacking hard data, control resources tend to be allocated on the basis of narrow interest group pressures that reflect the nation's interests only by chance.

In the absence of scientific environmental data that enables us to measure progress, Congress cannot claim to determine the effectiveness of pollution control programs. Showing declining pollution trends does not mean we are using our resources to best enhance our waters. The reduction in water pollution may result from changes in the mix of water-using industries, the rise of the services economy, and rising relative prices for energy and other inputs. A proper assessment of the effectiveness of pollution control regulation requires an "all else being equal" approach.

But, as important as knowing where problems may be most serious, and whether or not federal efforts to control pollution are effective, there are even more pressing reasons to have good data on pollution. The focus of the nation's pollution control programs must change from monitoring inputs, such as mandating technology, to measuring output—the protection of the environment. Indeed, knowing the state of the environment is fundamental to an effective pollution control program. Taking actions without information is like throwing darts blindfolded.

All innovative control programs that use market-based strategies must allow enforceable contracts that define what is being traded. Polluters cannot exchange treatment activities without knowing the agreed upon actions can be enforced. Citizens who seek to monitor the health of local waters cannot be effective without reliable data on pollution trends. The next CWA should provide funding for the expansion of the water quality monitoring system, an expansion of scientific research about the consequences of pollution, the systematic production of data on water quality trends on a state-by-state basis, and should require Congress to provide an annual report on the condition of the nation's water ecology. The report should document what has been accomplished with the resources devoted to pollution control efforts.

Having made this efficiency argument, we understand that the major actors in the federal pollution control arena do not have the incentive to send home regular report cards. Independent evidence to date indicates that an accurate report would show huge expenditures for little if any progress for many streams and lakes. The results of pork barrel patronage would be unveiled, and in some cases the fact that water quality in some locations is not all that bad would undermine the efforts of special interest groups to secure even more political leverage. Taking the environment seriously requires a factual presentation of data. Failure to provide a clear picture of where we are headed is a strong statement that the search for improved water quality plays second fiddle to special interests that drive the political process.

Final Thoughts on Part One

Building a water pollution control statute on a zero discharge, command-and-control foundation is like erecting a castle on the sand. The law may sound good, and the castle may appear solid, but it is doomed from the start. Enough has been written about the ineffectiveness of technology-based rules intended to protect the environment and their inappropriate focus on inputs to fill a large POTW. It is time to focus on the environment and human health, which requires sharply modifying the CWA.

Modification of the basic blueprint would do the following:
- Impose new data collection and reporting requirements that make it possible to define the water pollution control problem, to monitor progress, and to accommodate contracts that are written between organizations that trade pollution rights.
- Make performance standards the baseline instrument for controlling pollution, using technology-based standards only with public units that lack the economic incentive to minimize cost and protect the environment.
- Give states the full authority to manage the water pollution control problem, allowing them to use any control instruments available.
- Make EPA a consulting organization to states that provides technical expertise, establishes national water quality criteria to be met by state action, and monitors and reports progress.
- Eliminate all federal funding of water and sewage treatment works. Give full authority and responsibility for the provision of local services to state and local governments.

Common Law Remedies: The Path Not Taken

The Common Law of Water Pollution

Common law suits prior to the CWA addressed the issue of the right to pollute water. As a Texas court noted in 1965, "any corruption of water which prevents its use for any of its reasonable purposes is an infringement of rights of riparian owners."[18] Why did Congress find it necessary to pass the CWA when the common law appeared to protect water quality and quantity? Why was Lake Erie near "death" and rivers catching fire if the common law protected water quality?

It is likely that there is no definitive answer to these questions. But it is clear that common law rules were "mugged" by legislative actions that effectively monopolized water pollution control. We argue that the common law, not restricted by statutes, may have provided more strict and, hence, more ecologically sound pollution control than has occurred under the CWA. In addition, common law rules support market transactions that allow individuals to exchange rights to water quality.

Common law rules have long been relied on for protecting property rights. This includes the right not to suffer from the damaging effects of pollution inflicted on those who have a right to clean water. As Justice Jackson noted, "Rights, property or otherwise, which are absolute against the world, are certainly rare, and water rights are not among them."[19] Like other areas of the common law, some aspects of water rights changed as technology and social conditions changed. Had state and federal statutes not been passed, we believe that common law would have taken these changes into account. By reviewing the fragments of common law that have survived despite legislative interference, we can build an image of how pollution could be managed effectively by common law rules.

The Evolution and Erosion of Common Law Rules

Even before the CWA, various federal and state statutes reduced the ability and incentives of private parties to enforce common law restrictions on water pollution (Beck and Goplerud 1988, 204.2). However, an examination of cases before statutes and of cases that have been brought in pollution instances not covered by statutes provide evidence of the ability of common law actions to restrict pollution, even when state boundaries were involved.

The U.S. Supreme Court in 1907 supported the right of the state of Georgia to obtain an injunction against a Tennessee smelter that caused damage to Georgia property due to air pollution.[20] In 1971 a federal Court of Appeals held that federal courts had jurisdiction, under federal common law, when the state of Texas wanted an injunction to stop New Mexico farmers from using a pesticide that Texas alleged was polluting a river used by its citizens.[21] In 1972, before the CWA took effect, the U.S. Supreme Court supported this notion, holding that a federal common law basis exists for a water pollution action.[22] The common law worked, perhaps too well to suit some interest groups.

Statutory Preemption of Common Law Rights

The preemption of common law rights against polluters by various statutes has forced courts to dismiss common law actions. For example, common law actions against the dumping of toxic substances in coastal waters were dismissed because of the CWA and the Marine Protection, Research and Sanctuaries Act.[23] Milwaukee prevented Illinois from suing it for dumping its raw sewage into Lake Michigan because of federal pollution statutes.[24] Similarly, when Tennessee tried to stop a North Carolina company from polluting a river that flowed into Tennessee, its only recourse was to complain to the EPA that North Carolina should not have issued the water pollution permit to the company.[25] Again, a common law right of action was prohibited by a statute. The Clean Water Act explicitly eliminated common law actions for interstate water pollution. Statutes give regulators, who have no personal incentive to bring action, rather than those harmed, primary control of the environment.

We cannot know how common law liability rules for pollution would have developed in the last two decades had their evolution not been precluded by statutes. But other areas of law offer some clues.[26] We believe recent advances in pollution control technology, advances in understanding the consequences of pollution, and changes in society's attitude about the acceptability of pollution would have led to a rule of strict liability under the common law for polluters, as has occurred in product defect law. Even in its limited role, the common law often sets standards far tougher than those set by statutes.[27]

The common law does not evolve the most economically efficient of "just" rules. But the decisions of hundreds of independent judges, responding to thousands of independent cases filed by private parties seeking to protect their common law rights, are far more likely to produce sensible principles than are legislative bodies that produce rules influenced by special interests, or rules that reflect a crisis of the moment but make little sense otherwise.[28] The principled nature of the common law lies in its evolutionary and competitive nature. The weakness of statutes is in their being influenced by special interests and lack of competitiveness. Had common law pollution remedies, such as private and public nuisance actions, not been discouraged, litigation would have resulted in a more considered approach of the consequences of alternative rules of law.

What Might the Common Law of Pollution Be Today?

Because some common law actions have been allowed in areas not covered by federal statute, or in intrastate cases not prohibited by state statutes, we have some examples that give an indication of how the common law might have evolved on a broad scale were it not for statutes like the CWA.

In a 1982 Rhode Island Supreme Court case, neighbors sued a farmer who maintained a hazardous waste dump on his property. The neighbors (plaintiffs) claimed the dump emitted noxious fumes and polluted ground and surface waters. Holding for plaintiffs, the Court overturned a 1934 decision that would have held for defendant because ground waters were "indefinite and obscure." The 1934 Court had held that plaintiffs in pollution cases had to show that defendants should have "foreseen" the consequences of their action, that is, were negligent. The 1982 Court held that since 1934 "the science of groundwater hydrology as well as societal concern for environmental protection has developed dramatically. As a matter of scientific fact the course of subterranean waters are no longer obscure and mysterious.... We now hold that negligence is not a necessary element of a nuisance case involving contamination of a public or private waters by pollutants percolating through the soil and traveling underground routes."[29] That is, a rule of strict liability was imposed on polluters who cause damage to other users of ground and surface waters.

A rule of strict liability imposes a higher standard of care than negligence. It also shifts the burden of proof from plaintiff to defendant. Common law cases in the decades before statutes took control of pollution regulation closely tracked the development of common law standards for product defects. "As a general rule, any person who pollutes a natural watercourse to the injury of a riparian owner is liable for the damages resulting therefrom."[30] Contrast this result to the environmental protection under the federal system of command-and-control of what pollution control is sufficient. There is no way that an agency, such as EPA, can know as much about what level of pollution is necessary, desirable, or achievable compared to what individual polluters and recipients of pollution can know about such matters.

Problems with Statutory Enforcement of Pollution Damage

Our system of water pollution regulation is akin to a federal agency being mandated by Congress to study technology, then telling companies how to build products, and certifying the products as safe, thereby generally insulating producers from liability for defects. Regulatory determination of how much safety is legally correct may allow dangerous products to emerge that would have been prevented by competitors seeking to avoid common law liability by improving technology. Under the common law, those who cannot make products sufficiently safe, and incur liability for injuries inflicted, either cease production or, if the product is sufficiently valuable or danger free, build a premium into the price of the product that allows compensation of parties injured by the product.

The rights of citizens injured by water pollution to seek redress at common law have been restricted by the statutes supposedly designed to protect the environment and citizens from the effects of environmental degradation. While some class action and private party suits are allowed by the statutes, the remedies allowed are often trivial in comparison to remedies that would be found under common law liability rules. Suits filed under statutes like the CWA are complicated by requirements that plaintiffs comply with regulatory procedures before commencing suit against regulated polluters. This drives up the cost of litigation and reduces the incentives of plaintiffs to seek redress under the statutes or the common law. Finally, many people may assume that regulators are insuring environmental safety and do not consider the possibility of private action.

Federal environmental statutes allow private parties to sue polluters and regulators who are not complying with the statutes and their regulation.[31] Is this a good substitute for common law actions? Suits against regulatory agencies alleging that the agencies failed to do something required by the law are difficult and rarely successful. Courts defer to statutes and to regulators in their determination of how the law should be enforced. More common than suits against agencies are citizen suits against polluters alleged to be in violation of a statute. For example, a public or private water treatment facility may be dumping more pollution than allowed by permit and therefore be in violation of rules that should be enforced by a state regulatory agency.

The first difference with the common law is the presumption that the level of pollution allowed by the permit is the correct amount. Given the environmental consequences of the pollution, it may be that more pollution would not be harmful and so would be allowed under the common law, or it may be that the permit is not as restrictive as common law standards would impose. The statutory approach presumes regulators are correct in their knowledge about how much pollution is "right."

When a plaintiff believes a polluter has exceeded the pollution allowed by their permit under the CWA, the plaintiff must notify the regulators and the permit holder of the alleged violation and give them 60 days to correct the situation.[32] Common law rights allow no such grace period. Under the CWA, if the violation is ended upon notice, suit is precluded. If the suit goes forward because violations continue, the most likely result will be a court order to the violator to comply with the permit; the polluter may be required to pay some cleanup cost; and the polluter may be required to pay court costs and attorney's fees for the plaintiff. Unlike common law remedies, there is no statutory provision for payment of damages to parties injured by the pollution. This limitation reduces the incentive of injured parties to seek redress, which would have the benefit of obtaining a general reduction in environmental damage.

Under the common law, an injunction is a proper remedy in nuisance cases. If a court determined that pollution was a nuisance because it injured others' rights to clean water, it could order the pollution to be ended (reduced to a level so no damage was inflicted on other water users). In contrast, under the CWA, a polluter found to be dumping more pollution than allowed by permit would usually merely be ordered to get busy trying to comply with the law—not shut down—and might have to pay a trivial civil fine.

Further restrictions on the right of parties claiming to have suffered injury by pollution are imposed by the CWA provision that polluters cannot be sued for past violations. That is, even if a polluter has exceeded regulatory standards and caused environmental damage, if the polluter stops violating permitted levels before suit is filed (or during the 60-day warning period), citizen suit is precluded. In such instances, unless the regulators decide to sue, which is quite rare, there may be no legal consequences for having violated the CWA and imposed damage on others (Mann 1991, 184). Compare this to common law liability, which, except for statute of limitation rules, generally does not excuse one of liability for past actions that damage others, if one should have known at the time the action took place that it could damage others. Under strict liability, there is no question that liability would be imposed on the party who committed an act that injured others.[33]

Examples of Litigation

A South Carolina case illustrates the burden that pollution can place on plaintiffs. Three lakeshore property owners sued a sewer authority that for years polluted the lake on which they live. The authority was operating a licensed plant that dumped industrial and human waste into the lake, thus making the lakeshore owners' property substantially less valuable.

Plaintiffs sued, asking that civil fines be levied for violations of the CWA, and requesting damages for a taking of their property because of the nuisance. The authority claimed sovereign immunity. This claim was rejected by the court because, under South Carolina law, a public agency cannot be immune from a nuisance that is a constitutional taking. Plaintiffs were awarded $300,000 in damages. On appeal, the Fourth Circuit upheld the damages and also ordered that the sewer authority be fined for CWA violations, which allowed plaintiff also to recover legal fees from the defendant.[34] Private enforcement of common law rights, which was allowed only because of a constitutional hook for the case, generated more action than did years of regulatory oversight. Aware of the lake pollution, regulators never issued anything stronger than notices of violations to the sewer operators, which, quite sensibly, were ignored.[35]

In another case, the Illinois Environmental Protection Agency, backed by the U.S. EPA, supported the right of a chemical waste landfill to remain in operation. The Illinois Supreme Court found that the landfill was causing groundwater contamination and that there could be a chemical explosion given the disposal technique used. The Court held that in Illinois the rights of private landowners are presumptively superior to the public benefit or convenience from having a business operate at a particular location. The Court noted the need for toxic landfills, but held that they had to be constructed so as not to impose costs on surrounding noncompensated landowners.[36]

The point of this case is not who was right about the construction of the landfill, but that parties who may suffer the damages that can be imposed by toxic pollution have a lot more incentive to think carefully about the matter than do regulators, no matter how well intentioned or informed the regulators may be. As long as pollution can be imposed on communities because the state controls the process, rather than polluters having to contract with affected parties, the "Not in My Back Yard" (NIMBY) syndrome will always be a problem, making the whole process a political football. No market mechanism is at work that encourages parties to minimize environmental damage and pay for the damages for which they are responsible. Rather, at taxpayer expense, a regulator declares what is acceptable, and where, and mandates the action in the command-and-control approach.

Government Subsidies for Pollution

Common law liability for polluters has been restricted not only by environmental statutes like the CWA, which specifically set federal standards that take precedence over common law standards, but by other statutes that allow or subsidize environmental degradation. Federal agricultural law for decades has subsidized plowing land that would have been left as pasture or uncultivated, has subsidized drainage of wetlands to create more farm land, and has subsidized the development and spread of pesticide and herbicide usage (Bovard 1989; Stavins and Jaffe 1990, 337-52; Bosso 1987). As was discussed in Chapter 3, these statutes have contributed substantially to wetland erosion and nonpoint source water pollution.

States, often with federal subsidies, are involved in various drainage projects —drainage districts, reclamation districts, flood control districts, irrigation districts, mosquito control districts, and sewer districts. "Essentially all states give public entities doing drainage the power of eminent domain to condemn land and water rights for drainage purposes. Second, public drainage institutions are given 'sovereign immunity.'... For example, in New Jersey a suit cannot be brought against a public drainage body unless its action has been 'palpably un-reasonable'—a much higher standard than ordinary reasonableness" (Goldfarb 1988, 63).

Similarly, the "federal government is statutorily insulated from liability 'for any damages from or by flood waters at any place'" (Goldfarb 1988, 64). States and the EPA cannot regulate radioactive waste from nuclear plants. Congress has given sole authority to the Nuclear Regulatory Commission. This generally eliminates the right of injured citizens to seek redress from nuclear waste generators under traditional legal theories such as nuisance or negligence (Goldfarb 1988, 90). Similar restrictions exist in cases in federal power projects,

Army Corps projects, and so forth. Even when liable, there are statutory limitations on damages.

Final Thoughts on Clean Water Legislation

The pollution problem cannot be "solved." Just as no one can say what is the right amount of safety for consumer products, no one can say what is the right amount of pollution. What might be an appropriate answer for one group of people differs from the answer of others, especially when the people involved have to bear the cost of achieving their stated goals. In addition, knowledge about the effects of pollution evolves, as does technology for dealing with pollution control. What is reasonable today may not be reasonable 10 years from now. We also learn that things we thought to be harmful 10 years ago turn out to be less hazardous. We also know that the cost of dealing with pollution will fall, but we cannot know what technology will improve most in the future.

The statutory control of pollution is fundamentally flawed and, while it could be made more sensible, the basic framework of the law cannot be changed. As it stands, the CWA takes a command-and-control approach that basically destroys market incentives to reduce pollution in a least-cost fashion. The resulting costs are borne by the parties affected, not by unknown taxpayers.

Regardless of how well informed, how far removed from politics, and how well intended, regulators cannot determine the correct amount of pollution. Command-and-control economies cannot do simple things very well, such as grow wheat and make bread. Giving regulators the task of controlling something as complex as pollution—compounded by the real world of political influence, lack of knowledge, lack of incentives, and lack of resources—is doomed to produce worse results than would a market approach. Command-and-control costs more and produces less than the market approach.

The market approach to water pollution control requires the following: Federal and state statutes must be phased out, to be replaced with common law liability rules. Thousands of polluters and water users will struggle to determine what is to be allowed and how the market for water use is to work. The common law sets a tough standard. No one has the right to pollute water in ways that imposes harm on other water users, unless the receiver of pollution agrees to be compensated.

We do not know what the common law rules would be today if this law had not been cut short by statutory intervention. The judgments of independent judges reviewing thousands of individual cases would be far more likely to set pollution standards that make the rules of the game clear, than is a statutory process that involves constant pleading before Congress, state legislators, and regulators to modify the rules again and again.

Unfortunately, there is no special interest group likely to press for this "radical" proposal that would return us to our legal roots, which respects property rights and thereby protects the environment. Legislators want to keep control of the pollution regulation process. They are paid in votes and contributions for writing rules their constituents want. Regulators want to keep their jobs, which become more important and durable the stronger the regulatory process. Industry has learned to live under the current rules and fears an unknown alternative—and knows that judges, unlike members of Congress, are generally immune from promises of votes and financial reward.

Finally, environmental groups do not want the system to change. A major role of environmental groups is to lobby Congress and state legislatures to set rules. Common law courts have little interest in environmental groups' thoughts or election assistance. Environmental groups may well represent the wishes of many people who desire less pollution. But these groups, regardless of expertise, cannot know what the right amount of pollution is any more than can industry, members of Congress, or the EPA.

It is our guess, based on the development of product liability law, that the common law would provide more environmental protection for water and the rest of the environment than has the regulatory process, but we have never seen an environmental group call for a return to common law. The common law relies on individuals seeking protection of their rights, not on group lobbying before Congress. Environmental groups are threatened by such a change, even though it means that we would be more likely to achieve what they would like to see happen. Self-interest is a powerful motive that can be used to protect the integrity of our water. Unfortunately, it is driving us in the other direction because of perverse legal and political incentives.

The common law is not perfect. There are product defect cases that make little sense. But mistakes made by individual judges, subject to review by independent courts of appeal, are much more likely to be corrected, and less devastating in impact, than are mistakes by congressional mandates and national regulatory standards. Like markets, which evolve constantly to take advantage of new knowledge, technology, and desires of consumers, the common law is dynamic in its protection of individual rights. The environment is more likely to be protected by individuals seeking to protect their rights than when such matters are determined by obsolete technologically driven standards determined by legislators and regulators.

Notes

1. Current estimates of the annual cost of complying with environmental regulations, which do not account for the indirect effects of regulation that reduce demand because of price increases, are on the order of $90 billion, or 1.7 percent of GNP. Of this, $30 billion is attributed to the Clean Water Act. By comparison, the shares of GDP spent annually in other countries are France, 0.86 percent; W. Germany, 1.52 percent; Netherlands, 1.33 percent; Norway, 0.82 percent; United Kingdom, 1.25 percent; and Japan, approximately 1-2 percent. See Kopp et al. 1990, 3. Estimates that include the full cost to the economy indicate that the numbers here should be doubled. See Hazilla and Kopp 1990, 853-73.

2. The Sierra Club, National Wildlife Federation, Wilderness Society, Audubon Society, Natural Resources Defense Fund, and especially the Environmental Defense Fund are lending support for the use of economic logic in managing environmental use. See Hahn and Stavins. For a more pessimistic view, see Cook; he describes the internal struggle at EPA that arose when a few people at the agency began to push for the use of economic incentives.

3. See *Testimony of William K. Reilly, Administrator, U.S. Environmental Protection Agency*, before the Committee on Public Works and Transportation, U.S. House of Representatives, March 20, 1991. The General Accounting Office (GAO) also supports the use of economic incentives, along with improved data collection and reporting (1991c).

4. An interesting discussion of how to link economic decisions to environmental protection is found in Council on Environmental Quality 1991, Chapter 2.

5. Previous federal legislation provided funds to do research on environmental issues and to bring coordination to state efforts to resolve interstate pollution problems, but the 1972 CWA is the first extensive piece of water pollution control legislation.

6. Estimates of discharge prior to the 1972 CWA show nonpoint sources accounted for 57 percent of the total biological oxygen demand (BOD) imposed by pollution, which is a standard measure of biodegradable discharge. Nonpoint sources accounted for 98 percent of the suspended solids; 83 percent of the total dissolved solids; 80 percent of the total phosphorous loadings; and 80 percent of the nitrogen. See Freeman 1990, 109.

7. For discussion of the legislative history on this, see Leone and Jackson 1981, 231-71. Also see Maloney and Yandle 1983.

8. The discussion here is based on Leone and Jackson 1981, 240-41. At the time the legislation was being formed, Senator Muskie suffered a scathing attack for being soft on polluters. Recognizing the political importance of securing the support of environmentalists, he moved away from performance standards and

state management to one of zero discharge and federal control. See also Yandle 1989, 68-69.

9. Freeman 1990, 122-27. He draws on reports of the Council on Environmental Quality (CEQ) and EPA.

10. The CEQ's mid-1980s estimates of sources of key pollutants addresses the relative position of industrial and public sources of pollution. Some 6.1 percent of BOD nationwide comes from the metals and minerals industry. Municipal wastes account for 73.2 percent and agriculture, 21.6 percent of BOD discharge. For suspended particulates, municipal waste accounts for 61.5 percent of the total; industry, 26.6 percent; and agriculture, 13.3 percent. Id.

11. There is a massive literature on the topic, but the basic scheme was outlined congently in Dales 1968.

12. The Wisconsin situation is discussed later with documentation. On the Clean Air Act trading activity, see 56 *Federal Register*, May 23, 1991, 23744-23759.

13. The Wisconsin effort along the Fox River that began in the early 1980s has been described at great length in various reports. However, there has not been a single trade among the various polluters. Conversations with a Wisconsin official indicate that the command-and-control restrictions that must be met before any trading is allowed caused the market potential to vanish. (For an excellent survey of literature on permit trading and the use of other economic incentives, see Anderson et al. 1990. Also see Hahn and Noll 1990, 351-67.) The Wisconsin situation was described in a conversation with Gerald Novotny, State of Wisconsin, Bureau of Wastewater Management, on July 10, 1991.

14. Examples of the appeal are seen in the Testimony of Association of State and Interstate Water Pollution Control Administrators 1991.

15. See Testimony of Edward R. Ossan 1991 and Statement of Ron Pacella 1991. The survey of needs is presented in Apogee Research 1990.

16. Use of federal funds requires the recipient to meet various federal requirements for spending the funds, such as meeting the mandate of the Davis-Bacon Act, which sharply increases the cost of labor. (For discussion of this and other relevant points, see Statement of Richard L. Hembra 1991.)

17. Efforts to remedy this situation have accelerated, but more needs to be done. The CEQ assembled an Interagency Advisory Committee on Environmental Trends, which is working to improve data collection. CEQ was charged by the National Environmental Policy Act to report on the condition of the environment. Data are available for 300 rivers locations covering a decade. A consistent, reliable data set must be developed that goes beyond providing data on the "national" picture, which tells us little about local water pollution concerns. This problem extends to all pollution. See U.S. General Accounting Office 1988.

18. *Garland Grain Co. v. D-C Home Owners Improvement Assn.*, 393 S.W. 2d 635 (Tex. Civ. App., 1965). Riparian rights, which form the basis for water law in the eastern and mid-western states, are associated with the right to water that

flows over one's land or flows adjacent to one's land. Appropriation rights emerged in the west. These rights concern water use more than water quality. We disregard appropriation rights in our discussion, which focuses on pollution.

19. *U.S. v. Willow River Power Co.*, 324 U.S. 449, (1945).

20. *Georgia v. Tennessee Copper Co.*, 206 U.S. 230; 27 S.Ct. 618 (1907).

21. *Texas v. Pankey*, 444 F.2d 236 (10th Cir., 1971).

22. See, e.g., *Hinderlider v. La Plata River & Cherry Creek Ditch Co.*, 304 U.S. 92, 58 S.Ct. 803 (1938) (water apportionment); *Missouri v. Illinois*, 200 U.S. 496, 26 S.Ct. 268 (1906) (water pollution); and *Illinois v. Milwaukee*, 406 U.S. 91; 92 S.Ct. 1385 (1972), which discusses the federal common law of nuisance as a basis for pollution cases. The Court later dismissed this case because of passage of the CWA, which preempted the common law rights.

23. *Conner v. Aerovox, Inc.*, 730 F.2d 835 (1st Cir. 1984), *cert. denied*, 470 U.S. 1050 (1985).

24. *Illinois v. Milwaukee*, 731 F.2d 403 (7th Cir. 1984), *cert. denied*, 469 U.S. 1196 (1985).

25. *Tennessee v. Champion Int'l Corp.*, 479 U.S. 1061, 107 S.Ct. 944 (1987).

26. The evolution of rules of liability in product defect cases is instructive as to what might happen with water pollution. The modern rule of strict liability in tort for product defect cases is generally attributed to *Greenman v. Yuba Power Products*, 59 Cal. 2d 57, 377 P.2d 897 (Sup. Ct., Calif., 1963) and the *Restatement of Torts (2d)*, Sec. 402A. Critics of the rule cannot find a reason why the rule evolved and tend to blame it on antibusiness judges and juries. There is no evidence to support the notion that the court system has become more anti-business in the past two decades than it was in prior years. It is more likely that the rule evolved because technology now allows more safety at a lower price, better evidence about what technology can provide in the way of safety is available in recent years than was the case many decades ago, and, as a wealthier society, we demand more safety.

27. Consider the decade-long pleas by manufacturers to have a federal statutory standard for product defects that would replace the common law of strict liability and the judgments that attend those cases.

28. See Staaf and Yandle 1991. Regarding special interests in the regulatory process, see Meiners and Yandle 1989.

29. *Wood v. Picillo*, 433 A.2d 1244 (1982).

30. 93 *Corpus Juris Secundum* § 52.

31. For a source that encourages environmental actions, and so, if anything, gives more hope than may be justified to would-be plaintiffs, see Jorgensen 1989.

32. The Supreme Court has noted that if the sixty day notice is not given, suit must be dismissed. See *Hallstrom v. Tillamook County*, 110 S.Ct. 304 (1989).

33. Citizens claiming to be injured by a polluter who has exceeded regulatory standards are prohibited from seeking redress under the CWA if the EPA or state

officials are already "diligently prosecuting a civil or criminal action in a court of the United States." CWA §505(b)(1)(B). This might not make much difference in practice since, according to the GAO, "despite widespread significant noncompliance [with water pollution permits], EPA and the states rarely took timely enforcement actions." General Accounting Office 1991a.

34. *Stoddard v. Western Carolina Regional Sewer Authority*, 784 F.2d 1200 (1986).

35. This lack of regulatory enforcement of environmental law is normal according to the GAO. See General Accounting Office 1991b.

36. *Village of Wilsonville v. SCA Services, Inc.*, 426 N.E.2d 824.

References

Anderson, R., L. Hoffman, and M. Rusin. 1990. The Use of Economic Incentive Mechanisms in Environmental Management. Washington, DC: American Petroleum Institute.

Apogee Research, Inc. 1990. *America's Environmental Infrastructure: A Water and Wastewater Investment Study.* (December).

Beck, Robert E., and C. Peter Goplerud III. 1988. *Water Rights.* Charlottesville, VA: Michie Co.

Bosso, Christopher J. 1987. *Pesticides and Politics.* Pittsburgh: University of Pittsburgh Press.

Bovard, James. 1989. *The Farm Fiasco.* San Francisco: ICS Press.

Cook, Brian J. 1988. *Bureaucratic Politics and Regulatory Reform.* New York: Greenwood Press.

Council on Environmental Quality. 1989. *Environmental Trends.* Washington, DC: CEQ, 32-35.

Council on Environmental Quality. 1991. *Environmental Quality, 21st Annual Report.* Washington, DC: U.S. Government Printing Office.

Dales, J. H. 1968. *Pollution, Property and Prices.* Toronto: University of Toronto Press.

Freeman, A. Myrick III. 1990. Water Pollution Policy. In *Public Policies for Environmental Protection*, ed. by Paul R. Portney. Washington, DC: Resources for the Future.

General Accounting Office. 1988. *Improvements Needed in Controlling Major Air Pollution Sources.* Washington, DC: GAO.

General Accounting Office. 1991a. *Observations on the EPA and State Enforcement Under the Clean Water Act.* Washington, DC: GAO/T-REC-91-52.

General Accounting Office. 1991b. *Environmental Enforcement.* Washington, DC: GAO/RECD-91-166 (June).

General Accounting Office. 1991c. *Environmental Protection: Meeting Public Expectations with Limited Resources.* Washington, DC: GAO/RCED-91-97 (June).

Goldfarb, William. 1988. *Water Law.* Chelsea: MI: Lewis Publishers.

Hahn, Robert W., and Roger G. Noll. 1990. Environmental Markets in the Year 2000. *Journal of Risk and Uncertainty* 3: 351-67.

Hahn, Robert W., and Robert Stavins. 1990. Incentive-Based Environmental Regulation. *Ecology Law Quarterly* 18: 1-42.

Hazilla, Michael, and Raymond J. Kopp. 1990. Social Cost of Environmental Quality Regulation: A General Equilibrium Analysis. *Journal of Political Economy* 98: 853-73.

Ingram, Helen M., and Dean E. Mann. 1984. Preserving the Clean Water Act: The Appearance of Environmental Victory. In *Environmental Policy in the 1980s: Reagan's New Agenda*, ed. by Norman J. Vig and Michael E. Kraft. Washington, DC: Congressional Quarterly Press.

Jorgensen, Eric P. 1989. *The Poisoned Well: New Strategies for Groundwater Protection*, ed. by Eric P. Jorgensen. Washington, DC: Sierra Club Legal Defense Fund, Island Press.

Kopp, Raymond J., Paul R. Portney, and Diane DeWitt. 1990. International Comparisons of Environmental Regulation. Discussion Paper QE90-22-REV. Washington, DC: Resources for the Future. (September): 3.

Leone, Robert A., and John E. Jackson. 1981. The Political Economy of Federal Regulatory Activity: The Case of Water-Pollution Control. In *Studies in Public Regulation*, ed. by Gary Fromm. Cambridge: MIT Press.

Magat, Wesley A., Alan J. Krupnick, and Winston Harrington. 1986. *Rules in the Making: A Statistical Analysis of Regulatory Agency Behavior.* Washington, DC: Resources for the Future.

Maloney, Michael T., and Bruce Yandle. 1983. Building Markets for Tradeable Pollution Rights. In *Water Rights*, ed. by Terry L. Anderson. San Francisco: Pacific Institute for Public Policy Research.

Mann, David S. 1991. Polluter Financed Environmentally Beneficial Expenditures. *Environmental Law* 21: 184.

Meiners, Roger E., and Bruce Yandle, eds. 1989. *Regulation and the Reagan Era.* New York: Holmes and Meier.

Staaf, Robert, and Bruce Yandle. 1991. Common Law, Statute Law, and Liability Rules. In *The Economic Consequences of Liability Rules*, ed. by Roger E. Meiners and Bruce Yandle. Westport, CT: Quorum Books.

Stavins, Robert, and Adam Jaffe. 1990. Unintended Impacts of Public Investments on Private Decisions: The Depletion of Forested Wetlands. *American Economic Review* 80 (June): 337-52.

Statement of Richard L. Hembra. 1991. Water Pollution: Issues Concerning State Revolving Loan Fund Program. Presented before the U.S. House of

Representatives Water Resources Subcommittee, Public Works and Transportation Committee (April 17).

Statement of Ron Pacella, President, National Utility Contractors Association. 1991. Presented before the U.S. House of Representatives Water Resources, Public Works and Transportation Committee on Wastewater Treatment Funding (April 17).

Testimony of Association of State and Interstate Water Pollution Control Administrators. 1991. ASIWPCA Clean Water Act Reauthorization Recommendations on Municipal Compliance. Presented before the U.S. Senate Environment Subcommittee (June 12).

Testimony of Edward R. Ossan, National Wildlife Federation. 1991. Before the U.S. Senate Environment and Public Works Subcommittee (June 13).

Tietenberg, Tom. 1988. *Environmental and Natural Resource Economics.* 2nd ed. Glenview, IL: Scott, Foresman and Company.

Yandle, Bruce. 1989. *The Political Limits of Environmental Regulation.* Westport, CT: Quorum Books.

List of Cases

Conner v. Aerovox, Inc., 730 F.2d 835 (1st Cir. 1984) *cert. denied*, 470 U.S. 1050 (1985).

Garland Grain Co. v. D-C Home Owners Improvement Assn., 393 S.W. 2d 635 (Tex. Civ. App., 1965).

Georgia v. Tennessee Copper Co., 206 U.S. 230 (1907).

Greenman v. Yuba Power Products, 59 Cal.2d 57, 377 P.2d 897 (Sup. Ct., Cal. 1963).

Hallstrom v. Tillamook County, 110 S.Ct. 304 (1989).

Hinderlider v. La Plata River & Cherry Creek Ditch Co., 304 U.S. 92 (1938).

Illinois v. Milwaukee, 406 U.S. 91 (1972).

Illinois v. Milwaukee, 731 F.2d 403 (7th Cir. 1984) *cert. denied*, U.S. 1196 (1985).

Missouri v. Illinois, 200 U.S. 496 (1906).

Stoddard v. Western Carolina Regional Sewer Authority, 784 F.2d 1200 (4th Cir. 1986).

Tennessee v. Champion Int'l Corp., 479 U.S. 1061 (1987).

Texas v. Pankey, 444 F.2d 236 (10th Cir. 1971).

U.S. v. Willow River Power Co., 324 U.S. 449 (1945).

Village of Wilsonville v. SCA Services, Inc., 426 N.E.2d 824 (S.Ct., Ill., 1981).

Wood v. Picillo, 443 A.2d 1244 (S.Ct., RI, 1982).

Chapter 5

Superfund: The South Carolina Experience

Brett A. Dalton

Introduction

Congress passed the Comprehensive Environmental Response, Compensation and Liability Act of 1980 (CERCLA), better known today as Superfund, to address the health risks posed by abandoned hazardous waste sites.[1] Following on the heels of the much publicized Love Canal incident in Niagara, NY, there were high expectations that thousands of hazardous waste sites would be cleaned and made safe (Zuesse 1981; Yandle 1989, 108-12). Now, more than ten years later and with billions spent and $11.1 billion more expected to be spent, 84 Superfund sites have been cleaned (*Business Week* 1992). Literally thousands await their turn.

Much has been written on various aspects of the Superfund experience. Economists, legal scholars, policy analysts, and politicians have had plenty to say about the program's weaknesses and failures.[2] But the program continues to operate much as Congress designed it in 1980. Whatever its many flaws and documented ineffectiveness, Superfund seems to have a life of its own.

Unlike previous work on Superfund, this chapter focuses on the experience of one of the 50 states, that of South Carolina, where 23 Superfund sites are in various stages of being analyzed and cleaned. The chapter provides careful documentation of the 23 state sites on the priority list for cleanup. Indeed, some readers may become weary of the level of detail provided. But given Superfund's poor performance record, it is time to provide careful documentation of one state's experience. Failure to properly scrutinize implementation of laws often leads to prolonged error.

In the chapter, details drawn from EPA and other reports provide a picture of the risks posed, the estimated cost of cleanup, and the long slow process that typifies progress toward completion of specific Superfund projects. The chapter begins with a description of how the Superfund process works, explains the steps taken to place a site on EPA's National Priority List, and tells what happens from that point to the point of cleanup. The section that follows gives a description of the 23 South Carolina sites, using verbatim text from reports on file with the South Carolina Department of Health and Environmental Control (DHEC), the state's environmental control agency.

The chapter then turns to a discussion of seven sites that have progressed far enough to have been completely analyzed and approved for actual cleanup. In a few cases, cleanup activity is underway. Finally, after focusing closely on seven sites, their risk assessments, actual and planned expenditures, and their current status, a purely hypothetical but very practical question is raised. If the citizens of the Superfund communities had the funds obligated to Superfund and could use those funds for any other public purpose, would they spend the resources to clean away the designated sites? While the question can be raised, it cannot be answered definitively. Instead, details on current community needs and their costs are provided. The reader is left to weigh and ponder the evidence.

Superfund

An Outline of the Legislation

Stated in simplified terms, the 1980 Superfund legislation established a $1.6 billion cleanup fund for cleanup of hazardous waste sites, most of which were abandoned. Some 86 percent of the Superfund was provided by taxes on certain chemicals and petroleum products; the remainder was drawn from general appropriations.[3] The legislation specified a joint and several strict liability rule for firms and organizations charged with contributing hazardous materials to the sites and contained provisions for treble damages. In effect, any current site owner, past user of a site, firm engaged in moving waste to a site, or previous site operator, though operating legally at the time, can be held fully liable for all cleanup costs.

To become eligible for cleanup, a site must be placed on EPA's National Priority List, which follows an investigation of the relative risks and potential for damage. Once on the list, the site must be cleaned, following EPA-designated methods. The Superfund community has no choice but to go forward. The funds must be spent on cleaning the site. Upon completion, water runoff from a site must meet drinking water standards.

The 1980 legislation specified that at least 400 sites be chosen for the National Priority List, and that at least one site be selected from each of the 50 states, irrespective of relative risk. We note that Superfund contained the usual dose of pork-barrel politics (Bovard 1987). Higher risk sites that might be concentrated geographically were pushed to one side to make room for redistribution of funds.[4]

After operating for five years, Superfund was reauthorized in 1986 by the Superfund Amendments and Reauthorization Act (SARA). SARA increased the trust fund to $8.5 billion, with $2.75 billion in taxes on petroleum, a $2 billion tax on chemicals, $2.5 billion in additional corporate taxes, and $1.25 billion from general revenues. The remainder was to come from interest on the trust fund and recoveries of cost through litigation.

SARA authorized EPA to make early settlements with responsible parties and, if necessary, to apportion some liability. Disappointed with EPA's past cleanup record, which basically showed hardly any completions, Congress mandated a time schedule and the use of technologies that would assure permanent cleanup solutions. In addition, Congress urged EPA to obtain funds through suits against responsible parties and use those funds before tapping the Superfund.

The Superfund Process

An abandoned waste site may begin the long journey through the Superfund process to cleanup when an ordinary citizen calls a public official to express concern about a landfill or any other place where wastes have been stored or disposed. Sometimes public officials are already aware of a site that has troubled local citizens, or a site may emerge after reports of accidental spills or when a polluter reports that hazardous wastes have been stored at a particular location. Some sites have been discovered through tests of groundwater or soil at public landfills. In any number of ways, the EPA or its designated state agency, DHEC in South Carolina, receives notice of a potential problem site. Early in the process, a search begins to identify the potentially responsible parties, who may become liable for cleanup costs.

After a site has been identified, its potential risk is identified by EPA through a structured investigation known as the Preliminary Assessment/Site Inspection. The analysis uses an EPA ranking system that generates a risk index.[5] Any site that has an index above EPA's critical number is then placed on the National Priority List, which means that the site must eventually be cleaned up. However, a costly analysis first must be made to determine just how to proceed.

EPA's site investigation, which is generally conducted by agency contractors, determines the nature and extent of the contamination present at the site. Next, a feasibility study is conducted to determine alternatives that would permanently mitigate pollution and eliminate risk at the site. This study provides details on the costs and predicted results of these alternatives. In some cases, the firms and organizations that operated or used the site may carry out the investigations and studies and go forward with mitigation. In other cases, there is no identifiable party capable or willing to undertake the work.

In any case, a preferred alternative for action at the site emerges from the studies. After that, there will be a period of public comment on the studies and EPA's preferred alternative. Following the comment period, EPA chooses a final remedial plan and makes its decision known to all interested parties. This is when seemingly endless litigation often enters the process. Generally, there is more than one potentially responsible party. Because of the joint and several liability rule, with little chance of apportionment across polluters, each of the "accused" has an incentive to delay and deflect the liability.

With or without litigation there is a period open to negotiation between the EPA and the polluters. During this time, the parties may agree which polluters will carry out and fund cleanup activities, including the cost of the investigation and design of the pollution mitigation program. Once remediation is underway, the process is supervised by EPA or the designated state agency. Following completion of the cleanup, the site will be monitored as long as necessary to ensure the effectiveness and permanence of the remediation.

It is important to remember certain aspects about this process that are difficult to show clearly in a flow chart. For example, emergency cleanup or remediation may occur at any time during the process to ensure public safety and well being. For example, leaky barrels may be removed from a creek bank before a preliminary assessment is ever begun, if the risk posed is sufficiently high.

Superfund in South Carolina

In September 1990, there were 423 candidate sites listed for South Carolina by the EPA. The status of these sites ranges from those where no preliminary assessments have been done, and therefore are not on EPA's priority list for cleanup, to sites that have moved through the process and have almost been completely cleaned. In 1991, there were 23 South Carolina sites that had been assessed and placed on the EPA's National Priority List (NPL). According to statute, each of these sites will be cleaned eventually. The first site in South Carolina to be listed on the NPL was the South Carolina Recycling and Disposal Inc. Bluff Road Site in Columbia. The Para-Chem Southern Inc. site in Simpsonville, added to the NPL in October 1989, is the most recent addition. A list of the 23 South Carolina NPL sites is provided in Table 5.1.

Initial Site Details

A description is provided at the time a site is placed on the National Priority List. We use excerpts from EPA documents to describe the sites.[6]

Table 5.1
South Carolina Hazardous Waste Sites
on the EPA's NPL

Site Name	Town (County)	Date on List
1. Beaunit Corporation	Fountain Inn (Greenville)	June 1988
2. Carolawn, Inc.	Fort Lawn (Chester)	December 1982
3. Elmore Waste Disposal	Greer (Greenville)	June 1988
4. Geiger (C&M Oil)	Rantowles (Charleston)	September 1983
5. Golden Strip Septic Tank Service	Simpsonville (Greenville)	January 1987
6. Helena Chemical Co. Landfill	Fairfax (Allendale)	June 1988
7. Independent Nail Co.	Beaufort (Beaufort)	September 1983
8. Kalama Specialty Chemicals	Beaufort (Beaufort)	September 1983
9. Koppers Company, Inc.	Florence (Florence)	September 1983
10. Leonard Chemical Company, Inc.	Rock Hill (York)	September 1983
11. Lexington County Landfill Area	Cayce (Lexington)	June 1988
12. Medley Farm Drum Dump	Gaffney (Cherokee)	June 1986
13. Palmetto Recycling, Inc.	Columbia (Richland)	January 1987
14. Palmetto Wood Preserving	Dixiana (Lexington)	September 1983
15. Para-Chem Southern, Inc.	Simpsonville (Greenville)	October 1989
16. Rochester Property	Travelers Rest (Greenville)	June 1986
17. Rock Hill Chemical Company	Rock Hill (York)	June 1988
18. Sangamo-Weston Inc.	Pickens (Pickens)	January 1987
19. Savannah River Site (U.S. DOE)	Aiken (Aiken)	July 1989
20. SCRDI Bluff Road	Columbia (Richland)	October 1981
21. SCRDI Dixiana	Cayce (Lexington)	July 1982
22. Townsend Saw Chain Co.	Pontiac (Richland)	June 1988
23. Wamchem Inc.	Burton (Beaufort)	September 1983

1. Beaunit Corporation (Circular Knit & Dyeing Plant), presently BEM Holding Corporation, operated the Circular Knit & Dyeing Plant in Fountain Inn, Greenville County, South Carolina, during 1958-77. An abandoned lagoon used during that time is behind the Wilson Sporting Goods store at 206 Georgia Street. It is approximately 70 feet in diameter and varies in depth with rainfall. Roughly six feet of sludge are on the bottom. No barriers exist around the lagoon. This apparently unlined lagoon was used for treatment of waste from Beaunit's dyeing process.

   In June 1985, DHEC found volatile organic compounds, including 1,1-dichloroethane and 1,1,1-trichloroethane, in the lagoon and the nearby unnamed stream. PCBs and heavy metals, including chromium and lead, were present in soil and sediment at the site.

2. The Carolawn, Inc. site is an abandoned three-acre waste storage and disposal facility located near Fishing Creek, west of Fort Lawn, South Carolina. Several hundred drums of chemical wastes (including acids, bases, organic solvents, and contaminated soil) were stored both outside and inside the site, which is surrounded by a chain-link fence. Also on site was a diked lagoon filled with sludge. Heavy metals, phenols, and numerous volatile organic compounds have been detected. A significant amount of contaminated run-off from the site has migrated into a tributary of the Catawba River, which supplies drinking water for the town of Lugoff. Air contamination affects the nearest homes which are located 100 yards from the site.

3. The Elmore Waste Disposal Site is an open field covering approximately 0.5 acre in a residential area of Greer, Spartanburg County, South Carolina. According to DHEC, drums containing unknown liquid waste were deposited there in 1977. In response to citizen complaints of odors coming from the site, DHEC inspected the site and found an estimated 150 55-gallon drums (some leaking) and a 6,000-gallon buried tank. The liquid waste in the drums was reported to have come from the 1977 cleanup of the Jadco Hughes Facility in Belmont, North Carolina, which was placed on the NPL in June 1986.

   EPA found several organic and inorganic compounds, including 1, 1-dichloroethane, trans-1,2-dichloroethylene, ethylbenzene, xylene, vinyl chloride, lead, and chromium, in on-site soil, sediment, and surface water samples collected in August 1981 and June 1984.

4. The Geiger Site, previously known as the C&M Oil Site, occupies about five acres in the small community of Rantowles, South Carolina. The site, an abandoned waste oil facility, consists of seven unlined pits (each roughly 50

feet wide, 100 feet long, and 1 to 2 feet deep) containing about 35,000 gallons of a waste oil/water mixture. EPA analysis of the mixture indicated the presence of trichloroethane and dimethylbenzene. To the east of the pits is a pond with an outlet to the north. Run-off from the site flows through substantial hardwood swamps and estuarine marshes before emptying into Wallace River.

5. The Golden Strip Septic Tank Service, Inc. site consists of five abandoned lagoons covering two acres on a farm in Greenville County, South Carolina, near Simpsonville. The lagoons are unlined and have no structures to prevent rainfall run-off from leaving the lagoons. Between 1960 and 1975, the company deposited plating wastes and other liquids from nearby industries into the lagoons.

   Data collected by DHEC in 1981 and by EPA in 1984 indicate that chromium, copper, lead, and cadmium are in the water in the unlined lagoons, thus threatening groundwater and surface water in the area. An estimated 1,600 people draw drinking water from springs and private wells within three miles of the site.

6. Helena Chemical Company formulated pesticides in Fairfax, Allendale County, South Carolina, during 1971-78. The company disposed of pesticides and empty pesticide containers in an unlined landfill measuring approximately 100 by 150 by 8 feet. In the spring of 1984, the company removed some of the waste, transported it to an approved hazardous waste facility, and capped the site.

   In March 1985, DHEC detected 2, 4-dichlorophenoxyacetic acid and 2,4,5-TP (also known as Silvex) in shallow on-site monitoring wells. The shallow aquifer is hydraulically connected to the lower aquifer, permitting water to move to the lower aquifer. The lower aquifer provides water to Fairfax municipal wells within three miles of the site that serve approximately 2,200 people. The nearest municipal well is approximately 500 feet from the site.

7. The Independent Nail Company manufactures metallic screws on a site three miles north of Beaufort, Beaufort County, S.C. The company bought the site from Blake and Johnson in 1980. There is a one acre lagoon on the site into which Blake and Johnson placed waste water containing cyanide, chromium, cadmium, lead, nickel, zinc, copper, and iron. When Independent Nail bought the site, it asked Blake and Johnson to investigate the quality of groundwater. In response, Blake and Johnson installed three monitoring wells of intermediate depth. Analyses revealed that groundwater has been impacted by the lagoon. Further tests conducted by the state showed that the contami-

nated groundwater has moved outside of the area covered by the monitoring wells. Surface water has been locally contaminated by the lagoon, but it is not used as a source of drinking water.

8. The Kalama Specialty Chemicals Site covers about 16 acres in a coastal environment in Beaufort, Beaufort County, South Carolina. The company is no longer in business. Its primary product was Krinite, a herbicide. Wastes present on the site include methanol bottoms, laboratory wastes, distillation bottoms, phosphorus oxychloride, phosphorus trichloride, xylene wastes, Krinite wastes, spent oil, and methyl methacrylate. On-site is a lagoon that at one time overflowed into a tile field. In January 1979, an explosion of one of the reactors caused extensive spilling of various organic chemicals. State data indicate that the explosion, as well as the field operation, has contaminated shallow groundwater with lead, benzene, ethylbenzene, and toluene. The site is in the recharge zone of a primary aquifer. State analytical data also indicate surface water is contaminated with the same chemicals.

9. Koppers Company, Inc. treats and preserves wood with creosote and pentachlorophenol on a 20-acre site in Florence, Florence County, South Carolina. The company had numerous difficulties with contaminated run-off. The primary problem at this site, however, is an old evaporation lagoon closed since 1979. It has led to contamination of six of nine monitoring wells on-site, according to company data. The state has detected contamination in private wells off-site. At least 1,200 people use the shallow aquifer for drinking water. Surface water contamination has not been documented to date. In October 1981, the state issued a Consent Order requiring the company to conduct a groundwater study.

10. Leonard Chemical Company, Inc. stored wastes and disposed of process residues on the site. Numerous spills and leaks have occurred, threatening groundwater. The state ordered Leonard Chemical to install three monitoring wells at the site. The company's data indicate low levels of organic contamination in a shallow aquifer. In May 1983, a group of waste generators, in response to a state consent order, retained a contractor to remove surface wastes from the site. The operation was completed in June 1983. However, due to low estimates in the generators' bid proposal, not all of the surface wastes were removed.

11. The Lexington County Landfill Area is a 75-acre sand pit on US 321, two miles south of Cayce, South Carolina. In 1971, the county received a permit to operate the landfill from DHEC. Prior to 1980, local industries were allowed to dispose of wastes at the site. The wastes included asbestos. Adjacent to the county landfill are the old Cayce Dump, which was in

operation during the 1960s, and the old Bray Park Dump, which was an unpermitted dump used prior to 1972.

In 1987, EPA found arsenic, cadmium, mercury, selenium, and 2,4-D in on-site monitoring wells. An estimated 6,200 people obtain drinking water from public and private wells within three miles of the site. A local resident had to abandon a contaminated well that tapped a shallow aquifer. The shallow and deeper aquifers are hydraulically connected; water can move between them. Approximately 250 acres of farmland are irrigated by a well within three miles of the site.

12. The Medley Farm Drum Dump covers seven acres in Gaffney, a rural area Okee County, South Carolina. In about 1973, an unknown person buried about 5,400 drums and dug six lagoons in a clearing in the woods of the Medley Farm. On June 1, 1983, an anonymous caller informed state officials of the site. At the state's request, EPA investigated and found that all the drums were rusted and some had leaked or were leaking. EPA analyses indicated that the drums contained numerous flammable organic liquids, including toluene, benzene, vinyl chloride, and PCBs. The six unlined lagoons held 70,000 gallons of contaminated rain water and tons of sludge. On June 21, 1983, EPA started to clean up the site using CERCLA emergency funds. EPA removed 2,400 yards of contaminated soil and sludge plus the drums and their contents (25,000 gallons of liquids) and transported the materials to a hazardous waste facility regulated under Subtitle C of the Resource Conservation and Recovery Act. The liquids in the lagoons were treated on-site and discharged. The lagoons were then filled in.

Groundwater on and off the site is contaminated with volatile organic chemicals, including chloroform and 1,1,2-trichloroethane, according to tests conducted by DHEC. About 120 people draw drinking water from private wells within three miles of the site.

13. The Palmetto Recycling, Inc. site covers two acres in a rural area in Richland County about eight miles north of Columbia, South Carolina. The site is between US Routes 321 and 21 on the north side of Koon Store Road.

From 1979 to 1982, the company reclaimed lead on the site, primarily from lead acid batteries. In February 1981, DHEC denied the applications of Palmetto Recycling for permits to operate a hazardous waste facility and to transport hazardous wastes. The state alleged that Palmetto had not complied with the current operating permit, and that the facility had improperly treated, transported, and disposed of hazardous wastes. As a result of those denials, Palmetto requested an adjudicatory hearing on March 12, 1981. On June 25, 1981, a state order granted the facility a permit to operate for one year subject to certain conditions.

On February 11, 1983, Palmetto filed a voluntary petition for relief under Chapter Seven of the Federal Bankruptcy Code. DHEC determined that wastes remaining at the site included 1,800 gallons of acid wastes in an unlined 5-foot-deep pit, 100 drums of liquid caustic wastes, and an unstabilized 260-cubic-foot pile of battery casing scraps. In April 1984 fire damaged the roof over the operation, increasing run-off from rain. Subsequently, about 10,000 gallons of contaminated acidic waste were removed from the pit and transported to an EPA approved facility.

In 1983 DHEC detected lead, barium, cadmium, and chromium in on-site soil and in stream sediments both on and off the site. The site is surrounded by numerous lakes, streams, and rivers. The nearest surface water, the North Branch of Crane Creek, is about 1,000 yards east of the site and eventually flows into the Broad River. The creek is used for recreation.

14. Palmetto Wood Preserving occupies about 10 acres in Dixiana, Lexington County, South Carolina. Since about 1980, the company's process of pressure treating lumber has resulted in excess chromated copper arsenate solution being drained to the ground. The shallow aquifer, which supplies drinking water to some one to two thousand people, has been contaminated. The state has detected high levels of chromium in nearby private wells. Surface water contamination has not been documented to date (September 1983).

15. Para-Chem Southern, Inc. has manufactured organic solvents and adhesives on a 100-acre site near Simpsonville, Greenville County, South Carolina, since 1965. The area is rural and sparsely populated.

During 1975-79, over a thousand drums of organic and inorganic wastes were buried in unlined trenches in three parts of the site, according to information the company provided to EPA as required by CERCLA Section 103(C). Waste water from the plant was disposed of in two unlined lagoons until November 1984, when DHEC issued Para-Chem a permit under the Nation Pollutant Discharge Elimination System.

In October 1985, DHEC found manganese and several organic chemicals including chloroform, carbon tetrachloride, and 1,1,1-trichloroethane, in on-site groundwater; carbon tetrachloride and 1,1,2-trichloroethane in off-site groundwater and surface water; and arsenic, barium, manganese, nickel, and zinc in sediments in on-site surface water. Also, 1,1-dichloroethylene, 1,1-dichloroethane, 1,1,1-trichloroethane, 2-butanone, and tetrahydrofuran were found in on-site monitoring wells in tests conducted in July 1987 by a Para-Chem consultant. An estimated 1,500 people obtain drinking water from private wells within three miles of the site, the nearest within one mile.

16. The Rochester Property covers about two acres in Travelers Rest, a rural area in Greenville County, South Carolina. In 1971-72, the property owner permitted liquid industrial wastes containing volatile organic chemicals and arsenic to be buried in four 10-foot deep trenches in what had been farmland.

The wastes came from polymer industries of Greenville, South Carolina, according to DHEC. During an inspection in September 1982, state officials observed wastes seeping out of the ground.

In November 1984, DHEC detected arsenic and volatile organic chemicals, including trichlorofluoromethane, in on-site soils. Site soils are quite permeable. Thus, contaminants can move into groundwater, which occurs at depths of 10 feet and is the source of drinking water for about 1,000 people within three miles of the site. All drinking water is from shallow private wells; no municipal supplies are available.

17. Rock Hill Chemical Company operated a solvent distillation facility in the 1960s on approximately 4.5 acres on North Cherry Road in a light commercial and residential area of Rock Hill, York County, South Carolina. The company distilled paint solvents and reportedly recovered textile dye products. Some of the residue from the bottoms of the storage tanks and drums was placed in piles on the surface and later covered with dirt and construction debris. The facility was abandoned after it burned in 1964. The site is now owned by Rutledge Enterprise and First Federal Savings and Loan.

In an inspection in 1985, EPA discovered above ground tanks, an underground tank, a sludge pile, and an area of discolored soil. EPA analyses revealed lead, PCBs, chromium, methylene chloride, and 1,2-dichloroethane in waste and oil samples and trichloroethylene, 1,2-dichloroethane, trans-1, 2-dichloroethylene, and tetrachloroethylene in an on-site well. An estimated 1,100 people obtain drinking water from wells within three miles of the site. DHEC advised a nearby business to stop using its well. The owner of an adjacent trailer park (approximately 200 residents) hooked the park up to a municipal water system.

In 1986, DHEC detected PCBs and other organic compounds, including trichloroethane and tetrachloroethane, in the unnamed tributary to the Catawba River that drains the site. Fort Mill draws drinking water for an estimated 5,500 people from an intake into the Catawba River that is approximately two miles downstream of the site.

18. The Sangamo-Weston sites are located in Pickens County. As required by CERCLA Section 103(C), Sangamo notified EPA of its disposal of approximately 38,700 cubic yards of PCB waste on its plant site and an undetermined amount in seven satellite dumps, all in the Twelve Mile Creek Basin. Solid, sludge, and liquid wastes were stored or disposed of in piles, landfills, and impoundments. DPA is continuing to search for any additional sources of contamination, and may expand the site if contamination is found to extend further than currently identified. Sangamo-Weston has removed over 17,000 cubic yards of waste from past disposal areas on and off the plant property. These wastes are contained in an EPA-approved landfill on the plant property.

    EPA and DHEC detected PCBs in run-off leaving the Sangamo-Weston Pickens Plant tributaries of Twelve Mile Creek, Lake Hartwell, and the distribution system of the Easley-Central Water Plant, which provides drinking water to 14,500 people. The plant intake is in Twelve Mile Creek. A Clemson University intake in the Twelve Mile Creek arm of Lake Hartwell serves 18,000 students and employees. Since 1977, EPA and DHEC have monitored PCB levels in fish taken from Lake Hartwell. Levels have been declining, although the rate of decline appears to be slowing. After reviewing data from 1983 to early 1986, the Agency for Toxic Substances and Disease Registry said PCBs appear to present no imminent or substantial public health threat in Pickens County.

19. The Savannah River Site (SRS), formerly known as the Savannah River Plant, has produced nuclear materials for national defense on a 192,000 acre site near Aiken in Aiken, Allendale, and Barnwell Counties, South Carolina, since 1951. First operated by the Atomic Energy Commission, it is now operated by the US Department of Energy. The area around SRS is heavily wooded and ranges from dry hilltops to swampland.

    SRS operations generate a variety of radioactive, nonradioactive, and mixed (radioactive and nonradioactive) hazardous wastes. Past and present disposal practices include seepage basins for liquids, pits and piles for solids, and landfills for low-level radioactive wastes.

According to a 1987 US DOE report, shallow groundwater on various parts of the site has been contaminated with volatile organic compounds (degreasing solvents), heavy metals (lead, chromium, mercury, and cadmium), radionuclides (tritium, uranium, fission products, and plutonium), and other miscellaneous chemicals (e.g., nitrates).

Contamination has been found in the A-Area Burning/Rubble Pit, where degreasers and solvents were deposited during 1951-73. In 1985, trichloroethylene was detected in nearby monitoring wells. Soil in the A-Area Miscellaneous Chemical Basin, which reportedly received drums of waste solvents, also contains TCE. The 3,200 residents of Jackson, South Carolina receive drinking water from wells within three miles of hazardous substances on SRS.

A small quantity of depleted uranium was released in January 1984 into Upper Three Runs Creek, according to U.S. DOE. The creek and all other surface water from SRS flow into the Savannah River, which is a major navigable river and forms the southern border between South Carolina and Georgia. Along the banks of the river is a 10,000-acre wetland known as the Savannah River Swamp. A March 1987 U.S. DOE report indicates the swamp is contaminated with chromium, mercury, radium, thorium, and uranium which overflowed from an old seepage basin.

20. The South Carolina Recycling and Disposal, Inc. (SCRDI) Bluff Road site is on State Highway 48 (Bluff Road) about seven miles southeast of downtown Columbia, South Carolina. The property covers about seven acres, of which two acres are actually used for waste storage. About 7,200 drums of toxic, flammable, and reactive wastes are on-site, as well as numerous smaller containers. Two small ponds at the northern end of the site are remnants of lime slurry disposal ponds used by an acetylene manufacturer that once occupied the property. The storage area is partially fenced. Air, groundwater, and surface water are contaminated. In January 1992, this was the top priority site in South Carolina.

21. The South Carolina Recycling and Disposal, Inc. (SCRDI) Dixiana site covers two acres near Cayce, South Carolina. At one time, the site contained over 1,100 drums of materials such as paints, solvents, acids, waste oils, phenols, and dyes. In August 1978, the state filed a suit against the site owners. The resulting court order specified that the site no longer receive wastes and that the wastes on-site be contained. In May 1980, as a result of SCRDI's failure to contain the wastes, a state court found them in contempt, which resulted in the company being placed in receivership. Shortly thereafter, SCRDI removed all drums and some contaminated soil. As a

result of spillage of a dye (a suspected carcinogen), shallow groundwater is contaminated, and the state advised two families living nearby not to use their well water.

22. The Townsend Saw Chain Company site covers over two acres at the intersection of state Route 53 and I-20 in Pontiac, Richland County, South Carolina. Information the company provided EPA, as required by CERCLA Section 103(C), indicates that wastes containing heavy metals and solvents were disposed of at the site. During 1969-81, the company discharged large amounts of chromium waste onto the ground.

A July 1985 DHEC investigation revealed elevated levels of cadmium and chromium in groundwater at the site. Also, a surface water sample near a spring at the site contained high levels of chromium and volatile organic chemicals, including 1,1-dichloroethane, tetrachloroethylene, 1,1,1-tri-chloro-ethane, and trichloroethylene.

Private wells within three miles of the site provide drinking water to an estimated 1,400 people. The nearest well is less than 0.4 mile from the site. A private well near the site was closed in 1981-82 and the home connected to the public water system.

23. Until the late 1970s, Wamchem, Inc., synthesized organic chemicals and formulated color concentrates on 200 acres in Burton, Beaufort County, South Carolina. It disposed of its wastes (including phenols, lead, cadmium and solvents) in an evaporation lagoon. Then it switched to spraying its wastes onto two fields. State monitoring of wells on-site has detected lead, chromium, toluene, dichloronitroethane, and benzene. Some one to two thousand people get drinking water from the shallow aquifer within three miles of the site. Surface water is contaminated with the same chemicals but it does not supply drinking water at this time.

An In-Depth Examination of Selected Sites

Based on their status in the Superfund process, seven sites provide a basis for in-depth discussion. In each case, either the risk analysis and feasibility studies is complete or there are draft reports with enough detail to provide a fairly complete picture. EPA documents and conversations with DHEC officials provide the basis for the discussion. The Superfund history is traced for each site, and, in each case, a site description and discussion of the health risk assessment are provided. Following that, selected cleanup methods and their cost estimates are given. A current status report concludes the discussion of each site.

The Bluff Road Site

The Superfund History. According to EPA and state environmental officials, the Bluff Road Site is South Carolina's top priority site for cleanup. It ranked eighty-third of some 1,200 sites nationwide on the EPA's National Priority List. Consider the time it took for the site to reach the point for permanent cleanup activity to occur. According to EPA records, this site came to their attention in November 1979. The preliminary assessment was completed on February 1, 1980, and the site investigation was completed on November 1, 1984. The remediation plan was completed on October 19, 1989, almost five years after the site investigation was concluded. The feasibility study was completed in March of 1990. In sum, the trip from first notice to completion of plans for action took more than 10 years.

As of July 1991, work had not begun at the site. In short, the site has been studied, researched, litigated, and discussed for over 11 years without receiving any permanent cleaning as mandated by Superfund. Currently, the site is being prepared to receive remediation since EPA, DHEC, and the Bluff Road Group have settled on the methods for cleanup. The design of the work to be conducted at Bluff Road is expected to be completed around January of 1992.

The Bluff Road site has several features that merit and allow for close consideration. At the time of this study, the site was the top priority site in the state. In 1992 it was in a more advanced stage in the Superfund process than are most SC sites. The information available on the Bluff Road Site enables a closer examination of the parties who may be liable for the cost of cleanup. More precise estimates of the expenditures at this site can also be provided, including litigation costs and the cost to carry out EPA mandates and studies.

The Bluff Road site is located in Richland County about 10 miles south of Columbia, South Carolina, which is the state capital. The site encompasses about seven acres with just over two acres that were used for actual chemical disposal. Half the site is cleared of trees and vegetation; the other half is heavily wooded.

During the early 1970s, the site, which includes two lagoons, was used by an acetylene manufacturer. One lagoon contains lime, and the other lagoon contains lime sludge covered with about six inches of surface water. The lagoons seem to hold the only remnant of wastes left by the acetylene manufacturer.

In 1975 the site became the property of Columbia Organic Chemicals. A subsidiary of Columbia Organic Chemicals, South Carolina Recycling and Disposal Inc., used the site to store, recycle, and dispose of chemical wastes. The operation was closed in 1982 after tests of soil and groundwater conditions were conducted by EPA and DHEC in 1980 and 1981.

In 1982 and 1983, partial cleanup of the site was performed to limit further contamination. About 7,500 leaking drums were removed from the site, along with contaminated buildings and some visibly contaminated soil. Clean soil and gravel, brought from outside, replaced the excavated soil. The lagoons were left undisturbed.

A remedial investigation of the Bluff Road site was initiated in 1984 by Golder Associates under the direction of DHEC. The report was never completed, and there were some problems with the accuracy of the tests that were conducted. For these reasons, International Technology Corporation of Knoxville, Tennessee, began work on a second phase investigation, which was completed in October 1989.

International Technology was under contract with a subset of the potentially responsible parties known as the Bluff Road Group. As of December 1991, only the members of the Bluff Road Group have spent funds on cleanup, study, or planning with regard to the Superfund process at Bluff Road. However, other parties are being pursued to contribute to the cost of cleanup and design at the site.

The potential scope of the enforcement liability and settlement process can be seen by considering the number of potentially responsible parties at a given site. There are at least 288 such parties at Bluff Road, which indicates how complex the problem of hazardous waste remediation has become. Some of the polluters are agencies dedicated to improving the environment and public health and welfare. The U.S. EPA is ranked twentieth in amount of pollution disposed at the site. It is now negotiating with itself. In addition, DHEC is listed as a responsible party for pollution at the site. The two agencies that are responsible for enforcing Superfund are targets of their own enforcement. Despite their contributions, both EPA and DHEC are immune from prosecution.

A number of hospitals, as well as the Medical University of South Carolina, are being held liable for pollution at Bluff Road. In addition, the National Centers for Disease Control, which investigate the health effects of Superfund sites, are on the list as contributors to the waste at the Bluff Road site. The list of parties and their rankings, as established by DHEC, according to the volume of waste contributed are shown in Table 5.2. The names there suggest there are no obvious "white" and "black hats" in the lineup. Everyone, it seems, contributes to the pollution problem.

The Risk and Remediation Analysis. To understand the nature of the pollution contributed by these organizations, consider the scientific evidence of health risk and pollution at Bluff Road. The evidence reported here is taken from the Bluff Road technical reports prepared by IT Corporation. The data used to determine the nature and extent of pollution were gathered from groundwater, surface water, and soil samples.

In all, 23 monitoring wells were drilled, 29 soil borings were collected, and 39 surface soil samples were studied, along with numerous surface water, lagoon water and sediment samples. According to field investigations, the soil at the drum staging areas is contaminated by organic chemicals to a depth of three feet.

Table 5.2
The Bluff Road Potentially Responsible Parties
(Ranked by Volume of Waste Contributed)

Potentially Responsible Party	Rank
Warner Robbins Air Force Base	8
U.S. EPA	20
Centers for Disease Control, Atlanta	NA
University of Georgia	31
Georgia Institute of Technology	33
Charleston Air Force Base	39
West Virginia University	41
University of South Carolina	57
Fort Bragg	62
University of Louisville	77
University of North Carolina	90
Medical University of South Carolina	93
Georgia State University	97
Marshall University	102
St. Joseph's Hospital	111
Presbyterian College	113
Furman University	116
NC State University	117
Dreher High School	154
Erskine College	157
S.C. DHEC	189

The soil at the South Carolina Recycling and Disposal Incorporated (SCRDI) Site is contaminated with organics to a depth of 11 feet. There is no contamination of the deep water aquifer underlying the Bluff Road Site. There was no significant contamination found in the surface water drainage system or in the air samples. The shallow water aquifer, which is not used as a source of drinking water, showed limited contamination coming from the contaminated soil and the lagoons. Regardless of the pollution, according to the studies, the water in the area is not considered a good source of potable water. Myers Creek, which flows near the site, shows no contamination.

Current and future use scenarios were developed in the studies to determine the health risks posed by the site. At the time of the studies and since, the Bluff Road Site has been fenced and access is restricted. There have been no reports or observances of trespassing. The fact that the area is restricted, fenced, and the knowledge that the area may be hazardous has resulted in the area being undisturbed. Little if any human contact has been made with soil contamination at the site. Health officials indicate there are no trespassers to ingest the soil or to play in the contaminated lagoons. Furthermore, since there is no runoff contamination to Myers Creek, there is no exposure to people by this path. As mentioned, no one draws drinking water from the shallow water aquifer, and regulatory restraints could be employed to ensure that the aquifer is not used in the future.

Under the current use scenario reported in the remediation analysis, the only possible way for an individual to become exposed to carcinogens at the site would be for hunters and fishermen to consume wildlife, which contained concentrated levels of residual carcinogens they had ingested at the site. Under the current use scenario analyzed, a deer hunter was assumed to have consumed deer and fish at meals twice a week for a 70-year lifetime. The analysis assumed that all of the deer and fish eaten by this person came from wildlife living on or passing through the site. The assumption is farfetched, to say the least, since the waste disposal site encompasses only two acres. Further, the two acres are basically cleared of vegetation and therefore provide no food for deer or other wildlife.[7]

Even with these extreme assumptions, the estimated levels of public health or environmental risk associated with the chemicals at the site are negligible.

Following the development of the current use scenario, the contractor's analysis developed a future use scenario as required by the EPA that contains certain EPA-required assumptions. As the contractor's report to EPA put it:

> It should be stressed that these scenarios are *hypothetical* in nature with little likelihood of occurring.... They have been developed and evaluated at the agency's request to complete the intent of the agency's guidance documents for the conduct of an RI at a CERCLA site.... For the hypothetical future use scenarios, there appear to be concentrations of site-related chemicals in the shallow aquifer that may result in unacceptable levels of exposure *only* if all the health protective assumptions of the scenario are realized. (Remedial Investigation Report SCRDI, 1989, 6-3)

Despite effective fencing, the isolated location, and the absence of detectable trespassing, the RI is mandated to assume that children will use the area as a shortcut and as a playground. EPA also requires that the area be considered a common area for adult trespassers. Even under these assumptions, the pollutants at the site "do not present a potential risk to the health of potential adult or child trespassers on the site" (Remedial Investigation Report 1989, 6-4).

The official analysis of the site also assumed that the contaminated shallow aquifer would discharge into Myers Creek. Under this assumption, there was still no significant increase in the threat to either wildlife or humans. To meet the mandates of the EPA, the analysts included in its future use scenario the development of the area into a residential neighborhood in which inhabitants took their drinking water directly from the contaminated portion of the shallow water aquifer. Under this assumption, there was a significant increase in the incremental cancer risk faced by those drinking from the shallow aquifer.

An incremental increase in the lifetime cancer risk is an important term that is the basis for deciding whether a site needs certain cleanup activity. The IT Corporation report explained the excess standard this way:

> In weighing acceptable residential exposures to potentially carcinogenic compounds, an acceptable level of risk must be determined. Cancer is a significant cause of death in the United States with a background incidence of about three in 10 (280,000 cases in a population of 1,000,000) (American Cancer Society 1988). Approximately 80 percent of these cases result in death directly attributable to the disease. Incremental lifetime cancer risk (also referred to as excess cancer risk) is defined as the estimated increased risk that occurs over an assumed average life span of 70 years (EPA, 1986) as the result of exposure to a specific known carcinogen. Thus, an incremental lifetime cancer risk of one in a million (one x 10^{-6}) may be interpreted as an increase in the baseline cancer incidence from 280,000 per million population to 280,001 per million population.

> Based on the scientific evidence and the regulatory precedence of the acceptable risk ranges set for exposures to carcinogens in drinking water and at Superfund site cleanups, rigid adherence to an incremental lifetime cancer risk of one in a million (one x 10^{-6}) was shown to be clearly unwarranted in the exposure scenario developed in the current risk assessment. A more reasonable approach for a residential exposure scenario that maintains a level of health protection compatible with the rural environment surrounding the SCRDI site would be to use an incremental lifetime cancer risk of one in ten thousand (one x 10^{-4}). This implies that if 10,000 people were to be located in the zone of impact of the SCRDI site, one additional cancer occurrence might be predicted. (Remedial Investigation Report 1989, 6-4)

The risks are calculated based on individuals being exposed to selected carcinogens for a 70-year lifetime.[8] It is also assumed that all 10,000 people would be exposed to the maximum contaminate concentrations found on-site. For instance all 10,000 people would have to drink from the most contaminated well at the site every day for a 70-year lifetime to incur the risk of seeing one additional case of cancer during this 70-year period. The analysis assumes implicitly that if 10,000 people lived directly on the two-acre site for a 70-year lifetime, and they obtained their drinking water from the most contaminated shallow water aquifer, and they ingested the most contaminated soil, and inhaled the most contaminated dust, one additional case of cancer above the background levels could be predicted.[9] Understanding the incremental increase in lifetime cancer risk helps us better understand what can trigger a multimillion dollar cleanup.

Since the Bluff Road Site was already on the NPL, some cleanup activity was mandated. As a result of the analysis that showed an incremental increase in the lifetime cancer risk from drinking from the shallow aquifer, certain cleanup methods would now be thrust to the front. Alluding to the unrealistic scenarios that resulted in an increased incremental lifetime cancer risk and the resulting cleanup mandates, the authors of the EPA assessment stated that "the assumptions used in this assessment were health- and environmental-protective, and estimations of potential doses to both humans and wildlife were much greater than any potential exposures."[10]

Cleanup Alternatives and Their Costs. After completing the site analysis, IT Corporation developed a response to the pollution at the Bluff Road site, which included alternatives for remedial activity, their corresponding costs, and their advantages and disadvantages (Feasibility Study Report, 1990). The response analysis indicated that site contamination was limited to the soil at the site ranging in depth from 3 to 11 feet. In addition, the shallow aquifer, ranging in depth from 10-15 feet below the surface, is contaminated. The contractor estimated about 263 million gallons of water to be cleaned, about 28,000 to 45,000 yards of contaminated to be removed or treated. According to EPA mandates, the cleanup methods must provide permanent solutions and comply with all relevant statutory preferences for treatment. We summarize the alternatives and the estimate of costs provided in the analysis.

Groundwater Alternatives:

1. No Action: This alternative is required by statute to be examined as a reference point for other alternatives. This option would not attempt to actively remove pollution, it would rely on the natural forces of nature and natures renewing powers to cleanse itself. In addition, it would employ institutional controls to limit risk to individuals. For example, the option would require fences, deed restrictions, and limit access to the site. It would also involve sampling and monitoring of conditions. Estimated present value of all costs: $760,000.

2. Groundwater Extraction and Liquid Phase Carbon Adsorption: This alternative basically involves a complex method of pumping and filtering groundwater. Pollutants are contained and destroyed during the filtering. The estimated time for the completion of this process is 15.03 years. Estimated present value of all costs: $16,105,000.

3. Groundwater Extraction and Air Stripping with Off-gas Control by Vapor Phase Carbon Adsorption: This process is very similar to the previous

method. The estimated time for completion is again 15.03 years. Estimated present value of all costs: $4,339,500.

4. Subsurface Injection. Estimated present value of all costs: $250,000.

5. Discharge to Myers Creek. Estimated present value of all costs: $422,136.

6. Discharge to the Congaree River. Estimated present value of all costs: $3,321,069.

7. Spray Irrigation. Estimated present value of all costs: $452,685.

Treatment Alternatives for Contaminated Soil:

1. In-situ Soil Venting with Vapor Phase Activated Carbon Emissions Control: This would lower the toxicity of the soil by removing volatile organics which are the major pollutants at Bluff Road. The estimated time required to complete this project is 18 months. Capital cost: $1,070,000.

2. Soils Incineration: This process of soil incineration would remove contaminants from the soil at a rate of 20 tons of soil per minute. After decontamination the soil could be replaced. The total time to complete this type of cleanup would be one year. Capital cost: $28,260,000.

3. Thermal Desorption: This is a similar process to incineration. This process would take less than one year to complete. Capital cost: $18,250,000.

4. Soil Excavation and Off-site Disposal: This alternative would involve removing the contaminated soil, transporting it to an RCRA approved disposal facility, and disposing of it. The removed soil would be replaced, including a one foot layer of topsoil. This process would take four months to complete. Capital cost: $20,700,000.

5. Soil Excavation and Off-site Thermal Treatment: This combination of treatment alternatives would take four months to complete. Capital cost: $100,000,000.

In deciding on a remedial plan the EPA, state health officials and the group held liable for the cost of cleanup negotiated the methods to be used. Public notice and participation is a part of the decision process. Initially the EPA seemed firm on the choice of thermal desorption for treating the contaminated soil. This would have cost approximately $19,000,000. The chosen alternative for dealing with groundwater contamination was a combination of groundwater treatment alternatives three and four with a revised total cost of $4,500,000 to $5,000,000. After much negotiation, the EPA along with DHEC agreed to allow the Bluff Road Group to remediate the soil contamination with a new process known as in-situ soil vacuum adsorption at a cost of $1,070,000. This flexibility was granted by DHEC for research and development purposes. If the EPA is unsatisfied with the method, the process will be stopped and one of the other methods may again be chosen.

Despite the anticipated cost savings from this new technology, the total estimated cost of cleaning the three acres of contaminated soil and the underlying groundwater is estimated to be $7,000,000.[11]

The Estimated Bluff Road Expenditures. At $7,000,000, the cleanup of the Bluff Road site is well below the $29 million national average for Superfund site cleanup.[12] However, the Bluff Road estimate does not include the legal fees that are incurred during litigation. Nor are the costs of the engineering and remedial investigations included. Litigation costs, which can continue long after cleanup has begun, often exceed cleanup costs by severalfold. At the Bluff Road Superfund site, we learned "certain potentially responsible parties at the Bluff Road Site paid costs of $3,787,994 for a Remedial Investigation and Feasibility Study and related response costs at the site."[13] These potentially responsible parties are now in the process of suing several hundred other polluters at the site for their share of the cleanup and site investigation costs.

The Carolawn Site

The Superfund History. The Carolawn site is located in Chester County, three miles west of Fort Lawn, South Carolina. The total area of the site consists of 82 acres of wooded land; the three most polluted acres are contained with a fence. Since the outset of its Superfund history, which began in 1970, the property has been owned and managed by a number of different companies and individuals. From 1970-73, Carolawn was owned and used by the Southeastern Pollution Control Company (SEPCO) as a storage facility. The firm went bankrupt in 1974. In 1975, the Columbia Organic Chemical Company (COCC) received the property as payment for cleanup services provided to SEPCO. The entire site was maintained by a subsidiary of COCC until 1978, when the three acre fenced parcel of land was sold to the Carolawn Company, which hoped to construct and operate a waste incineration facility at the site. Their incinerator plans never progressed beyond a test burn at the facility. All evidence indicates that Carolawn never contributed waste to the site. In 1980 Carolawn went bankrupt.

Site investigations began in 1977. Between 1980 and 1981 federal money was allocated to remove some leaking drums, soil, and other wastes. In 1985, four nearby residents who obtained drinking water from underground wells were provided an alternate source of drinking water. During earlier tests, one of the four wells had been shown to be contaminated with volatile organic compounds. In 1984 the site was placed on the EPA's NPL. Following this, a remedial investigation was started in 1985. Due to incomplete data, additional testing was requested by the EPA. A second phase investigation was completed in February, 1989. The final draft report, completed in May 1989, provides details on the riskiness of the site.[14]

The Remediation Studies and Current Status. According to test results, the volatile organic contaminants methylene chloride and acetone are found in surface and subsurface soils at Carolawn. However, the report indicates that trace amounts of these chemicals were likely introduced in the testing process. They were not the result of polluting activities when the site was operated. The report explains that there is some groundwater contamination, which includes heavy metals that occur naturally in the area. The only contaminants found in the surface water were introduced by activities in the test laboratory where the water was tested. The report states: "The results of the Public Health Evaluation indicated that for present conditions there is no significant adverse impact to human health and the environment" (Revised Draft Report for Carolawn 1989).

Since four local residents who might have been affected by the groundwater now receive water from a municipal water system, there is no current human contact with the contaminants. However, the contractor, following EPA guidelines, obtained a higher risk outcome in the future use scenario. The analysts assumed the site would be developed for a residential community where all the residents are offered but refuse municipally supplied water. The new residents dig their own wells, and by choice, drink water from the contaminated aquifer. Under this set of assumptions, the report indicates that "the predicted exposure point concentrations would be unacceptable for human consumption based on total increased additional lifetime cancer risk" (Revised Draft Report for Carolawn 1989).

Since adverse health effects are possible under this unlikely hypothetical set of assumptions, the remedial design activity must address the pollution of groundwater. The recommended alternative action for this site was groundwater extraction, biological treatment, and discharge to an area creek. The estimated cost for this remedy is just over $1,000,000. However, South Carolina officials refused to accept the proposed remedy, indicating that the cleanup needed to include the acreage outside of the fenced portion of the site. As a result of the state's refusal to sign a release, litigation between the potentially responsible parties started a second time. It is conceivable that the entire investigation process could start over, with a new risk assessment and feasibility study to be conducted on the 82 acres outside the fence. It also is conceivable that the site will be tied up for years in litigation before this happens. Now, some 15 years since the first test, the future of the Carolawn site is still uncertain.

The SCRDI Dixiana Site

The Superfund History. The SCRDI Dixiana Site is located in Lexington County in the community of Dixiana, South Carolina. The site consists of two acres with a metal warehouse located near the center. The ground is sparsely covered by weeds and other vegetation, but the area has been disturbed due to previous waste disposal activities and the removal of some soil in previous cleanup activities. The two acres are surrounded by undeveloped forest.

In 1978 the site was leased from GMT Associates by SCRDI for storage of wastes that were required by court order to be removed from another site in Richland County. During the summer of 1978, SCRDI was refused a waste management permit by state health officials. Later that same summer, the state filed a suit to prevent any further storage of wastes at the site due to the poor handling and management practices. The court issued an order banning further storage at the site and requiring the removal of all wastes from the site. Chemicals stored in barrels were to be taken to the Bluff Road site to be disposed of by 1980. Visibly contaminated soil was transported to a facility in Pinewood, S.C., for treatment.

Basically, the site was used for less than two years to store wastes that DHEC and the courts had required SCRDI to remove from another site in the state. The stored wastes included paints, solvents, phenols, acids, oils, and dyes.

After demanding that the Dixiana site not be used for further disposal activities, and following the removal of the drummed wastes and the visibly contaminated soil, state health officials began investigations in 1980 to determine the extent of site contamination. At this point, the site still had not come to EPA's attention. In July 1982, the site was placed on the EPA's priority list. Investigations continued through the formation of a remediation analysis in 1986.

According to the earliest tests and the remediation study, a blue dye spill, which contaminated groundwater, was one of the chief concerns. Subsequent testing of the dye revealed it to be Food Drug and Cosmetic (FD&C) Blue 1, which is permanently permitted for use as a food dye in the U.S. The testing revealed no contamination of surface water or runoff, or of groundwater discharged from the site.

In addition to the spillage of FD&C Blue 1, tests revealed that "surface and subsurface soils are relatively clean as a result of the clean-up activities conducted in 1980. Current levels of contamination do not present an excessive risk from either dermal contact or ingestion of contaminated soils."[15] Tests revealed that there was some contamination of shallow groundwater aquifers. However, under current use scenarios this posed no excess risk of cancer or other illness to the small number of nearby residents who receive their drinking water from the City of Cayce municipal water system.

Under realistic future use scenarios, any new residents would also receive their water from the municipal source. However, to satisfy the EPA future use scenarios, risk must be calculated according to the assumption that the area directly on the hazardous waste site would be developed and that all residents would receive drinking water from contaminated on-site monitoring wells or wells nearby. Under this purely hypothetical set of assumptions, there is a possibility that the risk of contracting cancer might be increased. These results are best summarized in the conclusion of the report: "The only way that the site, as it exists today, could affect anyone is if the groundwater were to be used directly from the monitoring wells or the two nearest residential wells. This includes both ingestion and inhalation of volatiles in the groundwater. This activity would have to occur over an entire lifetime in order to present a significant risk."[16]

The remediation plan for the Dixiana site contained several alternatives for handling the contaminated soil that included capping the surface and various excavation and replanting approaches. These costs ranged from $31,000 to $162,000. The estimates for groundwater remediation were considerably higher. The cost of pumping and treating the groundwater and then recharging with clean water ranged from $1,700,000 to $2,000,000.

Current Status. Cleanup of Dixiana started in 1991, 13 years after the first site investigation. In 1992, the site was linked to a municipal sewer system; the initial steps toward groundwater pumping and treatment were being taken. Commenting on the flow of water from the site to the city sewer, a state health official stated: "The city sewer system is getting some awfully clean water."[17] The cost of consultant studies combined with the expected cleanup costs total $2,000,000 to $3,000,000.

The Independent Nail Site

The Superfund History. The Independent Nail site is located in Beaufort County, South Carolina, some three miles northwest of the town of Beaufort.[18] The site is immediately across from the air bases operated by the U.S. Air Force and Marine Corps. From 1969 until 1980, the site was used by the firm of Blake and Johnson in the manufacture of screws and fasteners. During that time, approximately 33,000 gallons of wastewater were pumped daily into unlined lagoons. Independent Nail Company purchased the property in the summer of 1980. From all reports, Independent Nail never contributed pollution to the site.

The documented pollution history of the site began in 1975 when waste from one of the lagoons leaked into a drainage ditch. State health officials then initiated groundwater testing.[19] The 1975 tests detected levels of lead, mercury, chromium, and iron that exceed drinking water standards. Subsequent 1980 tests found evidence of chromium and lead. The Independent Nail site was added to the national priority list in September 1983. Further 1985 tests revealed absolutely no contamination or elevated levels of metals or volatile compounds at the site. Soil tests indicated surface contamination in the lagoon and in two areas about 500 feet outside the lagoon.

The site risk assessment made the assumption that on-site workers would be exposed to carcinogens by eating and breathing certain daily doses over their entire employment lifetimes. Even with that assumption, the report indicated "that cumulative exposure ... would not pose health risks" (Remedial Investigation Report for Independent Nail 1987, 35). An even more extreme assumption was required to cross the risk threshold. In effect, the same person would have to ingest contaminated soil 250 times a year over a 70-year lifetime or that the same person would inhale contaminated air 250 days a year for 70 years (Remedial Investigation Report for Independent Nail 1987).

Current Status. Contamination at the Independent Nail site was confined to surface soil; there was no evidence of contaminated groundwater. The recommended remediation called for treatment of the soil and replanting at an estimated cost of $2,000,000. In 1991 when data was gathered on this site and some 16 years after the first soil tests, cleanup activity had still not started.

The Palmetto Wood Preserving Site

Superfund History. The Palmetto Wood Preserving site consists of approximately five acres, near the town of Dixiana, South Carolina, where a wood pressure treating facility operated from 1963 to 1985. The pressure treating process utilized three water-based solutions: a Fluoride-Chromium-Arsenic-Phenol solution, an Acid-Copper-Chromium solution, and a Chromate-Copper-Arsenate solution. Lumber to be treated was shuttled by narrow gauge rail car into a pressure vessel where it was treated with the solutions. The lumber was air dried in either a drip shed or in the lumber yard. The resulting pressure-treated wood is commonly used in patios, decks, boat docks, and other outdoor recreational structures exposed to weathering.

The documented pollution history at the site appears to have begun in the latter months of 1981. During this time, neighbors of the treatment plant complained about a greenish runoff from the site that was puddling on their land. In February of 1982, state health officials visited the site to investigate. Soil samples were gathered from the site, and groundwater samples were collected from nearby wells. The tests revealed no contamination of groundwater. Two of the three soil samples revealed elevated levels of chromium, one of the substances used to preserve the lumber. Because of this, DHEC declared the soil as a hazardous waste. Later in 1982, a local resident filed another complaint about the same runoff. This complaint resulted in the wood treatment firm being issued a notice of violation.

The next major occurrence near the site served as the main catalyst for major action against the firm. In 1983 a resident near the plant was drilling a new well and encountered yellowish water that did not clear after hours of pumping. The water samples revealed high levels of chromium in the water. Because of the findings of these tests, state health officials ordered the firm to conduct tests at the site and to begin a remedial plan to clean up the site. This evolved into EPA taking responsibility for the site and placing it on the Superfund list in September 1983. Follow-up tests indicated that the initial chromium found in the well was probably the result of vandalism, not pollution from the wood treatment plant.[20]

Consultant studies completed in 1985 reported arsenic, chromium, and copper contaminations at several site locations. Almost all shallow and deep wells on the site were found to have elevated levels of at least one contaminant. However, migration from the site appeared to be no problem. Wells of nearby residents were found to be clean.

Making the now familiar assumptions for current and future use, the risk analysts found an incremental increase in lifetime cancer risk. Again, ingestion of soil and breathing contaminated dust was the principal path to humans. In this case, the risk analysis addressed exposure of workers in a nearby pallet factory and assumed the site would be developed for industrial use, and workers would ingest the soil and breath concentrations of harmful waste raised by high winds. The risk analysis described the following hypothetical situation.

Potential human receptors include workers at the nearby pallet company, which is located immediately to the south of the site. (At least four residences are located within 200 meters of the site.) Workers at the pallet company work outdoors or in partially enclosed tin sheds, and therefore could be exposed to contaminated dust over much of the time they spend at work. Thus, exposure for these individuals will conservatively be assumed to be eight hours per day, 200 days per year, over a 30-year period of employment. Nearby residents could spend essentially all their time in the general vicinity of the site; thus, the period of exposure for nearby residents will be considered to be 365 days per year, over an entire lifetime of 70 years.... In the absence of institutional restrictions, the PWP site could possibly be redeveloped as an industrial facility at some time in the future. However, workers on site would not generally be expected to be exposed for longer time periods or to higher concentrations of dust than the pallet workers discussed above. (Final Remedial Investigation Report for Palmetto Wood Preserving 1989)

We call attention here to the mention of an "absence of institutional restrictions," which is an implied assumption in all the risk analyses we reviewed. The presence of zoning ordinance, the standard requirement for permits for drilling wells and operating water systems, and the operation of common law liability are assumed away. In other words, the standard EPA analysis makes the extraordinary assumption of writing off the rules adopted by communities to control environmental risks.

A number of alternatives were adopted for the cleanup. Although there was no groundwater risk reported, the cost of remediation action for groundwater contamination, depending on the technique applied, ranges from $2,483,000 to $975,000. The soil remediation treatment costs start at a low of $980,000 for capping the site and range as high as $9,258,000 for excavation and off-site disposal.

Current Status. At the time this site was reviewed, in July 1991, the site was in the design stage. A $4,000,000 combination has been chosen for treating the soil and cleaning the groundwater. Unlike the other sites we have discussed, the Palmetto Wood Preserving site has progressed from first complaint to the final design phase in less than 10 years.

The Sangamo-Weston Site

Superfund Background. The Sangamo-Weston Superfund site is actually seven different sites scattered through Pickens County in upstate South Carolina. One of these is the location of the Sangamo-Weston plant facility, which borders on the city limits of the town of Pickens. The six remaining sites are within a three mile radius of the plant.

The Sangamo-Weston plant was built in 1955 for the purpose of manufacturing electrolytic capacitors. PCBs were a standard component of the product. Indeed, government specifications required their use. The firm discontinued the use of PCBs in June 1977, just prior to a 1978 federal PCB ban.

In the earlier years of PCB use, long before the insulating fluid was recognized as a carcinogen, the firm disposed of PCB waste materials at on-site landfills; other waste was sent to public landfills. There is also some indication that PCB waste liquids were packed and shipped to the producer, Monsanto Chemical Company, for final disposal. Given research findings leading to the ban on PCB, the Sangamo site moved to EPA's priority list with little difficulty. Evidence of PCB contamination was found at all seven sites.

In the investigation of Sangamo-Weston, the plant site itself was listed as having the more significant problems. A wastewater stabilization lagoon, two related disposal basins, and the on-site landfill were the principal items of concern. Soils were found to be contaminated with capacitor debris and solvents.

Along with PCBs, trichloroethane, and tetrachloroethane, aluminum hydroxide sludge was detected in the landfill. Groundwater was not found to be contaminated by PCBs except in the immediate area of the firm's wastewater treatment facility and in two isolated areas at the plant site. However, volatile organic compounds were found in groundwater samples. Similar contaminants were found in the six related Sangamo sites. Again, there was no significant contamination of ground or surface water, nor was there evidence of migration from the six sites.

Sufficiently high risk was found in the investigation of the site to go forward with cleanup. As with the other sites discussed, ingestion of contaminated soil and water from contaminated wells over a 70-year lifetime was enough to cross the threshold.

Current Status. Because of difficulties confronted with disposing of PCBs, the cost of cleanup is considerably higher than that of the other sites we have discussed. They range from $5.1 to $271 million, depending on the approach taken. In 1991, thermal separation was chosen as the process for dealing with the contaminated soil, while the groundwater was to be pumped and treated. The least cost estimate for the two procedures totals $50 million.

The Wamchem Site

The Superfund Process. The Wamchem site is located about seven miles northwest of the city of Beaufort, South Carolina, on a small island in the middle of a salt marsh, where a dye research and manufacturing plant operated from 1950 to 1981. The plant was closed in 1982. In 1983, the site was added to EPA's priority list.

Investigations of the Wamchem site began around 1975, but these studies were crude and incomplete. In the early 1980s, investigations identified benzene and its variations as the chief contaminant.[21] In this case, contamination was found in the water table aquifer below the site. However, the site investigation indicated that the contaminated underwater plume was confined to its current location and would not migrate to a deeper more extensive aquifer. Soil and lagoon contamination was also identified, with the highest concentration found in waste disposal lagoons and in a former holding pond. The final consultant's report indicated that in spite of the contamination noted, "the Wamchem site is not currently a threat to human health or the environment" (Remedial Investigation of Wachem 1983, 7-2). However, this assessment was based on current use.

As noted before, the future use risk assessment requires extreme assumptions. In this case, it was assumed that individuals would live on the small island and ingest contaminated soil and water from the shallow water table, again over a 70-year lifetime. A marginal increase in cancer is associated with the future use scenario. Again, institutional restraints, such as zoning, government ownership that prohibits development, and rules of liability are assumed away.

Nine alternatives were considered for cleaning the site. Alternative costs range from as low as $210,000 for no action to a high of $9,500,000 for on-site treatment of soil and groundwater. Soil excavation, removal, and off-site disposal and pumping and monitoring of ground water were the recommended procedure. The cost estimate for remediation ranged from $322,000 to $749,000.

Current Status. At present, the groundwater at Wamchem is being cleaned. The soil is not being treated. The expected cost of the action is $1.3 million.[22]

Cost and Choice

Entry on EPA's priority listing means that a Superfund site will be cleaned. There is no turning back. On its face, the logic seems faultless. After all, acceptance of a site by EPA comes at considerable cost and after long delays. If a site is truly hazardous to human health, action is called for. But there is more to consider. Communities of people often confront a range of hazards they wish to overcome. Sometimes the hazard relates to environmental quality, narrowly construed, the sort of thing Superfund can handle. Other hazards relate to educational opportunity for children, the availability of sewage disposal systems and drinking water, and low levels of health care that lead to high infant mortality rates. In other words, if a community of people were given a bank account that had to be spent on a range of activities targeted to improve their collective welfare, would the community spend all the money on a Superfund site? That is the larger question to consider.

Some Other Needs

Consider Richland County, the location of the Bluff Road site. Richland is one of the state's wealthier counties.[23] Per capita income is 113 percent of the state average and 89 percent of the national average. Fewer than two percent of the houses lack complete plumbing, and the infant mortality rate is 15.1 per 1,000 births. Richland County has a good public health system, but the county has considerable public education needs. Their newest school was built in 1979; others, 40 to 50 years old, are in need of extensive repair, renovation, and expansion. The estimated cost of upgrading facilities comes to around $110 million. There are questions regarding the likelihood of the citizens supporting a facility improvement bond issue.

In Chester County, the location of the Carolawn site, there is a very different situation. Per capita income is 65 percent of the national average. Transfer payments make up about 20 percent of the county's personal income. According to the 1980 Census, 16.1 percent of the population had incomes below the poverty level. Almost half of these were below the age of 18. The infant mortality rate is 16 per 1,000 births. Aside from the low income problem and all it entails, Chester County has some of the poorest school facilities in the state. Each school has on average 10 portable classrooms. Some have built outdoor restrooms in order to expand space for classrooms. The county has been informed that it will lose accreditation if new facilities are not built. With plans to build several elementary schools, one middle school, and to expand the county high school, the school system needs $22 million. County voters rejected a bond issue referendum in 1991.

Lexington County, the location of the Dixiana and Palmetto Wood Preserving sites, is a populous county with relatively high income. There are no severe school needs. Their need for public facilities focuses on water supply. By the year 2005, the county projects a deficit of 3.9 million gallons a day. At present, the county needs $3.8 million to expand its water supply services.

Beaufort County, where the Wamchem, Independent Nail, and Kalama sites are located, has some of the wealthiest and poorest people in the state. Some 17 percent of the population has below poverty income. While school facilities are adequate, there are other needs faced by people in the county. Recent budget cuts eliminated part of the school system's cadre of social workers, reduced the provision of services by public health nurses, and eliminated the possibility of having a roving physician to provide preventative medical care to lower income people in rural areas. An additional $2.1 million would restore those services. The county also expects to run short of water by the year 2005. Some $2.2 million in capital funds are needed to expand the water system.

The Sangamo-Weston Superfund site, which involves six locations, is in Pickens County, located in the fast growing industrial upstate of South Carolina. Incomes there are just above the state average; 10.7 percent of the population had below poverty level incomes in 1980.

Pickens County needs additional school facilities and water supply. Currently, four elementary schools are scheduled for additions; three high schools are slated for renovation; and new science wings are needed at two high schools. The total price tag for these educational needs comes to $31 million. The county water system is running near capacity. Some $6.5 million is needed to meet projected demand.

What If Superfund Money Were Transferable?

The money spent on Superfund sites comes from the American people. The remediation funds spent by private firms are recovered in the form of higher priced products or lower payments to investors. The taxes that feed the Superfund, paid by chemical and petroleum firms, lead to higher prices. And of course, the general revenues that supplement Superfund come directly from taxpayers.

The funds earmarked for a particular community appear to be "costless" to the receiving community. To them, the cost of removing an ugly waste dump, even with little risk, is zero. At that price, the quantity demanded is large. Superfund incentives say that the number of the sites will always exceed the revenues available for cleanup.

But what if the receiving community obtained a cash balance and could then decide on the alternative uses and alternative remediation approaches? Instead of selecting the more costly cleanup option, like excavation and remote incineration of soils, the community might cap the site, fence it, and post guards. These actions could be combined with institutional restraints where zoning and permit restrictions could forbid residential construction and deny the right to drill wells. What would the community do with the savings?

If a magic wand were waved, and the people so decided, Pickens County could transform part of the Superfund expenditures and pay for its school system needs. Beaufort County could expand its public health program and its water supply system. The possibilities for Chester County are unknown, since the Superfund process there has not identified a cleanup method and cost.

To carry the mental experiment one step further, suppose each state were responsible for cleaning their own abandoned waste sites and there was no federal bureaucracy involved. Suppose further that the state had identified the approaches found in this report, and that the state had identified the community needs reported here. Would the state spend $57 million now estimated for Superfund cleanup and offer nothing to help the counties fund their $222 million in other needs? Or would the state husband the cleanup money and offer something to improve education, water supply, and health care in the affected communities?

Final Thoughts

This chapter has focused on South Carolina's Superfund experience. In developing this microview of one of the nation's more ambitious environmental programs, some things were learned that should be emphasized.

• The South Carolina Superfund experience is much like that of the nation as a whole; the state is typical. The state has one-fiftieth of the sites in the nation. As with other sites across the country, progress toward cleanup has been extremely slow, filled with litigation, and frustrated by bureaucratic concerns. Although some of the sites discussed have been identified for more than a decade, not one site had been cleaned when this study was completed.

• The science of Superfund analysis contains extreme assumptions. The future scenarios assume there are no community land-use controls, nothing to keep an unsuspecting citizen from building a home on a waste dump or drinking water from a monitoring well. Perhaps the assumptions are influenced by Love Canal and the apparent failure of public officials to protect citizens from building homes on the closed waste lagoons of Hooker Chemical Company, which the city had purchased.[24] Covenants and restrictions in the deeds were disregarded or lost. The city failed to protect public health.

• Even when extreme future-use assumptions are made, the risk of excess cancer is low for many of the surveyed sites. In some cases, like the Bluff Road site, it seems inconceivable that the assumptions for ingesting wastes could ever be met.

• The joint and several liability rule, with weak allowances for apportionment of damages, leads to protracted litigation and delays in cleanup, which would be funded by parties to a Superfund site, if a mechanism for gaining agreement and apportionment were developed and enforced.

Taking the Environment Seriously

There are no research findings that argue strongly in favor of Superfund. It is a program that does not work. If we are to take the environment seriously, the program has to change, or be wiped off the books. Which will it be? The results of this inquiry indicate the federal program cannot be salvaged. Cleanup of hazardous waste sites is logically the business of communities, counties, and rarely, the joint endeavors of adjacent states. There is no national interest to be satisfied by clearing away contaminated soil in Pickens, South Carolina, or at any other isolated site. The logic for Superfund is primarily political, not economic. The program is perfect for pork barrel politics. Politicians can promise something to the folks at home, like highways and dams years ago, and deliver what seems a costless package of benefits. The environmentalists support programs that reduce environmental risks, even when the risks are small. And firms that wrote environmental hazard insurance that cannot fund the liability claims coming later, welcome a substitute source for cleanup money. Clearly a coalition of interests is present to maintain the status quo. Otherwise, the program would go away, or at least be reduced in scope.

People who truly care about the environment and the health effects that spring from hazardous waste disposal want programs that work effectively. Ten to 15 years is too long to wait for cleanup, if risks to human health are present. And the alternative costs of protecting a community from a hazardous waste site has to be considered. After all, the use of lower-cost alternatives means that more sites can be cleaned. But cost effectiveness does not occur in a vacuum. It is a result of purposeful human action, where ordinary people find solutions for problems that matter to them and then participate in the completion and funding of projects. Once these responsibilities are shifted to hired bureaucrats incentives go awry.

After completing the research on which this chapter is based, we conclude that hazardous waste problems are community problems. If sites are abandoned and the previous operators are bankrupt, there is only one reason to go after firms that operated legally by contracting to have their waste products moved to disposal sites. The logic is simple. If someone can afford to pay, find a way to make them. But this says little for society that seeks to operate under rules of law. In a similar way, it makes no sense to hold current owners of a site liable for actions of a previous owner, unless the purpose is simply to get money.

Truly hazardous and abandoned waste sites should be cleaned, if the exposed community determines it is in their interests to do so. The exposed community, be it town, county, or state, can then decide how best to resolve and pay for such programs, using ordinary tax revenues. Ideally, the community that gets the collective benefit of risk reduction should pay. In other words, what is now Superfund should become a local public works program, a program that competes with others developed by people to provide services they value. When a hazardous waste site actually threatens a significant portion of the nation's people, then federal emergency action is called for. If we truly care about the environmental effects of abandoned hazardous waste, Superfund will become an abandoned federal program.

Notes

1. For background, see *Environmental Law Handbook* 1985.
2. For a sampling, see Huber 1988; Rea 1982; *Natural Resources and Environment* 1985; Florio 1986; and General Accounting Office 1987.
3. Background is found in *Environmental Law Handbook* 1985; Rea 1982; Huber 1987; Florio 1986; and Survey and Investigations Staff 1988.
4. For a review of related research on this point, see Yandle 1989c.
5. EPA uses the number 28.5 as the threshold index for entering the National Priority List. The number, which has no meaning outside the analysis and does not give a direct reading of risk, is interesting for one reason: it emerged early on as the value that generated the 400 sites required by Congress. A higher or lower number would have created either too few or too many sites. See Bovard 1987.
6. The descriptions here were provided by Mr. Kirk Lucius, Freedom of Information Coordinator, Atlanta Regional Office, U.S. EPA.
7. In the Columbia area, the most productive deer land yields 50 deer per square mile. If the two contaminated acres were wooded, covered with lush vegetation, and accessible to deer they could sustain one-seventh of a deer. Hence, the most radical assumptions of bioaccumulation make the health hazard an extremely remote and unlikely possibility. Bioaccumulation normally results in pollutant accumulation in the internal organs and fatty tissue of a deer, both of which are rarely eaten by hunters. The current use scenario does not presume deer would be fenced out of the area. Even assuming the worst case scenario, the lifetime incremental increase in risk of cancer was still not significant enough to call for cleanup action.
8. According to the EPA's National Contingency Plan, which sets forth the guidelines and mandates to be followed when conducting Superfund site assessments, an increase in the incremental incidence of cancer of one in one million may be unacceptable. The range of unacceptable increases may be as high as one in 10,000. When performing a Superfund assessment, the investigator must go to extreme measures to justify the risk level that is selected by EPA. (Conversation with James Dee, IT Corporation, Knoxville, TN.)
9. This interpretation is based on conversation with James Dee, IT Corporation, Knoxville, TN, September 5, 1991.
10. Ibid.
11. The cost includes administrative costs as well as the specific remediation costs provided above. (Based on conversation with Richard Haynes, DHEC manager of the Bluff Road project.)
12. Data for the national average were provided by the American International Group, Washington, DC; correspondence from Jan M. Edelstein, March 29, 1991.

13. This information was provided by the law firm of Edwards & Angell, New York, with the permission of the unnamed clients. Legal costs are not included.
14. Carolawn Steering Committee 1989. On file with DHEC, Columbia, SC.
15. *Draft Feasibility Study for the SCRDI Dixianna Site* 1986, ES-4. On file with DHEC, Columbia, SC.
16. *Remedial Investigation Report, Vol. 1, SCRDI Dixiana Site* 1986, 6-31—6-32. (On file with DHEC, Columbia, SC.)
17. Telephone conversation, August 1991.
18. The discussion here is drawn from U.S. EPA 1987, on file with DHEC, Columbia, SC.
19. This discussion is based on U.S. Environmental Protection Agency 1987, on file with DHEC, Columbia, SC.
20. See *Final Remedial Investigation Report for Palmetto Wood Preserving Site, Dixiana, South Carolina* 1987, 1-8. On file with DHEC, Columbia, SC.
21. The discussion here is based on *Remedial Investigation of Wamchem Site* 1983. The report is on file with DHEC, Columbia, SC.
22. Based on conversation with Gil Trentanovie, Wamchem project manager for DHEC, August 12, 1991.
23. The discussions in the section draw from a number of sources including U.S. Census data; conversations with U.S. Department of Commerce officials, who provided the most recent income and population data; and conversations with and reports provided by county officials. We will not provide detailed citations for the many items included here.
24. On this, see Yandle 1989a; Zuesse 1981; and Rea 1982.

References

Bovard, James. 1987. The Real Superfund Scandal. *Cato Policy Analysis, No. 89.* Washington, DC: CATO Institute, August.
Business Week. 1992. The Toxic Mess Called Superfund. (May 11): 32.
Carolawn Steering Committee. 1989. *Revised Draft Report of the Carolawn Feasibility Study,* October.
Draft Feasibility Study for the SCRDI Dixianna Site. 1986. (May): ES-4.
Environmental Law Handbook. 1985. Rockville, MD: Government Institute, Inc.
Feasibility Study Report, SCRDI-Bluff Road Site. 1990. Knoxville, TN: IT Corporation, March.
Final Remedial Investigation Report for Palmetto Wood Preserving Site, Dixianna, South Carolina. 1987. (January): 1-8.
Florio, James J. 1986. Congress as Reluctant Regulators: Hazardous Waste Policy in the 1980s. *Yale Journal on Regulation* 3 (Spring): 351-82.

General Accounting Office. 1987. *Hazardous Waste: Issues Surrounding Insurance Availability*. Washington, DC: GAP/RCED-88-2 (October).

Huber, Peter. 1987. The Environmental Liability Dilemma. *CPCU Journal* (December): 206-16.

_____. 1988. Environmental Hazards and Liability Law. In *Liability Perspectives and Policy*, edited by Robert E. Litan and Clifford Winston. Washington, DC: The Brookings Institution, 128-54.

Natural Resources and Environment. 1985. Superfund: A Game of Chance. 1 Fall (symposium issue).

Rea, Raymond A. 1982. Hazardous Waste Pollution: The Need for a Different Statutory Approach. *Environmental Law* 12: 443-67.

Remedial Investigation Report, SCRDI-Bluff Road Site. 1989. Knoxville, TN: IT Corporation (October): 6-3.

Remedial Investigation Report, Vol. 1, SCRDI-Dixianna Site. 1986. Draft R-34-1-6-140H (March): 6-31—6-32.

Remedial Investigation of Wamchem Site. 1983.

Survey and Investigations Staff. 1988. A Report to the Committee on Appropriations, U.S. House of Representatives, on the Status of the Environmental Protection Agency's Superfund Program, March.

U.S. Environmental Protection Agency. 1987. *First Operable Unit, Remedial Investigation Report for the Independent Nail Co., Beaufort, SC*, June 8.

Yandle, Bruce. 1989a. Can Superfund's Fatal Flaws Be Fixed? *National Environmental Enforcement Journal* 4 (October): 3-10.

_____. 1989b. *The Political Limits of Environmental Regulation*. New York: Quorum Books.

_____. 1989c. Taxation, Political Action and Superfund. *CATO Journal* 8 (Winter): 751-64.

Zuesse, Eric. 1981. Love Canal: The Truth Seeps Out. *Reason* (February): 17-3

Chapter 6

Acid Rain and the Clean Air Act: Lessons in Damage Control

David W. Riggs

Introduction

For more than two decades, acid rain has been a hobgoblin of air pollution control. It is presumably caused by sulfur dioxide (SO_2) and nitrogen oxide (NO_x) emissions that are transported, mixed to form acid, and then deposited far away from the source. The two high volume pollutants are common to a wide assortment of industrial and mobile sources that burn fossil fuels. Coal-burning electric utilities are the chief source.

The 1970 Clean Air Act (CAA) addressed SO_2 and NO_x as criteria pollutants to be controlled, and established related National Ambient Air Quality Standards to be achieved nationwide. The 1977 CAA tightened the standards, and in one of the most controversial and expensive regulatory episodes to date set costly technology-based standards to be met by coal-fired electric utilities, even where clean fuels were burned (Ackerman and Hassler 1981). Prevention of damage from acid rain was given as a principal reason for the tough regulatory action.

While legislation was certain, the scientific basis for linking SO_2 to acid rain was unclear. The extent to which acid rain caused damage to forests, lakes, agricultural land, man-made structures and people, was even more speculative. Finally, science had its day in court. In 1980, Congress passed legislation to fund an extensive investigation of acid rain. Some $500 million was appropriated and spent for the purpose, and a ten year research project commenced.

Just at the time the acid rain study was being completed, Congress was debating the 1990 CAA, which again contained more severe SO_2 controls, also based implicitly on the assumption of acid rain damage. Well before the final vote on the 1990 CAA, a preliminary acid rain report was released (National Acid Precipitation Assessment Program, 1990b). To the amazement of many, the NAPAP research found little basis for stiff SO_2 controls, at least with respect to acid rain. With the strong of several scientific pens, the foundation for federal control of SO_2 emissions was shaken. Nonetheless, Congress passed the law with even more strict acid rain standards intact, and the president signed it. In a word, the scientific study was disregarded.

This chapter focuses on the acid rain controversy as it relates to electric public utilities and the 1990 CAA. A review of the acid rain controversy and the actions taken to control SO_2 and NO_X raises a number of important questions. First, what can we say about acid rain? Just how significant are the damages? The first major section of the chapter summarizes elements of scientific findings that relate to these questions. Next, how does the 1990 CAA address SO_2? Are there special features in the law that might explain the reluctance of Congress to abandon the SO_2 control framework? Section three focuses on the 1990 CAA and features of special interest. Section four looks closely at the major industries affected by the acid rain portion of the Clean Air Act, putting some dimensions on the relative magnitude of impact. Still, an important question remains: Why might Congress choose to legislate in spite of contrary scientific findings? This central point is discussed in section five. A short summary concludes the chapter.

The Scientific Evidence

Chemistry and the NAPAP Study

The chemistry of acid rain may be defined as follows: Acid rain is a complex chemical and atmospheric phenomenon that results from the oxidation of sulfur dioxides (SO_2) and nitrogen oxides (NO_x). These compounds are transformed by chemical processes in the atmosphere, often far from their point of origin, and return to the earth in either wet or dry form. In 1980, Congress created the National Acid Precipitation Assessment Program (NAPAP), with a $500 million authorization, to assess acidic deposition damages.[1] Ten years later, the program found virtually no effect on agricultural output, forest devastation was limited to high-elevation mountaintops, and damage to exposed objects such as statues was negligible. Furthermore, it was difficult to measure and decipher whether utility companies, automobiles, or industry were responsible for the emissions (National Acid Precipitation Assessment Program 1990c). Although the program made significant advances in our knowledge of acid rain, it leaves unanswered many scientific and ecological questions.

Certainties do exist, however. There is little controversy regarding evidence that the acidic component of the atmosphere in the northeastern region of the country has risen significantly over the last 20 years. Consistent monitoring and measuring of acid levels in the region indicate that rise. In some Northeastern lakes, pH values were found to average 4.1.[2]

On a worldwide basis, it is estimated that half the sulfur in the atmosphere is a result of natural phenomena (volcanic eruptions and decomposition in bogs and marshes), but in the northeast United States it is estimated that only one percent of sulfur in the atmosphere results from natural processes (Harrington 1989). Two inferences can be drawn: (1) the rainfall in the northeastern region of the country is more acidic than it was in the recent past and (2) the increase in acidity is partly due to human activity.

The Apparent State of Knowledge

Scientific controversy clouds the second conclusion: Given the man-made SO_2 and NO_x acid precursors, where do they originate? Most of science and politics have pointed to the Midwest as the primary source of acid causing agents, but neither is 100 percent conclusive.[3] Controversy lingers over sources that are located near acid rain "damaged" sites and those that are farther away, e.g., the Midwest. Uncertainties with regard to meteorological processes are at the root of the problem. Specifically, "maritime tropical" conditions that bring moist, warm air from the Gulf of Mexico through the Midwest up to the Northeastern region, and "continental polar" conditions which move across Canada and into the Northeast United States are considered to be the conditions responsible for acidic particulate transportation. However, studies of trace elements such as vanadium (an element found mostly in fuel oil rather than coal), primarily emitted by New England utilities, reveal high concentrations in the Northeast, thus implicating local causation of acid deposition (Harrington 1989, 5-6).

The extent of acid-induced damage to ecosystems is another unsettled question. The most discussed ecological effect of acid rain is damage to lakes and streams. The EPA reports that "up to 15 percent of medium and large lakes (greater than 10 acres) are chronically acidic due primarily to acid rain; more than 25 percent of small lakes (2 to 10 acres) in the Adirondacks are likewise chronically acidic due largely to acid rain" (Helme and Neme 1991). In contrast, the survey by the aforementioned ten year federally funded study found only 240 out of 7,000 lakes (about 3.5 percent) in the Northeast region were chronically acidic (having a pH of 5.0 or lower). The controversy at hand is not between the discrepancy of figures in two reports—it is obvious that some lakes in the region are acidic beyond what is acceptable to maintain biotic life—but rather to what extent the acidity is attributable to man-made or natural phenomena.

Lakes in the affected region are in naturally acidic watersheds. The surrounding rocks are poor in limelike buffering substances, and the forest floors are very thick, peaty, and highly acidic because the soil provides a low nutrient environment, which, by the way, is ideal for acid-producing vegetation like sphagnum mosses (Krug 1990). NAPAP found that historically this region has always been acidic. Fossil organisms and chemicals buried in lake sediments indicate that fish have not lived in these lakes for most of their history.[4] These findings are consistent with Indian and European settlement records, which stated the waters were cold and unproductive (Krug 1990).

Another supposed impact of acid rain is damage to high-elevation red spruce forests in the Northeast region. In a survey conducted by NAPAP, damage to red spruce forests in the area was indicated. However, these forests make up only one percent of the total forests in the region, and the influence of acid rain was uncertain. This study concluded that other stress factors such as the prolonged drought during the 1960s and other pollutants, notably ozone, are also implicated in the forest depletion.

The effects of acid rain on agricultural productivity are better understood. Acidity could increase tenfold from current levels and still have no significant effect on the growth of crops (Kulp, 1990). Indeed there is little evidence to link acid deposition and damage to forests and crops: "Laboratory experiments suggest that neither trees nor agricultural crops are very sensitive to acid deposition until pH falls below 3" (Harrington 1989, 8).

There is also concern about the effects acid deposition might have on human health. Generally, acid rain affects health two ways: through contamination of water supply systems and by downwind derivatives of sulfur dioxides, known as acid aerosols. A higher than normal acidity in water can lead to toxic ions being leached from the soil and contaminating the drinking water supply. The inhalation of acid aerosols can lead to bronchitis in children and decreased lung function in adults, particularly asthmatics. The extent of health damages from acid rain is unknown, however, since quantification of any damages has yet to be collected.

A final area of concern is the reduced visibility that has been associated with acid rain. Sulfur dioxide has been recognized as a major contributor to regional haze and has been given a great deal of attention at the Grand Canyon and Virginia's Shenandoah Valley. But, again, due to meteorological uncertainty and the fact that damages have not been quantified, it is difficult to assess aesthetic impacts.

Summarizing What We Know

J. Laurence Kulp, who was the director of research of NAPAP, summarized the effects of acid rain in the following statement:

Acid rain has had demonstrable negative effects only on surface waters and atmospheric visibility ... little or no negative effects up to the present on the forests of the U.S., with the possible exception that it may, to a small degree, reduce the frost hardiness of red spruce in a narrow elevational band in the Northeast.... With the data at hand, it seems doubtful that acid rain will be shown to play a significant role in reducing the expected life of building materials. Researchers have hypothesized that acid rain has direct and indirect effects on health, but studies have not quantified these effects. (Kulp 1990)

Furthermore, Kulp concludes that benefits from acid rain reductions would, at best, be small. The most significant benefit would be to restore biotic health to a few lakes in the Adirondack area. The economic benefit from such action is estimated to lie in the range of $1 to $13 million, approximately one-tenth the cost of *one* electro-static precipitator (scrubber), which removes SO_2 and other pollutants from emissions.

In spite of the studies that have been done, a number of items of scientific uncertainty remain. These include:

- The source of acid rain and the extent to which the acidity in the atmosphere results from nature or man's activity (If man's activity, is it autos, coal-fired utilities, other industry or what?);

- Damage to red-spruce forests (How much is due to droughts or ozone?);

- Unquantified health effects, either through drinking water or downwind acid aerosols; and

- Visibility (To what extent does SO_2 contribute to haze?)

In the face of these uncertainties, Congress moved forward with even more stringent and costly legislation.

The 1990 Acid Deposition Control Law

Paying for Cleaner Air

Approximately $90 billion is spent per year by American consumers to cover the cost of environmental rules enforced by the Environmental Protection Agency. Of that $90 billion, $30 billion (approximately one percent of GNP) results from air pollution control efforts (Portney 1990). While consumers ultimately bear these costs, they are first imposed on products, such as autos, or on polluting industries. Some industries produce little air pollution and pass along small price increases to consumers. Other heavy polluters incur high costs and pass along larger price increases. Air pollution control expenditures cause changes in relative prices. Some products, such as steel, have a larger component of pollution control cost than others, such as shirts.

The Differential Effects

Since the federal rules are more or less uniform across industries, one gets the impression that there are few intra-industry effects. All firms face the same standard and meet it with the same stipulated technology. But that impression is incorrect. Firms in industries use different production techniques, have differing economies of scale and scope, and confront different levels of input pollution, which they must clean up. As a result, smaller firms generally suffer more than larger ones when meeting uniform standards; firms with low-polluting technologies suffer little, even when they are small. In short, uniform standards impose differential costs in an industry.

Electric Utilities: The Major Target

The electric utility industry bears the brunt of air pollution control.[5] But the producers in the industry are far from homogeneous. Some utilities are newer and cleaner than others. Some use low polluting natural gas or low sulfur coal technologies. Others use nuclear energy which has no SO_2 or NO_X emissions. Still others generate power from hydro sources. In addition, some are small; others are large.

Title IV of the CAA starts with a mandate to reduce the total amount of SO_2 emitted by all polluters, including electric utilities, by 10 million tons per year and also reduce NO_x by 2 million tons per year, from 1980 levels.[6] The aggregate constraint to be met has two phases. Phase I mandates controls to begin January 1, 1995, for plants emitting at a rate above 2.5 and 0.45 pounds per million British thermal units (lbs/mmbtu) of SO_2 and NO_x, respectively. Phase II begins January 1, 2000, with a total emissions cap of 8.9 million tons of SO_2 nationwide with mandates for plants to further reduce the emissions rate of SO_2 to 1.2 lbs/mmbtu.

Electric utilities are responsible for 67 percent of the total SO_2 emitted in the United States (National Coal Association 1989). Thus, Title IV of the 1990 CAA has an inordinate impact on the electric utility industry. Title IV establishes a market based approach for power plants to achieve clean air, i.e., tradable emission allowances. The tradable allowances goal is to allow utilities to meet standards at the lowest cost, or at least a lower cost, than previous legislation sanctioned.

Under the 1990 CAA, the EPA will allocate allowances during each phase, with each allowance permitting utilities to emit one ton of SO_2. The allowances are fully marketable, meaning utilities can trade allowances internally within their system and/or externally with other affected sources. Each utility must acquire enough allowances to authorize its emissions or face a $2,000/ton excess emissions fee and an additional requirement to offset excess tons in future years.[7] Phase I offers up to 3.5 million incentive allowances to high-sulfur coal plants that make reductions below a 1.2 lbs/mmbtu rate. Furthermore, during Phase I, an additional 200,000 annual SO_2 allowances are allocated to plants in Ohio, Illinois, and Indiana. During Phase II, an additional 50,000 allowances are allocated to ten midwestern plants. In addition, the EPA will hold special sales and auctions to enhance trading of allowances. The law does not allow trading for NO_x.[8]

While there are obvious redistribution effects associated with the special allowances for midwest utilities, the allowance system creates a cost-effective method for achieving the given standards. Consider two utilities, each allocated a certain number of allowances (one allowance = one ton of SO_2 annually) based on their 1985-87 emissions levels. Assume that both utilities are currently emitting above that level and that allowances are selling for $750 each. Furthermore, assume Company X can reduce one ton of SO_2 at half the cost of Company Y, $500 and $1000 respectively, due to economies of scale and/or superior clean coal technology efforts. It is in Company Y's best interest to purchase allowances. For Company X, the incentives exist to reduce emissions and sell allowances. Consequently, Company X better utilizes its technology. For Company Y, the cost of purchasing allowances from Company X is cheaper than attaining compliance on its own.[9]

Until the 1990 CAA, command-and-control regulation was the centerpiece of air pollution control. Practically speaking, coal-fired utilities were required to install scrubbers for the purpose of removing SO_2 and other pollutants from their emissions. Fuel switching was strongly discouraged; indeed the law required scrubbers irrespective of the sulfur content of coal. Cost effectiveness was hardly a goal of previous legislation.[10]

Tradeable emission allowances effectively endow property rights to existing utilities for an approved level of emission. Though the CAA specifically states that the allowances are not property rights, they will be treated as such. They are objects of mutually agreed upon contracts that can be enforced in a court of law. Expenditures on them will affect financial statements and allowed rates of return. But notice the effect of the endowment. Existing firms obtain wealth in the form of the new "property." Newly entering firms will be required to purchase allowances from members of the original emissions "club."[11] By endowing the new rights to existing firms and requiring new entrants to purchase rights, the 1990 CAA effectively maintained the regulatory cartel formed by earlier legislation.

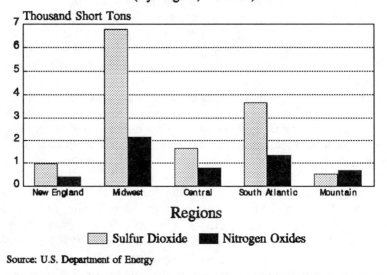

Figure 6.1 of text below:

Emissions from Electric Utilities
(By Region, for 1989)

Figure 6.1 Emissions of Electric Utilities by Region

The Effects of Acid Rain Legislation

The Electric Utilities

The first effects of the 1990 CAA can best be seen by considering the electric utility industry itself. Ten states, mostly midwestern, account for 51 percent of total SO_2 emissions and 65 percent of SO_2 emissions from utilities (Stuntz 1990). As the graph above illustrates, in 1989, the Midwest was responsible for a much larger proportion of emissions than any other region. The fact that emission tonnage is high in these states does not relate to a lack of past control efforts. Indeed, it is just the opposite. The midwest utilities produce clean electricity; it is just that they produce large amounts of it, and because of the features of the 1977 CAA generally burn high sulfur coal. In fact, the midwest is a major exporter of electricity to other regions. States like West Virginia, with little heavy industry, produce large amounts of electricity from ample coal supplies and wheel the electricity to eastern customers.

Given that the CAA speaks to tons of SO_2 to be reduced, it goes without saying that high tonnage producers will have to reduce more tons than low tonnage producers. It is not immediately clear that a large producer would bear a heavier proportional cleanup cost than a low tonnage producer. However, since the midwestern utilities already have a low SO_2 load per KW/hr. of electricity produced, they will inevitably encounter rising marginal costs. As indicated earlier midwest producers have received extra reduction allowances, so the owners of the utilities have reason to celebrate the redistribution from Washington. That is not the case for their customers.

The expected price effects are shown in Table 6.1, which shows the average electric bill by state for the heavily affected states, the national average electric bill, and the anticipated percent increase in electric rates due to the CAA. The ten states listed account for the majority of SO_2 and NO_x emissions in the country. Notice the position of West Virginia, Ohio and Pennsylvania, three major producers of high sulfur coal, electricity, and SO_2. With the exception of West Virginia, their current electricity rates are higher than the national average, and future rate increases are severalfold higher for all three states. The anticipated nationwide increase from the 1990 CAA in electricity rates is estimated in the 1-2 percent range. From all indications, the CAA allocation of emission allowances favored the owners of electric utilities, while the cleanup burden falls inevitably on the shoulders of the consumers.

Table 6.1 Future Percent Increases in Midwest Electric Rates

	$/Month	2000 High-Low	2005 High-Low
Kentucky	39.81	3.5-3.1	3.4-3.9
Tennessee	43.01	2.2-2.2	2.4-2.4
West Virginia	47.11	5.6-5.1	5.4-4.8
Georgia	49.49	1.8-1.5	1.5-3.0
Alabama	49.79	1.1-1.1	0.9-1.2
Illinois	50.89	0.8-0.1	1.4-2.9
Missouri	52.39	4.4-3.9	3.9-4.5
Indiana	58.49	3.8-3.6	4.0-3.8
Ohio	61.09	4.1-3.5	4.3-3.2
Pennsylvania	63.09	1.5-1.5	2.0-1.6
National Average	57.39	1.5-1.2	1.7-1.8

Source: U.S. Department of Energy

Coal and Coal-Carrying Railroads

In 1989, electric utilities consumed 766 million short tons of coal, an 86 percent share of total coal production. In 1965, western coal accounted for 5 percent of total coal production. By 1989, this had increased to 39 percent. The increase is attributable to environmental preference for use of the West's low-sulfur coal and the higher average productivity that surface mining in the West provides (Energy Information Administration 1990).

The graph below displays coal production bisected into east and west regions of the country. The years 1991 through 2010 are forecast estimates provided by the National Coal Association (National Coal Association 1989). Western coal production is expected to surpass eastern production by the year 2003. A resurgence in eastern coal, however, is expected after 2010, due to more new coal plants and clean coal technology incentive projects. Also, notice the dramatic increase in western low-sulfur coal production after 1970 when the first Clean Air Act was introduced.

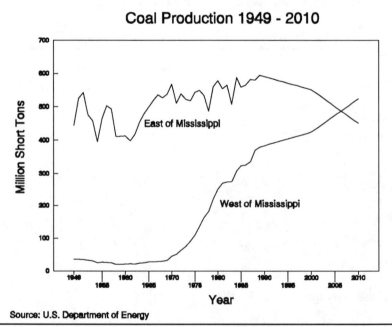

Coal Production 1949 - 2010

Source: U.S. Department of Energy

Figure 6.2 Coal Production in the U.S.

Most utilities are faced with the choices of scrubbing, switching to low-sulfur coal, or reducing output. Scrubbing will cost approximately $235 million for one 1,300 megawatt power plant, whereas switching to low-sulfur coal would cost $125 million (Cook 1991, 90-92). ICF Resources estimates that regional high-sulfur coal production from the Midwest and northern Appalachia would be reduced 35-42 million tons in Phase I from base case levels.[12] Estimated reductions of high-sulfur coal in Phase II range from 96-98 million tons. Overall, U.S. coal production should remain constant with reductions in high-sulfur coal being offset by gains in low-sulfur coal from central Appalachia and the West (ICF Resources, Inc. 1990).

The extent of fuel switching depends in large part on state regulatory agencies, some of which have incentives to protect local coal interests. High-sulfur coal production companies in Ohio, Indiana, Illinois, and Pennsylvania, where many utilities receive coal locally, risk the loss of production and jobs. There are also low-sulfur reserves in Kentucky, Virginia, and West Virginia, and utilities are certain to switch to some of this coal. Much of the low-sulfur coal production will have to come from the Powder River Basin in Wyoming and Montana, however. Western coal is cheaper to produce because mines are located at the surface rather than underground as with eastern mines. It is estimated that western coal, fuel plus transportation, shipped to the east would cost $1.30 per million British thermal unit. Eastern high-sulfur and low-sulfur coal currently cost $1.35 to $1.55 and $1.60 to $1.70 per mm/Btu, respectively. Acid rain legislation leaves utilities with no choice but to reduce their sulfur emissions.[13] The anticipated result will be increased low-sulfur coal traveling to the East.

Low-sulfur western coals have only two-thirds the Btu content of high-sulfur coals of the East.[14] This translates into more coal, in terms of weight, having to be shipped east. For every 10 tons of eastern high-sulfur coal demanded, 15 tons of western low-sulfur coal will have to be shipped to meet the energy demand (Cook 1991). The evidence overwhelmingly supports two conclusions: Western coal companies will gain at least a short-run increase in market share with eastern coal companies losing market share, and big revenue gains will occur for coal-carrying railroads.

U.S. coal production over the next two decades under the absolute worst case will remain constant.[15] The CAA delivers a bonus, however. Coal-carrying railroads stand to gain as much as 20 percent in total coal tonnage from acid rain legislation. While the same total tons of coal will be carried, the distance traveled will increase. Many eastern utilities will find switching to the West's low-sulfur coal a more cost-effective option than installing expensive scrubbers or reducing output. High-sulfur coal production will be reduced approximately 40 million tons over the next decade, but this coal has traditionally served only local utilities and never traveled far (ICF Resources 1990). Increased business for the railroads serving low-sulfur mines is inevitable.

The significance of this increase depends on the extent of high to low sulfur coal switching by utilities. Furthermore, high-sulfur coal companies will try and offset their losses by exporting their coal, giving further cause for increases in the use of railroads. The railroad upsurge has already started. In 1990, Union Pacific's coal revenue was up 8 percent, Burlington Northern's was up 5 percent, Norfolk Southern's nearly 8 percent, and CSX's 5 percent (Cook 1991).

The employment impacts from the CAA will primarily be felt by eastern high-sulfur coal companies. The number of coal miners nationally has decreased by about 40 percent since 1980, to its current level of 131,000 workers. Of that total, only 13 percent are employed west of the Mississippi River (National Coal Association, 1991). The 1990 CAA, through its clean coal incentives, will increase the closing of uneconomical high-sulfur coal mines. This, coupled with the increasing use of surface mining in the West (which requires much less labor compared to underground mining in the East), will result in fewer workers required in the coal industry.[16]

What Can We Conclude?

This survey of some of the major effects of the 1990 CAA leads to a clear conclusion: The effects are large and significant. Major producers of electricity nationwide are affected. Coal producers and carriers are affected in substantive ways. Consumers face significantly higher electricity bills. In short, the ripple effects are more like tidal waves.

Since the evidence of acid rain damage is so shaky, and since lower cost alternatives are available, such as liming lakes, why then did Congress pass the legislation?

Why Acid Rain Legislation?

Two Competing Theories

Generally speaking, there are two explanations for government regulation (Stigler 1971). The first holds that the purpose of regulation is to serve and protect the public at large, or at least a large subclass of the public. In theory, the gain received by those who benefit from regulation exceeds the costs to the rest of society of complying with the standards imposed; the cost of an unregulated market would be much higher. In this view, environmental regulation is considered to have an overall positive result. Bothersome features of regulation, like special allowances for midwest utilities and requirements of scrubbers for cleaning low sulfur coal, are evidence of errors of judgment. After all, politicians are human.

The second view, which is sometimes called the special interest theory of regulation, sees political leaders and regulators as brokers of rules that redistribute wealth, i.e., they serve special interest groups, not the general public at large. The theory also holds that special interest groups cannot have it their way without compromise. That is, consumers receive benefits, but special interests are in the driver's seat. Politicians find themselves directly benefiting from campaign contributions, endorsements, and votes that result from lobbyists or coalitions pushing for legislative measures. A bottom line in politics is continued employment for those in office and their appointees, thereby creating incentives for various forms of regulation that are not always socially optimal. In other words, politicians can use regulation as a tool for their own advancement.[17]

Applying the Theory to the CAA

The CAA's acid rain provisions appear to lead to a misallocation of resources by promoting the goals of interest groups and political actors with disregard for scientific fact and economic efficiency. An intrinsic problem is that the losses to the individual are small, but collectively they exceed the gains received by interest groups. As the losses to individuals are small, and the transaction costs of organizing these individuals into an effective opposition are quite high, the losses suffered by each will rarely provide sufficient incentive to express dissatisfaction (Stigler 1971). Therefore, on the surface, society appears to gain through emission reductions of acid precursors, but may in fact incur unnecessary costs to satisfy the goals of interest groups and politicians.

The costs of the acid rain legislation are borne primarily by electricity users; rates, on average, are expected to be 1 to 2 percent higher each year after the legislation. The benefits of regulation are concentrated on politicians and investors in the electric utility industry. In short, the regulation can be viewed as a mechanism that maintains and improves a costly barrier to entering the electric utility industry.[18] Legislation that fortifies existing state-enforced regulatory barriers is clearly beneficial to members of the utility cartel.

Some Evidence on Political Behavior

Benefits also accrue to politicians. The politician balances the competing interests of his constituencies so that his actions satisfy them and generate career benefits for himself. In doing this, the politician has a problem; he must have good information, which is costly to obtain. With information in hand, deals get made, and the politician moves to another transaction.

Financial markets provide objective information on the effects of political action. Sometimes unexpected decisions are made; at other times, external forces destabilize previous political actions. The results ripple through financial markets. The ten year long congressionally mandated acid rain study, NAPAP, was a destabilizing external event. It pronounced little need for further regulation of SO_2 and NO_X emissions. The report was not the result of careful congressional logrolling, but the developing Clean Air Act was. Evidence indicates portfolios of 98 electric utility stocks moved significantly when the report was made public (Riggs and Yandle 1992).

Why did investors react so dramatically? The special interest theory of regulation tells us a barrier to entry was at stake, one that had been bought in the political market. Of course, a politician watching the markets, or hearing from his constituents who watch, can take offsetting action.

The NAPAP study was made public on January 11, 1990, and a Senate subcommittee discussed the results on January 24 and 25, 1990. If the NAPAP results were taken seriously, plans for the new Clean Air Act would be completely undermined. Painful and costly political and regulatory deals would have to be renegotiated. Uncertainty clouded investor decisions.

There were 98 electric utility firms traded on the New York Stock Exchange at the time the NAPAP conculsions were made public. Some 73 of the 98 firms operated in the dominant acid rain control region, which borders on and is east of the Mississippi River. Investors in those eastern firms suffered negative abnormal losses in dividend adjusted returns in association with the report's release. The remaining stocks reacted negatively, but not at a statistically significant level.

Given the negative financial reaction, did the politicians take account of it? If so, were they motivated to repair the financial instability caused by NAPAP, or were they prompted to directly offset the financial losses experienced by their industrial constituency? That is, did politicians act as managers of a governmentally enforced cartel or were they motivated by traditional pork barrel politics?

The U.S. Senate voted on the entire 1990 Clean Air Act package on October 27, 1990.[19] A statistical analysis of the Senate vote, which adjusted for ideological, political, and other economic variables, included a variable constructed from the financial markets analysis of the 98 utilities. What did we learn? The larger the financial effect on investors, whether the effect was positive or negative, the more likely the senator voted for the CAA. The results tell us the greater the financial market reaction of a politician's industrial constituency, the higher the probability of that politician voting in favor of the CAA. Senators do behave carefully when reestablishing control of an industry's fate. They are not motivated to simply offset the financial losses of their constituency.

A follow-up study of financial market reactions to final passage of the CAA indicates the 73 eastern firms more than recovered the negative losses incurred by NAPAP. The remaining firms also experienced positive returns with final passage. The destabilizing effects of NAPAP were more than offset, and the evidence supports the Senate acting like a cartel manager. In short, the SO_2 and NO_X control features of the CAA are justified on cartel grounds, even if they cannot be justified on environmental grounds.

Some Final Thoughts

This chapter has focused on the important role sulfur dioxide emission control has played in the history of U.S. clean air legislation. If SO_2 suddenly disappeared, the CAA would be obsolete, or so it would seem. In a sense, the threat of disappearance surfaced in the 1990 release of the NAPAP study, just before Congress voted on the 1990 CAA. Science was disregarded; the new law contained even tighter and more costly standards. The law contained other things as well. The congressionally managed electric utility industry was kept in the regulatory straight-and-narrow, and a bonus was thrown in for good measure. Existing firms were given pollution rights that had to be purchased by new entrants.

This review of the legislative process tells us the acid rain control features of the 1990 CAA are vitally important. A large environmental lobbying coalition exists, pushing for stricter legislation on acid rain.[20] In general, efforts from these lobbying groups look to protect not only the environment, but also (at least indirectly) their own survivability.[21] Success on those fronts generates rents to certain industries.[22] There was, of course, a strong lobbying effort from the electric utility and midwestern/eastern coal industries. These groups were seeking to prevent increased costs and possible job losses. Furthermore, natural gas producers and western coal industries had lobbying efforts directed at protecting or creating rents for themselves. With such a diverse array of lobbying efforts, the resulting 1990 legislation proves to be quite intriguing.

But what can we say to a society that seeks to take the environment seriously? Is this the way to do it? If the 1990 CAA leads to the emergence of a free market for emission rights, we might celebrate it. But if it leads to a heavier bureaucracy that maintains a cartel while allowing members to be cost effective, we have little reason to celebrate. It is too early to tell just where the 1990 CAA will carry us. But we can conclude the trip will be slow and tortuous.

The evidence presented at the end of the chapter tells us the status quo is very valuable. Politicians will not easily revise major statutes, even when science says they should. All this suggests that science will not be politically compelling, unless it can be used to justify the status quo. Unfortunately, billions are spent to control phantom problems, like acid rain. Other real environmental problems, such as scarcity of community sewage treatment facilities and improved drinking water for the rural poor, will have to wait.

Notes

1. For more on this, as well as for the NAPAP report, see the three The National Acid Precipitation Assessment Program reports cited.

2. The pH scale ranges from 0 to 14, with 7 being neutral. Values below 7 are acidic and values above 7 are alkaline. Normal or "natural" rainfall has an average pH of 5.6. Furthermore, relatively few species of fish can maintain life under a pH level of 5.

3. Refer to the fourth and fifth sections of this chapter for details on the political mechanism deciding the Midwest to be at fault.

4. In the mid-to-late nineteenth century many of these lakes were prolific with trout and salmon because the area had become active in lumbering and slash and burn forestry. With "forests gone, spongy and water-absorbent mosses and the acidic peaty forest floor were burned off and replaced with alkaline ash. The ironic result was that sport fish could now survive in lakes that had previously been uninhabitable." Forest protection plans in 1892 were established ending slash and burn forestry, and the region has returned to its natural acidity. See Krug 1990.

5. Title IV of the Act regulates emissions from stationary sources, e.g., electric utilities. The distributional consequences, issues, and interest groups are considerably different under other titles of the bill, so that a combined analysis is neither desirable nor feasible.

6. In 1980, 27 million tons of SO_2 and 21 million tons of No_x were emitted in the U.S. See ICF Resources Inc. 1990.

7. The penalty is calculated "on the basis of the number of tons emitted in excess of the unit's emissions limitation requirement or, in the case of sulfur dioxide, of the allowances the operator holds for use for the unit for that year, multiplied by $2,000." The fee of $2,000 appears to be an arbitrary assessment to the marginal damage cost of SO_2 (1990 CAA, §411, 42 *United States Code* 7651j).

8. Initially under both the House and Senate versions of the bill, trading of SO_2 for NO_x and vice versa, was allowed. However, due to skepticism about the feasibility of the tradable emissions market, trading of NO_x was disallowed in hopes of reducing risk.

9. This scenario, however, assumes a market for allowances exists. Many speculate that problems will arise in the market such as regulatory hoarding of allowances, anticompetitive behavior, market barriers, and other problems associated with local, state, and regional electric utility regulatory agencies. For a more complete assessment of the feasibility of the market for allowances, see Bumpers 1991 and Coggins 1991.

10. Estimates indicate that command-and-control techniques would increase cost, in this section of the 1990 bill, by 50 percent in Phase I and 20 percent in Phase II. See Stuntz 1990.

11. Please note that EPA has reserved a certain quantity of allowances for later revision, which can be sold at auction level prices. However, as a practical matter, the allowances market will be the logical place to seek allowances.

12. The EPA provided base case assumptions which specify future high and low ranges for emissions, electricity rates, and fuel use under the regulations that existed prior to the 1990 CAA.

13. Sulfur content has been declining in coal since the early 1970s due, in part, to the CAAs but also to increases in receipts of low-sulfur coal to new power plants located in the central and western United States. In 1989, coal receipts from Wyoming contained the lowest sulfur content, 0.38 percent by weight, while Missouri contained the highest with 4.5 percent sulfur content by weight. Utilities that received their coal from Montana, Wyoming, Utah, and certain parts of Virginia, West Virginia, and Kentucky report the lowest sulfur content, usually under 1 percent. Whereas, utilities receiving coal from Ohio and West Virginia reported the highest sulfur content at 3.81 percent (Energy Information Administration 1990).

14. Coal originating in Virginia ranks the highest in Btu content with 12,896 Btu per pound of coal. Lignite coal, mined in Texas ranks the lowest with 6,272 Btu per pound and subbituminous coal from the Powder River Basin in Wyoming and Montana ranged from 8,500 to 9,500 Btu per pound, approximately 2,000 to 3,000 Btu per pound less than bituminous coal mined in the East (Energy Information Administration 1990).

15. The National Coal Association estimates the annual increase in coal production to lie in the range of 1 to 1.9 percent. Also, refer to Figure 6.2 (National Coal Association 1991b).

16. ICF Resources Inc. (1990) estimates job-losses in coal mining to be 5,000 to 6,000 through 1995 and 14,000 to 15,000 through the year 2000 for the Northern Appalachia and Midwest coal mining regions. ICF estimates job-gains through the year 1995 in central and south Appalachia to be approximately 6,000 to 7,000 and job-gains in the West to be about 500. In Phase II job-gains are expected in central and south Appalachia to be 13,000 and in the West to be 2,000 to 4,000.

17. Politicians must continue to behave in this manner or lose to a superior political actor who will work to advance various interests at the expense of the general public. Political leaders and regulators are endogenous to the regulatory system. They are not exogenous actors who serve to maintain the standards and promote efficiency as many social scientists like to view government.

18. For example, state regulation requires an electric utility to have a certificate of convenience and public necessity before entering the industry. The Clean Air Act adds a feature for those firms that expect to produce SO_2 and NO_x emissions. They must purchase allowances from existing holders of rights.

19. The Senate voted in favor, 89 to 10. The House floor vote occurred on October 26, 1990, with 401 favoring, and 25 opposing the bill. The president signed the bill into law on November 15, 1990.

20. It would appear that environmentalism has grown to a level of religion. Casual observation indicates grass root movements across the nation coalescing into larger, politically effective groups, with many advocating "blanket" regulatory measures as alleged solutions. This is often in spite of scientific conclusions to the contrary. Although the objective of a cleaner environment is substantive, the causes of an environmental ill and the means of correcting it are equally important. The tables seem to have turned on the old adage, "blinded by science" to "blinded by religion."

21. There have been numerous studies in the area of environmental economics expanding on special interest theory. Yandle (1989) describes the political economy of regulation with his chapter "Bootleggers, Baptists and Political Limits." Here bootleggers and Baptists are generic terms used to describe industry and special interest groups, respectively. Baptists push for legislation restricting the sale of alcohol on Sundays and, likewise, the bootleggers support this legislation which increases the demand for their illegal alcohol on Sunday. Thus, both groups seemingly on opposite sides of the issue, are in actuality supporting the same cause. Furthermore, the bootleggers reap the benefits, while sitting idle, of the Baptists' lobbying activities.

This scenario translates directly into electric utilities and special interest groups. Consider the 8.9 million tons of SO_2 emissions cap, under the acid rain provisions. Environmental groups were strong proponents of the cap, and one of their main concerns was with infant industries, or industries that do not exist yet, to ensure lower emission rates in the future and protect areas with clean air from becoming polluted. The existence of the cap causes higher costs of entry and expansion for the electric industry. Clearly, some existing firms within the industry are in strong support of such an action because this acts as a barrier to entry, or in some cases, a barrier to expansion for their competition. Therefore, profits may result for existing utilities while they reap the benefits of environmental groups' lobbying activities.

22. For a discussion of the capture theory of regulation in regard to the PSD ruling under the 1977 CAA, see Maloney and McCormick 1982.

References

Ackerman, Bruce, and G. Hassler. 1981. *Clean Coal/Dirty Air.* New Haven, CT: Yale University Press.

Anderson, Terry L., and Donald R. Leal. 1991. *Free Market Environmentalism.* San Francisco, CA: Pacific Institute for Public Policy Research.

Brady, Gordon L., Michael T. Maloney, and Alden F. Abbott. 1990. Political Limits of the Market for "BAT Medallions." *CATO Review of Business and Government.* (Winter): 61-4.

Bumpers, William M. 1991. Property Rights Associated with Allowances Under the Clean Air Act Amendments of 1990 and Impediments to an Efficient Trading System. Presented at the National Regulatory Research Institute Workshop on Acid Rain, May at Chicago, IL.

Clean Air Act of 1990, Pub. L. No. 101-549, 104 Stat. 2399.

Coase, Ronald H. 1960. The Problem of Social Cost. *The Journal of Law and Economics.* 3 (October): 1-44.

Coggins, Jay S. 1991. Economic Analysis of Emission Allowance Trading: A Regulatory Economic Approach. Working Paper, Dept. of Agr. Econ. and Economics, Montana State University, April.

Cook, James. 1991. Rain from Heaven. *Forbes.* (March 4): 90-92.

Energy Information Administration. 1990. *Annual Energy Review 1989.* Washington, DC: U.S. Department of Energy, May 24.

_____. 1990. *Cost and Quality of Fuels for Electric Utility Plants 1989.* Washington, DC: U.S. Department of Energy, July 13.

Hahn, Robert W. 1990. The Politics and Religion of Clean Air. *Regulation.* (Winter): 22.

Hammond, Claire Holton. 1986. An Overview of Electric Utility Regulation. *Electric Power: Deregulation and the Public Interest.* San Francisco, CA: Pacific Research Institute for Public Policy, 31-60.

Hardin, Garrett. 1968. The Tragedy of the Commons. *Science.* 162: 1243-1248.

Harrington, Winston. 1989. *Acid Rain: Science and Policy, A Primer.* Washington, DC: Resources for the Future.

Helme, Ned, and Chris Neme. Acid Rain: The Problem. *EPA Journal.* (January/February): 19-25.

ICF Resources Inc. 1990. *Comparison of the Economic Impacts of the Acid Rain Provisions of the Senate Bill (S.1630) and the House Bill (S.1630).* Washington DC: U.S. Environmental Protection Agency, July.

Kulp, J. Laurence. 1990. Acid Rain: Causes, Effects, and Control. *Regulation.* (Winter): 41-50.

Krug, Edward C. 1990. Fish Story: the Great Acid Rain Flimflam. *Policy Review.* 52 (Spring): 44-49.

Maloney, Michael T., and Robert E. McCormick. 1982. A Positive Theory of Environmental Quality Regulation." *The Journal of Law and Economics.* 25 (April): 99-123.

The National Acid Precipitation Assessment Program. 1990a. Integrated Assessment: Questions 1 and 2. Washington, DC: U.S. Government Printing Office, August.

_____. 1990b. *Interim Assessment: The Causes and Effects of Acidic Deposition.* Washington, DC: U.S. Government Printing Office.

_____. 1990c. *1989 Annual Report to the President and Congress.* Washington, DC: U.S. Government Printing Office, June.

National Coal Association. 1989. *Coal: Energy for the Next Decade and Beyond.* Washington, DC: The National Coal Association, February.

_____. 1991a. *Coal Data 1990 Edition.* Washington, DC: The National Coal Association.

_____. 1991b. *Facts About Coal, 1991.* Washington, DC: The National Coal Association.

Navarro, Peter. 1981. The 1977 Clean Air Act Amendments: Energy, Environmental, Economic and Distributional Impacts. *Public Policy.* Spring: 121-46.

Office of Technology Assessment. 1984. *Acid Rain and Transported Air Pollutants: Implications for Public Policy.* Washington, DC: U.S. Congress, Office of Technology Assessment, OTA-0-204, June.

Pashigian, Peter B. 1985. Environmental Regulation: Whose Self-Interests Are Being Protected? *Economic Inquiry.* 23 (October): 551-84.

Portney, Paul R. 1990. Economics of the Clean Air Act. *Journal of Economic Perspectives.* 4 (Fall): 173-81.

Pytte, Alyson. 1990. *The Congressional Quarterly Almanac.* Oct. 27: 3587-92.

Radigan, Kyle. 1991. Dam It All. *Trout.* (Summer): 28-46.

Schwert, G. Williams. 1981. Using Financial Data to Measure Effects of Regulation. *Journal of Law and Economics.* 24 (April): 121-58.

Stigler, George J. 1971. The Theory of Economic Regulation. *The Bell Journal of Economics and Management Science.* (Spring): 3-21.

Stuntz, Linda G., Deputy Under Secretary, U.S. Department of Energy. Testimony before the Committee on Energy and Natural Resources, U.S. Senate. January 24, 1990.

Yandle, Bruce. 1989. *The Political Limits of Environmental Regulation: Tracking the Unicorn.* New York: Quorum Books.

Chapter 7

Fishing for Property Rights to Fish

Terry L. Anderson and Donald R. Leal

Introduction

Much progress has been made toward understanding how market processes can be applied to environmental problems if property rights are well defined and enforced (Anderson and Leal 1991). For example, when water rights are well specified, water-use efficiency can be greatly enhanced if impediments to water marketing are removed. Similarly, protecting endangered species can be achieved much more efficiently by purchasing or leasing habitat from private landowners.

On the other hand, the air, water, and sea resources have eluded market processes because of the greater difficulty in defining and enforcing property rights. In the absence of any property rights, access to these resources is open to all, and the "tragedy of the commons" results (Hardin 1968). No one individual has the incentive to conserve the resource simply because there is no way of preventing others from capturing the gains from better management. Given the difficulty of specifying property rights, these resources become the domain of the political process, which is subject to a myriad of collective action problems discussed by others in this volume. The challenge in tackling these tougher problems is to devise property rights regimes that can move us out of the political arena and into the market where individuals face the opportunity costs of their actions.

There is no better example of the tragedy of the commons than ocean resources. Outside the territorial limits of sovereign countries, only weak treaties limit access to fisheries, and inside those limits costly regulations are the norm for limiting entry into fisheries. In the race to capture rents (profits), expenditures by fishermen drive up total costs and drive down the marginal productivity of additional fishing effort. From his study of New England's northern lobster fishery, Bell (1966, 156) concluded that "over 50 percent of the capital and labor employed in lobstering represent an uneconomic use of factors." Higgs (1982, 82) concluded, with respect to the Pacific Northwest salmon fishery, that rent seeking has made the net value negative:

> Today, from a comprehensive point of view, the Washington salmon fisher almost certainly makes a negative contribution to net national product. The opportunity costs of the *socially unnecessary* resources employed there, plus the *socially unnecessary* costs of governmental research, management, and regulation, are greater than the *total value added* by all the labor and capital employed in the fishery.

Profit-seeking commercial fishermen are not the only ones exploiting the commons. The Sport Fishing Institute reported that the number of days devoted to marine recreational angling each year in the United States nearly tripled between 1955 and 1985. In fact, scientists contend that the catch of some species by sport fishermen has had a greater impact on fishery stocks than the activities by commercial fishermen (Bryant 1989; Maranto 1988).

Table 7.1 lists species in United States coastal waters that were either fully utilized or overfished according to the biological criteria of maximum sustainable yield. Of the overfished species, seven were fished by foreign fleets and six by U.S. fleets. Today, declines such as these continue but they can no longer be blamed on foreign vessels because their numbers have dropped dramatically in recent years (National Oceanic and Atmospheric Administration 1987).

Historically, the fishery commons problem has been treated with regulations on season, allowable catch, fishing areas, vessels size, and equipment. The results have often been absurd. For example, at one time Maryland oystermen could use dredges but had to tow them behind sailboats on all but two days of the week when motorized boats were allowed (Christy and Scott 1965, 15-16). While such regulations drive up the costs and discourage some fishing effort, they also encourage fishermen to explore other margins for capturing rents. For instance, limits on vessel size encourage investment in more boats and in more sophisticated equipment; specifying which days of the week one can fish encourages more intensive effort on those days; and so on. Christy (1976) estimated that the over-capitalization and overuse of labor in American fisheries cost $300 million per year or, at a 6 percent discount rate, the equivalent of a $5 billion investment. In the final analysis, excessive fishing effort still results due to the absence of property rights.

This paper briefly reviews the economics of property rights and then examines various approaches for fisheries in light of this theory. Cases of relatively complete privatization of fisheries are contrasted with examples of individual transferable quotas (ITQs) used in some selected commercial fisheries in the United States. We conclude that ITQs can improve fishery management and enhance returns but that complete privatization can generate even greater returns.

Table 7.1
Status of Selected United States Fisheries, June 1974

Fully Utilized

Atlantic Mackerel	Pacific Hake
Red Hake	Atlantic Cod
Silver Hake	Atlantic Ocean Perch
Atlantic Herring	Bluefish
Atlantic Squid	Menhaden
Bering Sea Cod	American Lobster
King Crab	Gulf Shrimp
Tanner Crab	Eastern Tropical Pacific
Yellowfin Tuna	

Overfished

Yellowfin Sole (Foreign)	Haddock (Foreign)
Alaska Pollock (Foreign)	Yellowtail Flounder (U.S./Foreign)
Pacific Ocean Perch (Foreign)	California Sardine (U.S.)
Pacific Halibut (U.S.)	Pacific Mackerel (U.S.)
Atlantic Halibut (Foreign)	Atlantic Sea Scallop (U.S.)
Bering Sea Herring (Foreign)	Northwest Atlantic Shrimp (U.S.)
Bering Sea Shrimp (Foreign)	Atlantic Bluefin Tuna (U.S.)

Source: U.S. Senate, Committee on Commerce and National Ocean Policy Study, *A Legislative History of the Fishery Conservation and Management Act of 1976*, 94th Congress, 2d Session (Washington, DC, October 1976): 358–59.

The Economics of Property Rights

The establishment of private property rights to the fish stock and/or the area in which it resides can increase rents by optimizing the number of fishing inputs and by providing an incentive to conserve the stock. The basic problem with open access to a fishery is that fishermen must overinvest in fishing effort in order to catch fish before they are caught by others. The race requires bigger boats, more nets, more labor, and so on, each of which reduces net returns. Moreover, fish are taken regardless of size and reproductive capacity because a fish returned to the water will be caught by another fisherman. If private property rights can be well defined and enforced, there is no incentive to race to fish; there is an incentive to enhance stocks because the owner can capture future returns.

The net effect on rents depends on two important dimensions of the property rights definition and enforcement process. First, greater rents will result if private property rights to a fishing territory (e.g., oyster beds) can be well defined and enforced. The owner will neither race to take fish nor deplete stocks which can enhance future catch; if the owner does either, he bears the cost. On the other hand, if only the rights to a share of the season's catch are established, as is the case with individual transferable quotas, there may still be some incentive to catch quota while stocks are large and an incentive to cheat on the number of fish taken. Consequently, the cost of enforcing the quotas can be high. Moreover, since the catch over time usually is set in a bureaucratic framework, there is less incentive to optimize catch over time. Hence, if the quota is too large or too small, rents will not be maximized.

The second determinant of rents from privatizing the commons is the amount of resources consumed in the establishment of property rights. There are the direct costs of defining and enforcing rights such as fencing, recording deeds, court fees to prosecute trespassers, and so on (Anderson and Hill 1975). In cases where property rights are handed out by government, there are also rent-seeking costs that arise as individuals attempt to convince bureaucrats that they should get the rights (Anderson and Hill 1983). In the final analysis, the net effect of privatizing the commons depends on how many resources are consumed in the process of privatization.

Rent Creating or Rent Seeking

Anderson and Hill (1983) hypothesize that residual claimants in the process of establishment of property rights will have an incentive to conserve on the costs of definition and enforcement, but that politicians and bureaucrats may have an incentive to encourage rent seeking. Small, clearly identified groups of individuals who recognize the rents from private ownership can gain by conserving on the resources used in definition and enforcement. For example, private land claims clubs on America's western frontier wrote constitutions that discouraged wasteful investment in establishing property rights. On the whole, Anderson and Hill (1983, 444) found that

... the definition process of land claims clubs followed a relatively low-cost method, and the available evidence on enforcement activity is also consistent with the hypothesis that residual claimant associations will discourage rent seeking.

On the other hand, since politicians and bureaucrats generally had no claim on residual rents, homesteading legislation required expensive rent-seeking expenditures in the form of irrigation, residence requirements, cultivation, and timber harvesting.

These hypotheses carry over to the establishment of property rights in fisheries. If residual claimants have a hand in the way property rights are established, we can expect a more efficient property rights process. On the other hand, if property rights are doled out through a political/bureaucratic process, rent seeking may negate some or even all of the benefits of privatizing the commons. The following examples illustrate how alternative means of eliminating the fishery commons affect the net rents from privatization.

Cooperation Without Government

While state and federal governments have monopolized modern management of most fisheries, there are significant historical examples of private cooperation to overcome the commons problem. These efforts generally minimized costly rent seeking by depending on local customs and culture.[1] These private efforts also tended to establish territorial rights that gave individuals the greatest incentive to maximize fishing rents.

Indians and Salmon

Indians along the Columbia River offer a prime example of how indigenous people were able to establish effective private rules for controlling access and ensuring future harvests from the salmon fishery. Robert Higgs found that Indians had well-established rights to fishing sites long before whites came to the area (Higgs 1982). The Indians had private rights to fishing sites along the river and had intertribal agreements to allow sufficient upstream migration to ensure recruitment. Unfortunately, state and federal governments allowed newcomers to circumvent these rights by placing nets across the mouth of the Columbia, ultimately decimating salmon populations and leading to state regulation. As Scott (1988, 19) notes, such political action runs counter to a long history of recognizing private rights in coastal fisheries:

... when we consider that there were already, in 1200 AD, in tidal waters, territorial fishing rights in England and a form of territorial salmon rights throughout the world in the 19th century, the legislative process can only be said to have reduced the characteristics of individual fishing rights.

Lobster Gangs

Some parts of Maine's lobster fishery continue to offer an example of private control of access. Acheson (1992, 2) describes the 100-year-old territorial system as a system "under communal control" and at the same time "owned by the State." In order to harvest lobsters in a particular territory fishermen must be a member of a "harbor gang." Nonmembers attempting to harvest lobsters are usually sanctioned by these extralegal harbor gangs which destroy gear. Though this territorial system is not sanctioned by the state of Maine, it is recognized by Maine lobster fishermen and does have a significant impact on productivity.

Private Oyster Beds

Oyster beds along some portions of the U.S. east coast provide additional evidence for the efficacy of private property rights. Since adult oysters attach permanently to rocks or shell deposits located in intertidal zones, exclusive user rights to subaqueous parcels are feasible. Moreover, where exclusive rights exist, owners have an incentive to enhance beds by providing bottom material such as rock or shell deposits to which oyster larva can attach. In a study comparing oyster production from open access and private oyster beds, Agnello and Donnelley (1975, 528) concluded that the latter can "generate substantial increases in production." Agnello and Donnelley (1979, 260-61) tested the hypothesis that private ownership of oyster beds would generate higher returns for fishermen than open-access beds. Comparing private leasing in Virginia with open access in Maryland and controlling for other variables, they found that annual average income for fishermen in Maryland was slightly less than two-thirds the average income of Virginia fishermen. Despite this significant difference, only 9,000 acres of Maryland's oyster grounds are privately leased while 280,000 acres remain subject to open access. Moreover, because of weak enforcement and therefore extensive poaching, only 1,000 private acres are in production. Not surprisingly, investment in the Maryland oyster fishery is declining (Leffler 1987).

Cooperation or Collusion

Even in the absence of private territorial rights along the Gulf coast, Johnson and Libecap observed that from the 1930s through the 1950s fishermen "resorted to informal contracting and the use of unions and trade associations to mitigate open access conditions" (1982, 1007). Such efforts eventually met their demise in the courts, which refused to exempt the collective actions of these groups from antitrust prosecution.

> A cooperative association of boat owners is not freed from the restrictive provisions of the Sherman Antitrust Act ... because it professes, in the interest of the conservation of important food fish, to regulate the price and the manner of taking fish unauthorized by legislation and uncontrolled by proper authority. (*Gulf Coast Shrimpers and Oystermens Association v. United States*, 236 F. 2nd 658 (1956))

During the time they were controlling entry, these groups negotiated price agreements with wholesalers and canneries, and succeeded in internalizing the cost of regulation and conserving the stock of shrimp (Johnson and Libecap 1982, 1008). But establishing property rights to resources is difficult to maintain if the government declares it illegal.

These examples illustrate that property rights to the ocean fishery commons have been applied in the past and that they can have a dramatic impact on resource allocation. In spite of this track record, property rights solutions have not been readily accepted by bureaucratic managers who stand to lose control and budget if fishery management is decentralized. In some instances, however, growing inefficiencies inherent in current regulatory regimes have prompted managers to consider a new direction in fishery management.

Homesteading the Oceans

ITQs

Individual transferable quotas (ITQs) are a property rights approach to fishery management that is slowly gaining acceptance among managers and fishermen. With ITQs, each fisherman is issued an individual quota entitling him to a specific share of the harvestable fish for a season. The quota is usually set by a governmental agency, but fishermen are free to adjust their share by buying, selling, trading, or leasing quota. They may even be able to carry the unused portion of a quota over from one season to subsequent ones. The constraints on quota transfers and carryover vary across bureaucracies.

If the primary problem confronting fishermen is racing to catch fish before the season's legal harvest is caught by others, then ITQs provide a means of reducing costly competition. This approach can allow fishermen to respond better to market conditions by adjusting the nature, timing, and scale of operations to produce a more profitable harvest. In order to improve efficiency, the rights to quota must be well defined, enforced, and tradeable; if not, the opportunity costs to individual fishermen will not reflect the actual costs of their action.

Potential Drawbacks

Despite their growing acceptance, ITQs are not without criticisms. Copes (1986) points out that ITQs do not work well in bycatch fisheries. These are fisheries in which the harvest of one species almost inevitably results in the harvest of other species. In New Zealand, problems remain in bycatch fisheries where ITQs have been implemented (National Marine Fisheries Service 1991). In addition, Copes argues that ITQs will not solve "high-grading," the tendency of fishermen to discard smaller fish in hopes of catching larger, more valuable ones. He also contends that ITQs fail to resolve the race for fish problems because the quota owner does not have to take into account the costs his efforts imposes on others. Boyce (1991, 1) argues that the circumstances under which an ITQ system will reduce costly competition are "exceedingly narrow."

There are two other potential problems with implementing ITQs that can negate their beneficial effect. First, given that ITQs are generally set by a bureaucratic regime, there is the question of what incentive or ability they have to establish the efficient level of harvest. The standard is to approximate the maximum sustained yield. Knowing this, however, is difficult at best. Moreover, as numerous economists have demonstrated, maximum sustained yield is a biological rather than an economic standard which may be greater or less than the quantity which maximizes the rental value of the fishery (Tietenberg 1988, 260). To the extent that fishermen can carry quota over into the next season or catch more in the current season by borrowing against future quota, they may adjust toward the economic optimum, but these options may not be available because of restrictions on quota transfers.

The second problem with ITQs stems from the fact that would-be quota holders are willing to invest time and money to secure claims to valuable quota rights. In other words, the race to catch fish will be replaced by a race for the quota.[2] If the quota are allocated at random, by auction, or on the basis of historical catch prior to any anticipation of ITQs, rent seeking will be minimized. However, if quota are allocated on the basis of historical catch which anticipates the allocation, fishermen will overfish in an effort to increase their share of the quota. Alternatively, if bureaucratic discretion determines the allocation, fishermen will invest in influencing the decision. In either case at least some of the rents from the fishery will be dissipated through the race for property rights.[3]

Case Studies

The following examples illustrate how ITQs have been implemented in the United States, how effective they have been in increasing the rental value of fishery resources, and what problems exist with implementation.

Wisconsin

Wisconsin appears to have more experience with ITQs than any other state in the country (Wisconsin Department of Natural Resources). Individual quotas were issued to commercial fishermen in 1971 for lake trout on Lake Superior; in 1983, for yellow perch and chub on parts of Lake Michigan; and in 1989 for several other commercial fisheries. The later applications resulted from fishermen satisfaction with the initial program.

The degree of rent seeking to secure quota is limited because the number of fishermen who can enter Wisconsin's commercial fisheries is limited by state law and not easily changed. Currently, 21 commercial fishing permits are issued for Lake Superior and 127 are issued for Lake Michigan. Permits may be purchased or obtained as a gift from an existing permit holder as long as the purchaser is either active as a crew member on a holder's vessel or is a family member of existing holders. These permits give their holders the right to operate in any commercial fishery on the lake for which they are issued. The holder can operate more than one vessel and need not be present on the water with any particular operation. A person without a permit may only participate in the fishery as the employee of a permit holder. The permits restrict holders to operate within the gear constraints set by the Wisconsin Department of Natural Resources. On Lake Superior, for example, a permit holder may only fish with 10,000 feet of drift gill net at a time, no matter how many separate vessels he has fishing.

For commercial fisheries, the Wisconsin Department of Natural Resources determines the annual total allowable catch. Once this amount is set, the decision whether to use an individual quota program rests with the Lake Michigan and Lake Superior commercial fishing boards. These boards also decide how the quota will be divided among fishermen and set the rules governing quota transfers. Each board is composed primarily of commercial fishermen, but also contains a fish processor and a public representative.

The initial experiment with lake trout on Lake Superior in 1971 provides an illustration of the problems with ITQs when high grading is present. This valuable bycatch fishery provides fresh fish to local restaurants and to markets in distant urban areas, primarily Minneapolis-St. Paul and Chicago. In the 1950s the trout stocks in Lake Superior were being depleted by the sea lamprey, and by the early 1960s the stocks were so badly depressed that commercial fishing for lake trout was closed. In the late 1960s, population studies by state biologists indicated that lake trout stocks had recovered enough to allow a commercial fishery. In 1971, the commercial fishery in lake trout was reopened with a total allowable catch established for the season.

Since 1971, the Lake Superior Commercial Fishing Board has elected to divide the total allowable catch for lake trout equally among permit holders, the number of which has fallen from 32 to 21 due to tighter eligibility requirements. Currently, permits are transferable to qualified fishermen. Fishermen are prohibited from owning more than one permit and associated quota share, however. Each fisherman who receives individual quota is issued a plastic tag for each fish in his quota for the season. These tags must be attached to the fish when they are caught. Permit holders are allowed to lease all or part of their quota for the season by selling their tags to other qualified fishermen.

Total allowable catch and individual quota were once designated in pounds but were changed to number of fish following a 1986 agreement with local Indian tribes. This, in turn, increased the incidence of high-grading. Because of high-grading, Wisconsin Department of Natural Resource officials believe that reported landings may underestimate mortality by 30 to 50 percent making total catch greater than total allowable quota.

Another problem that arose in the late 1970s was the landing and selling of untagged fish. In 1981, the state of Wisconsin reached an agreement with the U.S. Fish and Wildlife Service and the state of Illinois to conduct a sting operation to collect enough evidence to prosecute fishermen and fish buyers who were dealing in untagged trout. The operation proved successful and a number of Lake Superior fishermen who were caught smuggling fish received fines and several served jail sentences. State officials believe that since the sting operation, smuggling has become less of a problem.

While there continues to be a problem with high-grading, the lake trout individual quota program is apparently favored by fishermen, indicating the program may be creating market benefits. Since 1971, the Lake Superior Commercial Fishing Board has renewed the individual quota program every year.

In the early 1970s, Wisconsin's Lake Michigan chub fishery produced 4 to 6 million pounds of chubs per year, the bulk of which were smoked. A declining stock of chubs forced severe restrictions on chub catch during the mid-1970s during which time the Department of Natural Resources was assessing the fishery. Fish populations eventually recovered and the commercial fishery was reopened in 1979 with a total allowable catch set for the season.[4]

In 1983, after several years of market gluts and shortened seasons, the Lake Michigan Commercial Fishing Board assigned individual quotas (expressed as percentages of the total allowable catch) to 32 of the top chub fishermen.[5] To overcome the rent seeking problem, allocations were made on the basis of a complicated formula which gave fishermen with higher historical landings more quota, but which did not increase quota holdings in strict proportion to landings. Quotas in most other Lake Michigan fisheries have been allocated with simple formulas giving each recipient a quota proportional to his share of the total catch caught during a base period. Ninety percent of the total allowable catch was composed of individual quotas while the remaining 10 percent was left for use as a common property fishery. Fishermen not falling in the top 32 category were placed in the common property fishery with the restriction that each could not catch more than 10 percent of the available common property quota (*Wisconsin Administrative Code*, NR 25.07).

A position among the 32 individual quota recipients, and the quota associated with that position, can be sold, but such sales have been rare. A person who has the right to receive one of the 32 quota allocations cannot permanently increase his quota by buying a percentage of another quota or permanently decrease his quota by selling a percentage of it. A person may lease up to half of his quota to one or more other individual quota holders for the season in which the quota has been issued, and several leases take place each year.[6] The limitation on the amount of quota that can be leased is apparently out of concern that individuals could own quota and never fish it themselves. Leases must be approved by the Lake Michigan Commercial Fishing Board and by the Wisconsin Department of Natural Resources. Weekly landing reports from chub fishermen are compared to lease requests to make sure that the individual disposing of the quota has quota to lease (Muse and Schelle 1989, 73-74).

From the standpoint of eliminating market gluts and dispersing harvest over the season, the program has worked well. In 10 of the 12 fishing quarters before the program began in 1983, the bulk of the quarterly harvest was taken in the first month of the quarter, resulting in depressed prices. In the quarters following the introduction of the program through 1985, landings became more evenly distributed throughout the season (Muse and Schelle 1989, 76-77).

The impact of ITQs on chub marketing is harder to determine beyond 1985. The stock of chubs increased so much that the growth rates of individual fish has slowed and the average size of fish has decreased. Hence many fishermen have found it hard to harvest the chub profitably within an existing net mesh size restriction. Also, the expansion of a valuable yellow perch fishery has directed fishermen's attention to this fishery. Based on these changes many fishermen have elected not to harvest all of their quota (Muse and Schelle 1989, 75-76).

Notably, the increase in the stock and the decline in fish size easily could have been reversed by the state either by increasing quotas or changing the net mesh size to accommodate catching the smaller fish. For whatever reason, such a move was not taken, however. This is indicative of the potential problems that exist when bureaucracies, who are not residual claimants, and thus are not affected by changes in profits, ultimately determine the number and size quotas as well as the method of catch.

The yellow perch fishery is centered in Green Bay, a large bay off Lake Michigan, with vessels using gill and drop nets. Increased fishing effort and indications that most of the fish harvested were from one age class prompted a decision by the Wisconsin Department of Natural Resources to establish a total allowable catch for the 1983 season. In response, the Lake Michigan Commercial Fishing Board adopted ITQs in the hope of avoiding the problems initially experienced in the chub fishery.

Each of the 157 fishermen with valid commercial fishing permits on Lake Michigan was eligible to receive quota for yellow perch. Allocations were made on the basis of a simple formula which gave a permit holder a quota proportional to his share of the total fishery catch during a base period. Several persons protested the landing figures on which their quotas were based, but only one was able to change his quota (*Wisconsin Administrative Code* NR 25.07; Muse and Schelle 1989, 66).

Quota shares can be sold to persons holding Lake Michigan commercial fishing permits. From the start of the program through mid-May 1988, there appear to have been 37 separate transactions in which shares were sold. The smallest separate transaction involved the transfer of 0.01 percent of the total allowable catch, while the largest involved 4.85 percent. The number of separate operations in the fishery has declined from 105 to 75 as quota has been sold to more efficient fishermen.

Quota also may be leased, with all lease transactions approved by the Department of Natural Resources. The agency checks lease requests to make sure the person disposing of the quota actually has the unfished quota to lease. In the 1987-88 period, there were 15 lease transactions involving 39,500 pounds of fish out of a total allowable catch of 400,000 pounds (Muse and Schelle 1989, 66-67).

Fishermen and fish dealers are said to be satisfied with the yellow perch ITQ program with some exceptions. They believe that the harvest is more dispersed over the season which means less volatility in prices. In addition, fish consumers are provided with a greater amount of fresh, as opposed to frozen, yellow perch most of the year, and the smaller inventory of frozen fish has reduced costs. On the other hand, some fishermen are concerned that large amounts of quota may become concentrated in a few hands. The Lake Michigan Commercial Fishing Board has the power to adopt aggregation limits but has not yet done so (Anderson personal communication; Wisconsin Department of Natural Resources; Muse and Schelle 1989, 69-70).

The program would be even more successful were it not for illegal harvesting. Fishermen are able to avoid the carefully monitored wholesale market by selling directly to retail outlets. This situation has retarded conservation efforts and resulted in poorer knowledge of the fish stocks. According to fisheries managers, fish stocks have been rebuilt, but they might have been rebuilt faster in the absence of cheating (Muse and Schelle 1989, 67-68).

In sum, ITQ programs in Wisconsin have met with varying degrees of success. The lake trout fishery has shown the least amount of success because of the persistent high grading problem. The Lake Michigan chub fishery ITQs have been effective in eliminating market gluts and dispersing the harvest more evenly over the season, even though the state has not responded well to changes in the fish stock. The yellow perch fishery has also shown a more rational harvest schedule with ITQs, benefiting both fisherman and consumers. Because of monitoring problems, illegal harvesting remains a problem in this fishery.

Mid-Atlantic Surf Clams and Ocean Quahogs

In November 1977 the National Marine Fisheries Service (NMFS) approved a plan limiting total catch and restricting fishing effort for the Mid-Atlantic surf clam and ocean quahog (a deepwater clam) fisheries.[7] At the time, the surf clam resource was substantially lower than historical levels and, as a result, the industry was economically unstable. Also, declines in surf clam stocks were stimulating fishing for the deeper dwelling ocean quahog (Mid-Atlantic Fishery Management Council 1991, 2-7).

While the plan did restore surf clam stocks and stabilize quahog harvests, its failure to establish individual quotas drove up fishing costs. Without individual quotas, fishermen invested in more gear to catch a larger share of the annual total allowable catch. A moratorium on fleet size did not alter the harvesting capacity of each vessel and actually kept outdated vessels afloat because they represented the right to fish. It became clear to managers and fishermen that a new system had to be implemented if these fisheries were to be economically viable (Mid-Atlantic Fishery Management Council 1990, 11).

In 1989, the Mid-Atlantic council recommended and NMFS approved ITQs for the surf clam and quahog fisheries, the first ITQs for a federally regulated fishery in the United States. Managers used different formulas to determine a fisherman's share of the total allowable catch in each fishery.[8] For the surf clam fishery, 20 percent of a fisherman's share of the total allowable catch was based on vessel hull size, and 80 percent was based on his total catch of surf clams from 1979 to 1988. For the ocean quahog fishery, a fisherman's share of the total allowable catch was based solely on his total catch of ocean quahogs between 1979 and 1988. For both fisheries, two of the worst years during this period were disregarded (*Federal Register* 1990, 24193-4).

Unlike other fisheries where fear of monopoly power has limited the amount of quota any individual can hold, managers of this fishery elected not to impose such limits. Instead they have chosen to let the courts under the antitrust laws deal with issues of market power (National Marine Fisheries Service 1991, 2).

A monitoring system is in place which predates the quota program. When a 32-bushel "cage" of surf clams or ocean quahogs is landed, it must be accompanied by a numbered tag issued to the quota holder by the government. Log books are also required from fishermen, dealers, and processors. In conjunction with ITQs, each fisherman is allocated enough tags to land his quota. While there have been some tagging violations reported recently, Dave Keifer of the Mid-Atlantic council does not believe this is a serious problem. He is concerned, however, with stopping fishermen who fish both the state and federally regulated surf clam fisheries off the New Jersey coast from smuggling clams. Some of these fishermen harvest larger clams in federal waters and tag them with state tags. The inability to enforce quota allocations between the two fisheries means that federally controlled resources are being overharvested (Keifer, personal communication).

Fishermen are free to sell or lease their quota or sell all or part of their tags to other licensed fishermen. An active quota market emerged almost immediately, and in the last quarter of 1990 and the first quarter of 1991 about 380 quota transfers took place, about 70 percent of which were leases. Anecdotal evidence suggests that while a bushel of clams could be sold by fishermen for $8 to $9 (ex-vessel price), surf clam quota could be purchased for $15 to $18 a bushel. Additionally, while a bushel of ocean quahog could be sold for $3 to $3.75, ocean quahog quota could be sold for $3.50 to $5 a bushel, and could be leased for 40 to 50 cents a bushel (National Marine Fisheries Service 1991, 2). Apparently, the degree of uncertainty existing in the early phase of the program depressed quota prices. Part of the uncertainty resulted from lawsuits filed in June 1990 by some disgruntled fishermen following publication of the initial rules of quota allocations. The suits claimed that fishery managers had exceeded their authority in using individual quota. These suits were defeated in April 1991.

According to an article in *National Fisherman*, fishermen are divided over how well the new program was implemented. The initial allocation was supposed to favor fishermen who wanted to continue clamming. But critics charge that there is not enough quota to keep small independent vessel owners in business. Part of the problem, some argue, is that the government's determination of total allowable catch levels was based on outdated surveys of clam populations. Another criticism is that allocating quota on the basis of vessels allowed some fishermen who were not efficient because they committed more resources than were necessary to be rewarded with extra quota. Another criticism involved fishermen who built new vessels to harvest the deepwater ocean quahogs. They claimed that their quotas are not large enough to allow them to meet their financial obligations because the initial allocations were based on years when the resource was being underharvested (Moore 1992, 20-21).

Overall, ITQs have reduced the costs of fishing. Mid-Atlantic council director John Bryson says that the program expedited the retirement of vessels that were either too old or unneeded. Clam fisherman Bill Gifford, who added to his allocation by buying quota from retiring fishermen, says before the quota program was initiated, "I had to operate seven boats to catch what I do with one now" (Moore 1992, 22-23). Efficiency was also improved when the quota system eliminated a complicated regulation that limited each fisherman to six hours of clam fishing every two weeks (National Marine Fisheries Service 1991, 2).

While providing a more rational approach to the harvest, ITQs fall short of providing the same economic incentives that prompt the sole owner of an area to conserve fish stocks for future use (Boyce 1991, 4). Hence it is reasonable to ask whether establishing private property rights in the fishing grounds might not be a better approach. Privately leased oyster beds and salmon farms are cases that illustrate that when exclusive ownership exists, owners are willing to invest in improving the productivity of the resource.

Like oysters, surf clams and ocean quahogs are immobile and thus appear to be amenable to a similar arrangement. In any attempt to establish property rights, however, one must consider the costs of establishing those rights. While surf clams and ocean quahogs are certainly stationary, their habitat lies 30 or more miles offshore. As such, they are not as easily monitored for poaching as are the privately leased oyster beds which typically reside less than three miles from shore.

Of course, one could argue that new technological developments have enhanced the feasibility of assigning area rights to the fishing grounds of surf clams and ocean quahogs. The combination of a navigational system such as LORAN and plotter control of vessel operation make it possible to direct a vessel with considerable accuracy to a specific area, and confine fishing operations to that area. However, these technologies also make it easy for poachers to exploit their neighbor's claim. Unfortunately, no simple technology exists to exclude or detect the presence of trespassers on the high seas. Since the surf clam and ocean quahog fisheries are well offshore, subject to trespass, pollution, and weather, the clam fisherman today probably sees little to gain by factors beyond his control which could have significant effect on his investment.

Of course, that does not mean new developments in the future cannot dramatically lower the cost of establishing property rights on the high seas. Technology provided the means to change dramatically the face of the American West. In the 1870s, homesteaders and ranchers capitalized on the low costs of barbed wire to define and enforce their rights to rangeland (Anderson and Hill 1975).

It is important to stress that the evolution of technology will be closely related to the incentives faced by potential resource owners. Consider the development of barbed wire on the American frontier (Anderson and Hill 1975). Anyone who could effectively exclude others from the range could capture the rents from private ownership. Since wood and stone were prohibitively expensive for fencing, there was a ready market for an economical alternative; barbed wire filled the niche. Imagine how different the West would have been had a regulatory agency been charged with controlling grazing. There would not have been much incentive to invent barbed wire had private exclusion not been allowed. Given that regulatory agencies control access to most fisheries and leave little room for the evolution of private property rights, there is not as much incentive for entrepreneurs to develop the equivalent of barbed wire for the oceans.

West Coast Herring Sac Roe

Oregon's Yaquina Bay herring sac roe fishery provides the only American example of a privately managed individual quota agreement (Butler, personal communication). As it did before the program in 1989, the state limits the number of participants in the fishery and sets the season's schedule and total allowable catch, but it was the fishermen who recognized the efficiency gains inherent in establishing transferable quotas.

Prior to the agreement, competition among the nine fishermen had become so intense that the risks were unmanageable and the net returns low. On opening day, fishermen would rush out to the fishing grounds to capture as many fish as possible. According to Oregon fisherman Eugene Law, it was not unusual for the season to end in a matter of hours because fishermen had harvested the season's total allowable catch. Under intense competition, an equipment breakdown on opening day spelled financial disaster for the season, and each of the nine fishermen experienced such a disaster. Safety also was sacrificed; if a storm was forecast, a fisherman might lose his share of the season's catch if he stayed ashore while others ventured out. The race for the commons meant that fish were of lower quality because fishermen landed every fish they netted, including immature ones with little roe. This lowered the value of the catch by as much as 20 to 25 percent, according to Law (Law, personal communication).

In 1989, the nine fishermen agreed to individual shares in the total allowable catch for each of the next three years. Each fisherman agreed to try to catch one tenth of the total allowable catch set by the state. To allow for a margin of error, a tenth permit owned jointly by all nine fishermen was established. Income from landings made on this permit was distributed equally among the fishermen. A transfer of share to a new entrant in the fishery can only occur through the sale of one of the nine state issued permits to fish in this fishery. One such transfer has taken place since the program began (Butler, personal communication).

The program apparently has alleviated the tragedy of the commons and improved returns for fishermen. Fishermen can now choose the most opportune time to fish. When immature fish with low amounts of roe are netted they can be safely returned to sea to mature in approximately seven days and enhance the stock. This ability to land fish with higher yield has, in turn, led to higher annual profits for fishermen. Also, there is no longer any need to invest in annual equipment upgrades since fishermen are no longer competing with one another to catch fish. Savings have also resulted from economies of scale as some fishermen have teamed up on one vessel to catch their shares. Equipment breakdowns are no longer a catastrophe as they were before the individual quotas (Law, personal communication). State fishery managers are pleased with the program because it helps keep the harvests in line with the total allowable catch (Butler, personal communication).

Interestingly, the nine fishermen were able to come to terms despite differences in fishing ability. Prior to the start of the program, two of the nine fishermen were catching 30 percent of the total catch while the others caught roughly 10 percent each. Apparently an agreement to split the harvest equally among the nine fishermen produced enough benefits in terms of lower risks, guaranteed returns, and more flexibility to fish when they wanted to satisfy everyone. The small number of participants made it possible for the group to enforce the agreement on their own. Although fishermen are alert to the possibility that only poorer quality fish will be put into the tenth commonly held quota, there has been little indication that this is a problem. Satisfaction with the program prompted fishermen in 1991 to renew it for three more years (Law, personal communication).

If the number of participants increases, the cost of reaching and enforcing a private agreement may become prohibitive. Two herring sac roe fisheries in California's San Francisco Bay with 42 and 375 participants, respectively, provide interesting case studies of what happens when numbers increase. For the roundhaul (seine and lampara nets) fishery, the cost of reaching an agreement among the 42 participants apparently was not prohibitive, but the cost of enforcing the agreement was. For the gill net fishery, a consensus has not been reached among the 375 fishermen over the last decade (Maxwell, personal communication).

At the start of the 1980s, fishermen in the roundhaul fishery concluded that they needed an individual quota program to overcome the rising costs of competition and the low roe recovery rates. They solicited the California Department of Fish and Game to implement an individual quota program, which the agency did for the 1982-83 season. The program is now in its sixth year of operation. As in the Oregon fishery, shares of the total allowable catch are divided equally among the 42 fishermen, but there is not an extra permit to cover overages. The permits can be bought and sold.

The individual quota program has enabled fishermen to land fish with higher roe percentages and given fishermen greater operational flexibility. For example, some fishermen who fish for other species do not have to be on the herring grounds at the onset of the season. When poor weather occurs, fishermen have the option of waiting until it blows over. Overall, fishermen are quite pleased with the program (Maxwell, personal communication)

Enforcement is imperfect but state officials do not think the violations are serious. Cases of high-grading and fish smuggling by some fishermen have been reported by other fishermen, but managers think they have more significant enforcement problems with the gill net fishery which has an overall catch limit without individual quotas. Individual quotas have given fishermen more opportunity to catch and release fish in search of fish with higher roe percentages, but this may have resulted in unacceptably high mortality. As to why this happens in this fishery and not in the Oregon fishery where immature fish are also released, one can only speculate. Possibly, since the nets are larger and the catch is bigger it takes longer to select and release immature fish from the net.

Wreckfish

In March 1992 the National Marine Fisheries Service implemented ITQs for the rapidly developing wreckfish fishery in the South Atlantic region. This is a relatively new fishery with little evidence to date that the fish population is under stress from over fishing. A rapid rise in the number of fishermen and signs that the fishery is falling short of its economic potential, however, led managers and representatives of the fishing industry to agree to try ITQs (Gauvin, personal communication). From two vessels in 1987, the fishery has grown to an estimated total fleet for 1991 of 83 vessels though fewer than 50 are full time.

Prior to ITQs, there were emerging signs that the fishery was falling short of its economic potential. Prices paid to wreckfish were low during times of short-run oversupply.[9] This problem was exacerbated by the nature of total allowable catch management, which forced fishermen to fish when the season opens rather than when prices are expected to be higher or fishing costs are expected to be lower. Also, efforts by fish houses to augment consumer acceptance of wreckfish was being hampered by shortened seasons and limited times when fresh fish was available. Typical of fisheries without ITQs, fishermen were adding harvest capacity to their vessels or purchasing larger vessels in order to catch a larger share of the total allowable catch (South Atlantic Fishery Management Council 1991, 14-15).

Although it is too early to assess the impact of ITQs, there are a number of features worth noting. To be eligible for the fishery, applicants must have documented evidence of landings above a threshold amount of 5,000 pounds. The reason for this is apparently to limit entry to full-time wreckfish fishermen and thus avoid dilution of the initial quota shares. Of the 100 shares allocated initially, 50 shares are divided equally among the eligible fishermen while the remaining 50 are divided based on participants' percentages of total wreckfish catch between January 1, 1987, and August 8, 1990. This method of allocation is designed to strike a balance between rewarding those who have been more active in the fishery with larger percentage shares and allowing later entrants a chance to participate.

A shareholder's right to harvest wreckfish is defined in terms of a fixed percentage of the total allowable catch set for the season. This percentage does not vary from year to year but can be modified through trade. For example, an individual allocated a 4 percent share initially can sell all or part of it, or he can add to it by purchasing all or part of a share from another fisherman. Individual quota, given in pounds, is the quantity of wreckfish a percentage share translates into each year. For example, in a given year a percentage share of 4 percent and a total allowable catch of 1 million pounds translates into an individual quota of

40,000 pounds. If in the following year the total allowable catch is changed to 1.5 million pounds, then the individual quota rises to 60,000 pounds.

Whether shares are denominated as percentages of total allowable catch or as fixed quantities of fish is an important aspect of how well the ITQ system functions. When shares are expressed in terms of percentages, the amount of fish associated with each share automatically varies as total allowable catch varies. Managers are relieved of the burden associated with shares expressed in fixed quantities of having to reduce the shares outstanding or share size if the population is under stress. This is something which has caused problems with a few New Zealand ITQ programs (Muse and Schelle 1989, 93-94). In either case, the traded value of shares will reflect the degree of uncertainty associated with the fishery. In the case of the wreckfish fishery this can be a potential problem. Because biological information is lacking there could be significant adjustments in the total allowable catch and this, in turn, will affect the value of shares and the ability to trade shares.

In terms of transfer, all or portions of percentage shares can be sold to anyone without restriction. This contrasts with the Wisconsin chub ITQ program which subjects transfers to management approval. In Wisconsin this rule is used as a *de facto* provision to prevent percentage shares from being purchased by outside entities, i.e., fishermen or investors who are not a part of the original program. Although there is often public support for such restrictions, managers in the wreckfish fishery realized that such restrictions hamper market forces and prevent the flow of fishing rights to those with lower fishing costs or the ability to produce a higher value product. On the other hand, the transfer of all or portions of annual individual quota are restricted to holders of percentage shares only. Hence, to be able to buy or lease individual quota a person outside the program must first purchase some portion of a percentage share from someone in the program. Managers believe that restricting the sale of individual quota to vested shareholders strengthens the current enforcement strategy which relies on stiff penalties to deter violations. Under this strategy, a shareholder caught taking more than his quota can forfeit his share. The incentive behind such a penalty would be weakened dramatically if nonshareholders were allowed into the program through purchase of individual quota. These nonvested participants could violate their quota and not face the same consequences shareholders vested in the fishery face.

Summary Thoughts

This paper reviews a number of property rights structures in U.S. fisheries in the context of the economics of property rights. Several nongovernmental solutions to the fishery commons problem illustrate the efficacy of private ownership of fishing territories and/or fish stocks. Before such solutions will evolve, the economic benefits must outweigh the costs of definition and enforcement. But as the case of the Pacific Northwest Indian salmon fishing rights illustrated, private solutions will fail if the government fails to enforce them.

The cases in the United States where individual quotas have been applied long enough to evaluate the outcomes are few in number. The Lake Michigan chub and yellow perch fisheries, the Oregon herring sac roe fishery, and the herring sac roe roundhaul fishery in California's San Francisco Bay have produced notably positive results. While various restrictions in transferability have prevented these programs from attaining additional market benefits, the fact that individual rights to harvest are specified does relieve pressure to race to fish. Market gluts that plagued the fisheries prior to the quota programs have been eliminated as fishermen have spread fishing effort over the season.

If we are to move beyond the traditional regulatory regimes for managing resources where specifying property rights is more difficult, we can learn important lessons from the fishery experience. ITQs take us part way toward market allocation by assigning rights to a share of the harvest. This is similar to the establishment of tradeable pollution permits which give the permit holder a claim on a share of an air or water shed. Both cases, however, take us only part of the way toward a full market solution because the decision regarding how much will be harvested or how much pollution will be allowed remains in the political arena.

The assignment of transferable permits to fish or to pollute is an improvement over standard regulatory approaches, but prospects for more complete privatization should not be ignored. Since the rights are in the harvest and not in the stock of fish or in the fishing grounds, ITQs do not replicate the incentives a sole owner has to protect the resource (Keen 1991, 21). In the case of the surf clam and ocean quahog fisheries, it appears that private rights to beds would be a better approach if the costs of monitoring and enforcing these rights could be lowered. Allowing private fishing organizations to restrict entry also may provide better results than ITQs, but this will require that courts reconsider antitrust rulings in the context of the tragedy of the commons.

Finally, as barbed wire revolutionized private ownership on the America frontier, new technology may help "fence" fish. NASA satellites are already able to monitor fishing vessel locations. Such monitoring could help enforce against trespass if fishing grounds were privatized. While such technological fixes may seem like science fiction, they are also the stuff from which property rights evolve. Care must be taken not to construct bureaucratic impediments to this evolution.

Notes

1. For a more complete discussion of the role of customs and culture in overcoming the commons problem, see Anderson and Simmons 1993.
2. For a more complete discussion of the "race for property rights," see Anderson and Hill, 1983 and 1991.
3. Hide and Ackroyd (1990) describe this rent seeking in the context of New Zealand's efforts to establish ITQs.
4. In 1988, the total allowable catch was set at 2,688,000 pounds.
5. This division was based on fishing histories which indicated that there was a considerable difference between the landings of the thirty-second and the thirty-third persons; enough to conclude that there had only been 32 professional chub fishermen.
6. In 1987, there were nine leases of about 10,000 to 20,000 pounds each.
7. These fisheries provide the single greatest source of clam meat in the United States used in fried clam strips, chowders, sauces, and other products. In 1984, 70 million pounds of surf clams were landed, valued at $34 million.
8. Total allowable catch for the surf clam and for the ocean quahog fisheries was based on biological survey data collected annually from the 1960s through the early 1980s and on records of previous harvests (Mid-Atlantic Fishery Management Council 1991, 2-7).
9. In 1991, prior to the ITQ program, prices to fishermen for wreckfish varied from $1.00 to $1.30 a pound.

References

Acheson, James J. 1992. Capturing the Commons: Legal and Illegal Strategies. In *The Political Economy of Customs and Culture: Informal Solutions to the Commons Problems*, ed. by Terry L. Anderson and Randy Simmons. Lanham, MD: Rowman & Littlefield.

Agnello, Richard J., and Lawrence P. Donnelley. 1975. Property Rights and Efficiency in the Oyster Industry. *Journal of Law and Economics* 18 (October): 521-33.

_____. 1979. Prices and Property Rights in the Fisheries. *Southern Economic Journal* 42 (October): 253-62.

Anderson, Dan. Wisconsin fisherman. Personal communication (1992).

Anderson, Terry L., and P. J. Hill. 1975. The Evolution of Property Rights: A Study of the American West. *Journal of Law and Economics* 12 (October): 163-79.

_____. 1983. Privatizing the Commons: An Improvement? *Southern Economics Journal*, 50 (October): 438-50.

182   *Taking the Environment Seriously*

_____. 1990. The Race for Property Rights, *Journal of Law and Economics* 33 (April): 177-97.

Anderson, Terry L., and Donald R. Leal. 1991. *Free Market Environmentalism*. San Francisco, CA: Pacific Research Institute for Public Policy.

Anderson, Terry L., and Randy Simmons, eds. 1993. *The Political Economy of Customs and Culture: Informal Solutions to the Commons Problems*. Lanham, MD: Rowman & Littlefield.

Boyce, John R. 1991. Individual Transferable Quotas and Cost-Reducing Behavior in a Fishery. Unpublished manuscript. University of Alaska, Fairbanks (January 14).

Butler, Jerry. Oregon Dept. of Fish and Game. Personal communication (1992).

Chandler, Alfred D. 1988. The National Marine Fisheries Service. In *Audubon Wildlife Report 1988/1989*. San Diego, CA: Academic Press, Inc.

Christy, Francis T., Jr. 1986. The Flaw in the Fisheries Bill. *Washington Post*, April 13.

Christy, Francis T., Jr., and Anthony Scott. 1965. *The Common Wealth in Ocean Fisheries*. Baltimore: Johns Hopkins University Press for Resources for the Future, Inc.

Copes, Parzival. 1986. A Critical Review of the Individual Quota as a Device in Fisheries Management. *Land Economics* 62 (August): 278-91.

Federal Register. 1990. June 14.

Flaherty, Peter. Wisconsin Department of Natural Resources. Personal communication (1992).

Gauvin, John. Fishery economist. South Atlantic Fishery Management Council. Personal communication (1992).

Hardin, Garrett. 1968. The Tragedy of the Commons. *Science* 162: 1243-48.

Hardy, J.D., Jr. 1978. *Development of Fishes of the Mid-Atlantic Bight, Vol. III, Aphredoderidae through Rachycentridae*. U.S. Fish and Wildlife Service, F.W.S./OBA 78/12, pp. 106-12.

Hide, Rodney P., and Peter Ackroyd. 1990. Depoliticising Fisheries Management: Chatham Islands' Paua (Abalone) as a Case Study. Working Paper. Centre for Resource Management, Lincoln University, Christchurch, New Zealand.

Higgs, Robert. 1982. Legally Induced Technical Regress in the Washington Salmon Fishery. *Research in Economic History* 7: 82-95.

Johnson, Ronald N., and Gary D. Libecap. 1982. Contracting Problems and Regulation: The Case of the Fishery. *American Economic Review* 12 (December): 1005-22.

Keifer, Dave. Mid-Atlantic Fishery Management Council. Personal communication (1992).

Law, Eugene. Oregon fisherman. Personal communication (1992).

Leffler, Merrill. 1987. Killing Maryland's Oysters. *Washington Post*. (March 29).

Maxwell, Bill. California Department of Fish and Game. Personal communication (1992).

Mid-Atlantic Fishery Management Council. 1990. *Amendment #8 Fishery Management Plan for the Atlantic Surf Clam and Ocean Quahog Fishery.* Dover, DE, June 20.

_____. 1991. *1992 Optimum Yield, Domestic Annual Harvest, Domestic Annual Processing, Joint Venture Processing, and Total Allowable Level of Clams and Ocean Quahog FMP.* Dover, DE, September 6.

Moore, Kirk. 1992. New Plan Shakes Up Surf Clam Fishery. *National Fisherman* 72 (March): 20-3.

Muse, Ben, and Kurt Schelle. 1989. Individual Fisherman's Quotas: A Preliminary Review of Some Recent Programs. CFEC 89-1. Juneau, AK: Alaska Commercial Fisheries Commission.

National Marine Fisheries Service. 1991. Survey of Individual Quota Programs. In *Environmental Impact Statement: Initial Regulatory Flexibility Analysis for Proposed Individual Fishing Quota Management in the Gulf of Alaska and Bering Sea/Aleutian Islands.* Anchorage, AK; July 19.

Nichols, Bruce. 1986. The Past, Present, and Future of Magnusen Act Surf Clam Management. In *Fishery Access Control Programs Worldwide: Proceedings of the Workshop on Management Options for the North Pacific Longline Fisheries.* Alaska Sea Grant Report #86-4. Orca Island, AK: University of Alaska.

Scott, Anthony. 1988. Market Solutions to Open Access, Commercial Fisheries Problems. Paper presented at A.P.P.M. 10th Annual Research Conference, October 27-29.

South Atlantic Fishery Management Council. 1991. *Amendment 5 (Wreckfish), Regulatory Impact Review, Initial Regulatory Flexibility Determination and Environmental Assessment.* Charleston, SC, September.

Tietenberg, Tom. 1988. *Environmental and Natural Resource Economics,* 2nd ed. Glenview, IL: Scott, Foresman and Company.

Wisconsin, State of. *Wisconsin Administrative Code.* Chapter NR 25: Commercial Fishing-Outlying Waters.

Chapter 8

Community Markets to Control Agricultural Nonpoint Source Pollution

Bruce Yandle

Introduction

The regulation of environmental use in the United States is changing. It has to change. Past approaches are just too costly. Aside from cost, the micromanaged technology-based standards of the past cannot readily be applied to pollution that comes from streets, construction sites, and farms.

Instead of hard and fast input regulation, where central authorities mandate cleanup technologies for each and every source of pollution, more flexible performance standards that allow for cost minimization are emerging. The new emphasis is on the result, not the technology.

The quiet revolution now occurring in a few out-of-way places is not the result of scholarly studies or efforts by brilliant bureaucrats to engender more effective control. The change is driven by ordinary people who face the direct cost of meeting stringent and, in some cases, impossible pollution control standards. As it turns out, farmers are leading an effort that could bring common sense to federal water pollution control strategies.

Until recently, the burden of federal command-and-control regulation was felt heaviest in the industrial sector. That is where pollution control started. Ordinary consumers and investors paid for this in the form of higher prices and reduced dividends, but few individuals faced the full cost head on. The costs were widely dispersed. Agriculture escaped the heavy burden of meeting federally dictated rules for cleaning up farm wastes and limiting the runoff of nutrients, sediments, and animal wastes.

Of course, the agricultural sector bore the burden that came with controls on pesticides and other agricultural chemicals, wetland legislation, and meeting tougher standards for food products. But the burden of direct control continued to be postponed. That has changed. Today, federal coastal zone management statutes and state regulations require farmers to implement management practices intended to improve the water quality of streams, rivers, and aquifers in their regions of operation. The costs are high, and the number of farm operators is large.

Unlike industrialists, who generally speak for particular industries, such as steel, computers, and textiles, farmers speak for farming, all of it. Regardless of what farmers produce—corn, soy beans, sugar beets, or wheat—the newly imposed nonpoint source pollution standards hit them all. Their political voice tends to be heard. And unlike industrialists, farmers usually are part of a well-rooted community. They are wed to the land. Exit costs are high. Political muscle and community orientation combine to yield an interesting possibility. Property rights and community-based trading of rights to water use will likely emerge.

How This Chapter Is Organized

This chapter examines certain features of the newly emerging regulation of pollution from agriculture. Its principal purpose is to examine institutional arrangements that could support market transactions among farmers who seek to reduce discharge from their operations. Related to that are interactions with industrial polluters who continue to face increased pollution control requirements. Other polluters, such as cities that must deal with storm runoffs and construction firms that face erosion controls, may also become a part of a trading community that seeks to minimize the cost of hitting water quality targets.

The next part of the chapter briefly examines the old command-and-control approach that is still the dominant form of pollution control. Turning quickly to market approaches, the section offers a rationale for permit trading, illustrated by a highly simplified example. The section also explains why elements of command-and-control are likely to be observed in the new institutions that emerge. A discussion of point and nonpoint source pollution is included in the section, along with a summary of potential cost savings from trades that involve the two kinds of sources.

Section three considers some of the major problems assumed away in section two. These have to do with some serious scientific questions about the linkage between farm discharge and runoff and the quality of receiving streams, the tendency for environmental protection, which has to do with improving the quality of water and air, to be transformed to pollution prevention, which may have little effect on environmental quality. The section also discusses other policy conflicts that affect the agricultural sector.

The next major section focuses on permit trading, first discussing the situation where trade occurs between point and nonpoint sources of pollution. An analysis of trade among nonpoint sources ends the section.

Section five explores methods that might be used to progress from the current control regime to one that emphasizes market instruments. The discussion begins broadly, then narrows. It first focuses on institutions that have emerged for managing natural resources in a market context. Property rights and contracting are crucial to that process. The discussion narrows to the current environment and then provides a summary of traits and characteristics that appear to be necessary for permit trading to emerge.

The last major section is the most applied. It builds a discussion of permit trading in the current environment. The list of ideal characteristics developed in the previous section are folded into a world that compromises the ideal. Finally, the chapter concludes with some brief final thoughts and recommendations.

The Old and New Control Strategies

Command-and-Control Versus Marketable Permits

Command-and-control regulation works. Install enough machinery, hire enough inspectors, and eventually the amount of waste discharged into rivers will be reduced. But the approach is unnecessarily burdensome and basically at odds with American traditions and social norms. While regulation has practically always been a feature of the American enterprise system, the nation's economy is based fundamentally on the operation of free markets where owners of property rights follow price and cost messages received from markets. The messages provide the basis for economizing actions and mutually beneficial trade. By contrast, command-and-control is part of an authoritarian tradition, where politicians and their appointees manage economic behavior.

While the spur of market competition rewards lower cost producers and yields variety, command-and-control pays less attention to the costs borne by the consumers of regulated firms and producers; command-and-control goes for uniformity. Politicians and bureaucrats understandably seek to maintain their positions and minimize their own costs. Widely dispersed costs borne by consumers and investors hardly have a bearing on the politics of control.

Eventually, however, even the bureaucrats receive the message. Pressure to improve the effectiveness of regulation and to accomplish more with fewer resources causes them to consider market alternatives. Indeed, EPA Administrator William K. Reilly recently had this to say about the benefits of harnessing market forces:

The forces of the marketplace are powerful tools for changing individual and institutional behavior. If set up correctly, they can achieve or surpass environmental objectives at less costs and with less opposition than traditional regulatory approaches.[1]

Marketable Pollution Permits

Interestingly enough, Mr. Reilly was referring to the possible use of property rights and marketable pollution permits for the control of water pollution. What was he getting at when he pointed to the market alternative? Instead of writing more and more detailed regulations defining technologies to be applied at each and every outfall and then mandating proportional reductions in waste discharge from each and every source, a system of marketable permits simply sets the amount of discharge allowed by the holder of the permit. Market forces take hold from there. But there is more to the story than just saying the market takes hold.

Suppose ten firms are located in the same river basin and for some reason seek collectively to reduce the discharge of a specified pollutant now received in the river. To really simplify things, suppose that the discharge from each of the ten firms is known, and the effects of discharge on the river are identified. After a meeting attended by all the dischargers, each firm agrees to reduce pollution by half. Property rights to the remaining 50 percent, the allowed discharge, are defined and enforced. The property rights can be exchanged.

If one permit holder can reduce pollution at a lower cost than its neighbor in the same watershed, the higher cost operator can buy pollution discharge rights from the operator with lower cleanup costs. The low-cost producer cleans up far more than stipulated by the community agreement. The higher cost producer cleans up less. The total amount of waste discharged does not exceed the amount allowed. The idea seems so simple that one wonders why it is not been implemented with great frequency.[2] However, the simple description here assumes a lot about knowledge of pollution, its sources, and complex community and legal institutions that will be discussed later.

Whatever the institutional arrangements, the possibilities for trade hinge fundamentally on differences in pollution control costs and the value of pollution control. First off, if all pollution sources have identical cleanup costs, there are no potential gains from trade associated with cost reductions. Each and every producer might as well be told by a government regulator to cleanup specified amounts. Of course, if there are differences in control costs, the possibilities for gains from trade shrink if the methods for cleaning waste are mandated by regulation and all negotiations are managed by a bureaucracy that has little incentive to help other people save money.[3]

The magic of the market relates to the discovery incentive. If ordinary people with common sense can make money by finding cheaper ways to treat waste, they will find and apply new technologies. The discovery incentive is blunted when control techniques are dictated by command-and-control rules. Net gains from trade are reduced even farther when parties to a transaction are required to endure lengthy administrative hearings and engage in costly legal transactions when they seek to engage in trade. Of course, if pollution control costs are subsidized with tax money, polluters tend to accept the bureaucratic costs that bring them the revenues, even if the rules make little sense. Like all other ordinary people, polluters seek to minimize *their* net costs, which are not generally the same as society's net costs.

The value of pollution reduction, which is partly based on potential cost savings, is also related to the market price of goods and services produced by different polluters. Suppose the ten firms in our example include industrial plants, municipal waste treatment plants and farmers who generate waste that consumes dissolved oxygen in a particular river. To simplify things further for the sake of making a point, assume each polluter may be able to apply the same management practice to reduce the amount of waste received in the river. That is, their control costs are identical. There are still potential gains from trade in a polluter permit market.

If the market value of the farmer's product, per unit of waste sent to the river, is larger than that of the industrial plant, the farmer can gain by buying rights to discharge from the industrial plant. The industry will vacate its rights by cleaning up more waste. The farmer will expand discharge. The resulting trade leads to an increase in the total value of goods produced by the two trading parties.[4]

Grappling with the Problems

Ignorance and Uncertainty

There are immense problems hidden in this simple example. In general, agricultural waste is generated from a wide-ranging set of activities that are not specialized to one particular location. They are "nonpoint source" pollution. By contrast, industrial pollution generally emerges from the end of process pipes or other well-identified points. Those are referred to as "point source" pollution. There is another complicating factor. The linkages between environmental effect and point source discharge are often easier to identify. The gains from control can be estimated with greater accuracy. Identifying the environmental consequences of wide-ranging runoff of sediments and nutrients from hundreds of acres of land presents a more difficult task. Even when controls are implemented, it is difficult and costly to identify specific water quality changes and where they might originate.

Uncertainty is the problem. The direct linkage between agricultural "discharge" and the water quality of receiving streams is just not there. As one researcher put it: "The standard solutions that have been successful in controlling point source problems are unworkable for ... nonpoint pollution partly because it is generally not possible to observe (without excessive costs) the level of abatement or discharge of any individual suspected polluter or to infer those levels from observable ambient pollutant levels."[5]

The same issue surfaces in other research (Milon 1987, 387-95). Referring to nonpoint source pollution, a USDA report described the problem this way: "[O]ffsite damage associated with water pollution cannot be measured directly and links between farming and affected water uses are not well defined. Many assumptions are made to estimate offsite damage, and both methods and data for estimating damage need to be improved" (Crowder et al. 1988, 2).

Research on nonpoint source pollution in other countries indicates that phosphorous stream loadings from intense agriculture operations are quite low, in spite of the fact that phosphorous loadings are high in the fields (Loigu 1989, 213-17). The field-generated phosphorous combines with sediment to prevent stream damage. However, phosphorous loadings from industrial and municipal sources are highly interactive. On the other hand, high levels of agricultural nitrogen do reappear as stream nutrients. Taking rather simple steps, such as establishing sod filter strips between fields and streams, offers a viable remedy to this problem.

The uncertain linkage between what happens in a farmer's field and what occurs to the water quality of streams and rivers is a fundamental problem that stands in the way of any effective water quality management approach. Note the choice of words here. Water quality management is different from pollution control. Maintaining some level of water quality is the result, the output. Reducing pollution is an input. We can obviously find ways to reduce sediment and nutrient runoff, that is pollution control. What we cannot do is state emphatically that such actions improve water quality, and that presumably is what environmental protection is about.[6]

The Goal Shift: Water Quality Improvement to Pollution Prevention

It is far too easy for regulators to shift environmental goals. Such shifts can be extremely costly. The important goal of improving the quality of streams, rivers, and aquifers can be transformed to pollution prevention, which sounds good but is fundamentally at odds with science and economic logic. Improved water quality enhances life and brings economic benefits. Pollution prevention does not necessarily improve anything but the pocketbooks of machinery manufacturers and the employment of bureaucrats and regulators. Unfortunately, pollution prevention tends to become the goal, and water quality tends to be forgotten.

Instead of monitoring the quality of streams and reporting regularly to concerned people, regulators monitor inputs, whether or not controls are in place, and how production is managed. Almost inevitably, the problem becomes a technical one, and the policy debate gets focused on which technology to use. All along, little attention is paid to environmental protection.

The Conflict of Policies

A major policy conflict between environmental and agriculture price stability further complicates the problem. U.S. agriculture policy encourages production through a system of loan guarantees and target prices. The farmer is given strong incentives to bring fragile land into production (McSweeny and Kramer 1986, 159-73). In other words, the production effects of improved loan and target prices can completely swamp the effect of soil conservation and pollution control programs, causing the farmer to steer away from pollution control.

Permits, Point, and Nonpoint Pollution

The U.S. Experience

The story of U.S. pollution control has been largely one of command-and-control regulation where technology-based standards are specified for each source of pollution. Permit trading has been the exception to the rule. By and large, the cost of controlling private sector pollution has been borne by consumers who pay more for final goods and services. Special tax treatment of investment in pollution control capital is a relatively common feature, but generally speaking, there has been little in the way of direct subsidies to industrial polluters.

There are exceptions to the command-and-control regime. Marketable pollution permits have been used in limited ways in the United States for at least 15 years.[7] But their use has been confined primarily to air pollution from stationary point sources. Indeed, the 1990 Clean Air Act extends the use of marketable permits to the control of sulfur dioxide emissions from well-identified electrical utilities. Under the statute, electrical utilities are given a fixed number of sulfur dioxide emission allowances, which are fewer in number than their current emission levels. EPA coordinates trades among utilities. The very first trade under the new legislation illustrates the possibilities for gain (Davis 1992, 12F).

In 1992 the Wisconsin Power and Light Company found that it could exceed EPA's cleanup goals and operate well within its allocation of sulfur dioxide allowances. Doing so, the firm sold the annual right to emit an additional 25,000 to 35,000 tons of sulfur dioxide to the Tennessee Valley Authority and the Duquesne Light Company. The transaction was clearly profitable: Wisconsin Power added between $10 million and $20 million to the bottom line.

Tradeable permits have been allowed for the control of water pollution from industrial and municipal sources that discharge into the same river, but trade has been very limited. In all cases thus far, marketable permit systems have related to point source pollution. That is, the source of the pollution was easily identified and controls could be specified.

The fact that it is easy for regulators to identify machines to be controlled in industrial plants or in publicly owned treatment works is just a partial explanation of the dominance of technology-based command-and-control standards. Though cost effectiveness and flexibility are denied to operators of industrial plants, command-and-control makes life easier for regulators and simplifies life for firms that operate plants in multiple locations. Once implemented, command-and-control is assumed to achieve pollution reduction goals. If the control machinery is installed and operating, it is assumed the environment is protected. From industry's standpoint, one set of regulations to be met by all firms in a competitive industry is more desirable than uncertain approaches that might offer a competitive advantage to new and old firms alike.

The point about competitive advantage deserves a little more emphasis. The command-and-control approach generally favors larger more sophisticated operators who have technical expertise and scale of plant to operate effectively in the regulatory system.[8] Smaller operators are frequently forced out of business; output goes down and price rises. In other words, command-and-control regulation can be used for anticompetitive purposes. A system that relies on property rights and market forces cannot.

From a regulator's standpoint, the pollution from a coal-fired boiler at an electrical utility or a petroleum unloading dock can be identified, monitored, and controlled in reasonably well-specified ways. Emission reductions from one source in an airshed can be recognized, and those reductions can be used to offset another well-identified pollution source. Enforceable contracts can be executed. With some degree of workable accuracy, buyers and sellers can tell when the work has been done.

The development of control institutions for point-source pollution is one thing. Implementing controls for waste that washes from streets, construction projects, and agricultural operations is quite another. While the principle involved is the same, the institutions to support trade are quite different. At the same time, it is possible to conceive of arrangements where operators of point and nonpoint pollution sources in the same control region would be able to trade pollution permits (EPA Office of Water 1992). The gains from trade can be substantial.

Just How Large Are the Potential Gains?

It can be far more costly to control the same pollutants by means of command-and-control than by allowing polluters to minimize cost across sources of the same pollutants.[9] An excellent offering of such evidence is found in the work reported by Magat, Krupnick, and Harrington, who analyzed a raft of EPA background documents related to effluent limitations for the control of biological oxygen demand (BOD), a basic measure of pollution. The data analyzed covered a large sample of industry and subindustry groups.[10] But while the coverage is extensive, we must bear in mind that administrative, monitoring, and enforcement costs are not considered in the analysis. In other words, the single focus is on the cost of operating pollution control equipment.

The three analysts identified the incremental cost of removing a unit of BOD across many sources and found the cost varied from 10 cents per kilogram to $3.15 per kilogram, more than a thirtyfold difference in costs (Magat et al. 1986). A survey of capital costs for the same sample of industries found the incremental annual cost of capital for removing a unit of BOD varied from $59.09 per kilogram to once cent. The capital cost data indicate that a unit of BOD reduced at the cost of one penny in one plant can save $59.09 at another plant. The wide-ranging costs offer potential opportunities for significant cost savings if the polluters are allowed to trade permits.

Another glimmer of the possible gains from such an arrangement is reported in an EPA study that focuses on the prospects for permit trading in the control of nutrient runoffs from agricultural operations. The report, which in this case considered the cost of establishing a market framework, described a situation for the Tar-Pamlico estuary in North Carolina, which required estimated expenditures of $2 million to cover administrative personnel, the development of an estuarine and nutrient computer model, and for monitoring costs (EPA Office of Water and Office of Policy 1992). In this case, an industrial point source polluter that faced even higher control costs paid the cost of organizing and managing the institution. At one location in the estuary, further pollution reductions from industrial point sources would cost from $860 to $7,861 per pound eliminated. Nonpoint source reductions of the same pollutant from farms in the same location would cost between $67 and $119 per pound. The potential for gains from trade is obvious. But the institutional hurdles are still high.

How Do We Get to Permit Trading from Where We Are?

The Mandate

According to EPA, there are 18,000 bodies of water that will not attain water quality standards if every point-source polluter meets the letter of the law but nonpoint sources maintain their current methods of operating (EPA Office of Water and Office of Policy 1992). But a 1987 Conservation Foundation report indicates that the nonpoint source pollution problem reaches beyond surface water. At the time of the report, 34 states reported nitrates (generally assumed to come from agricultural runoff) as the most common groundwater contaminant.

Agriculture was listed as the "predominant source of the problem for both surface water and groundwater"; state government officials listed agriculture as the most widespread source of water pollution for 60 percent of the states, "causing problems in 64 percent of the river miles and 57 percent of the acre areas assessed" (Conservation Foundation 1987). But that was the state of knowledge, or ignorance, in the late 1980s.

Whether fully correct or not, something will be done to control agricultural nonpoint source pollution. Indeed, much is already being done. It is not that agricultural runoff is unchecked. It is the fact that the goals of the Clean Water Act cannot be met unless more is done. To some degree the mandate to clean up is a paper chase. The law requires pollution to be reduced, whether or not our knowledge supports specific actions. Substantial regulation of nonpoint source pollution is on the way.

In addition to what might be called the legislative necessity of doing so, which is to say that attainment of the goals of other legislation require the action, there are cost savings to consider. The Council on Environmental Quality's mid-1980s estimate of sources of key pollutants tells us about the relative position of various sectors. Some 6.1 percent of BOD discharge comes from the metals and minerals industry (Council on Environmental Quality 1989, 32-35). Municipal wastes account for 73.2 percent. Agricultural waste adds another 21.6 percent to the total. For suspended particulates, municipal waste accounts for 61.5 percent of the total; industry, 26.6 percent, and agriculture, 13.3 percent. However, since 1970, industry has reduced its level of pollution by some 71 percent. After many years of imposing ever tighter controls on industrial point sources, the incremental cost of additional reductions becomes quite large. That is, larger amounts of pollution may be avoided for lower costs if nonpoint sources are controlled. Amendments for doing so are being debated in Congress.

Can Command and Control Be Avoided?

Granted that the legislation train is headed toward agriculture, is it possible to load the cars with cost-effective rules and allowances for trade that will enhance overall efficiency? Will transaction costs overwhelm the control cost savings? Will the train carry a load of command-and-control regulation?

A naive forecast of any social activity says past behavior is the best predictor of the future, and a naive forecast is hard to beat. That being the case, one can say with confidence that command-and-control, technology-based regulation will dominate the control of nonpoint source pollution. A review of related documents supports the forecast.[11] There are several reasons for this regulatory dominance. First off, all environmental regulation has evolved in the form of centralized command-and-control; the bureaucracy understands it and is geared to produce it. It is cheaper for the bureaucracy to expand this product line.

Next, command-and-control appeals to planners, and the regulation of natural resources is largely the domain of public sector employees and officials who have little, if any, private market experience. They are a part of the socialized sector of the U.S. economy. When confronted with a problem, they understandably see a challenge to establish committees and commissions, to seek tax money, and then to establish a bureaucracy for dealing with the problem. The notion of leaving a problem in the hands of private citizens and the market is often antithetical to their views of how the world should work and is at odds with their personal experience. Problems are to be solved. Solutions are seen as written documents and reports to be adopted by or imposed on groups who implement the plan. Indeed, if marketlike instruments are used, they will likely be wrapped in bureaucratic clothing that limits their full play.

The tendency to regulate with command-and-control goes even deeper. The management of natural resources in the U.S. is largely a public sector activity. Still organized under the rules of feudalism, the environmental sector is managed by the "lord of the land" (Yandle 1992, 601-23).

Finally, there are the anticompetitive features of command-and-control discussed earlier. Put simply, command-and-control regulation that requires a reduction in pollution also leads to a reduction in product output.[12] The regulator becomes a cartel manager who enforces the restriction. Prices and profits rise so long as command-and-control rules the day.

The habit of applying command-and-control regulation is well ingrained, but the prospects for doing so in traditional ways for agricultural pollution is not so bright. Nonpoint source pollution simply does not lend itself well to the system developed for point source pollution. Even the above mentioned rules of best management practices allow for more flexibility than seen in point source regulation. Put differently, there is an opportunity to develop trading. Doing something different will require building institutions that support permit trading.

The Necessary Institutional Characteristics

In a 1991 report based on the experience of the major industrialized nations, the Organization for Economic Cooperation and Development (OECD) focused on how to apply economic instruments in controlling pollution. The report examined a full range of economic incentives, including marketable permits, which are described as being applicable to point and nonpoint sources.[13] Assuming that pollution is a known quantity that can be measured, preconditions for marketable pollution permits noted in the report include the following:

- Marginal control costs differ across pollution sources.
- Command-and-control standards impose excessive costs.
- The environmental goal is fixed.

- Incentives to discover and implement improved control approaches are needed.
- The number of pollution sources is large enough to support a market where transactions can occur.

All but the last item in the OECD list emerged in the earlier discussion of trading. Even that item was considered less than crucial by OECD. Just one willing buyer and seller will make the market function. Concern about market thickness introduces a focus on transactions and the practical aspects of trading. But that presupposes a willingness to trade that must be based on property rules or the force of law. Legal institutions do not emerge out of thin air.

Property Rights: A Central Issue

Markets can generate cost reductions, but markets are costly to operate. Once in place, they move spontaneously. The definition of property rights is a crucial piece to the puzzle. To bring a focus on property rights and motivation for trade, consider how pollution, including that from agriculture, was controlled under common law prior to the development of national statutes (Yandle 1989, 41-63; Meiners and Yandle 1992).

Under the common law doctrine of nuisance, owners of land downstream had a right to beneficial use of water that was of an undeteriorated quality. In the event of pollution from an upstream user, those damaged downstream could sue the upstream user. Proof of harm was required; injunction, not damages, was the remedy. The polluter was forced to cease polluting. Where more than one polluter was involved, all polluters were held jointly and severally liable, under a rule of strict liability. The common law also allowed for the enforcement of contracts between water users. An upstream discharger could purchase the right to reduce the quality of a receiving stream from downstream users. The party upstream was motivated to do so by rules of property. The burden of control of contract rested with the polluter, who consumed water quality belonging to others.

Common law rules developed from within communities, and they were based on well-specified property rights and measurable damage to those rights; they were not developed by external governments and imposed on communities. Common law courts, organized by communities, enforced the rules. And in ancient times, members of a common law community were ultimately liable, jointly and severally, for one another's actions. If one member imposed costs on the community and skipped town, any other member of the community could be held liable.

Under common law, a nuisance could be ruled private or public. If public, a local or state government official would bring suit on behalf of a group of harmed citizens who could prove damages. The remedy was the same. The polluter would have to stop the harmful action. Again, polluters had the option of contracting with the harmed citizens. Their rights could be purchased.

Sometimes communities moved to collective action and agreed to require all property owners to own nontransferable rights to a common-access resource, such as a common pasture or park (the commons). The rights went with the land; acquiring land meant acquiring an undivided proportional share of the commons. Separate courts were operated for the purpose of settling grievances among the land owners. If one land owner abused the commons, the others could bring action, since the value of their interest was affected by abuse of the commons.

Going beyond the common law tradition, communities sometimes developed associations for managing rivers. The modern experience with the Ruhr (Ruhrverband), Wupper, and Emscher river basin associations (genossenschaften) in Germany is a case in point where cities that discharge treated sewage, park operators that impose loadings, and industrial plants that affect a common watercourse, are required to own shares of the association and to be assessed the cost of maintaining water quality. Systems of fees and charges for discharge and recreational use are a part of this community water quality system. Operators who wish to increase their use of water quality are required to pay the association the cost imposed on other users of the stream or to take steps to reduce discharge, whichever is cheaper. If they pay discharge fees, they effectively pay the cost of maintaining the stream's quality. In effect, the expanding user is buying the right to use the river. No one specifies how a polluter will run a plant or manage a business. The "owner" of the river is interested in one thing: maintaining the quality of his asset. What might be termed "best management practice" is determined by market forces.

Consideration of these historical approaches, and recent experience with marketable permits, suggests there are certain characteristics common to the decentralized approaches that rely on established property rights. The following list contains what might be termed an ideal set of such characteristics:

- *Motivation:* Rules of property and liability are developed by members of a community who seek to improve their health and wealth. A surety system is developed that requires each community member to be liable for the costs imposed by any other member. If the system fails, the community must take offsetting action. Gains from trade under a rule of law motivate transactions.

- *Management:* The resulting property rule causes an affected river to be managed with ownerlike concern; its asset value is maintained. Management can be decentralized, under a rule of property law, or centralized, as in a river basin association.

- *Goal Certainty:* Baseline conditions are described for the river and for all uses that affect water quality; agreement is obtained regarding the level of quality to be maintained. Certainty regarding the level of quality to be maintained provides a scarcity parameter that motivates trade and quality controlling activities.

- *Transactions:* The property rule means that all water quality users deal with the owner/manager of the river. A decentralized system, like the land ownership system in the nation, means that individual buyers and sellers seek each other or operate through brokers when developing a permit trade. In a centralized system, the river basin manager is the broker.

- *Monitoring:* The water quality manager monitors water quality; members of the community have an incentive to do the same, since their investments are based on maintaining the asset. Monitoring certainty means that what is bought and sold is delivered. Those who poach on the system will be prosecuted.

- *Trading:* Mutually beneficial trade is allowed among members of the community who own rights to use water quality where the effects of the trade are confined to the trading parties. The water quality manager monitors trade and use of the stream. The terms of contracts are enforced. Members of the association have an incentive to the same, since they are liable for any excessive expenditures required to offset the behavior of cheaters.

- *Accountability:* Water quality managers are required to provide annual reports to each member of the association describing water quality conditions, levels of activity, and steps taken to maintain the asset.

- *Flexibility:* Unless transaction costs dictate it, there are no mandated methods for controlling pollution. Economic incentives and property rules interact to help water quality users find their least cost approach.

- *Entry:* New users of water quality must purchase rights from existing owners or pay the water quality association the cost of offsetting their discharge.

In considering this list, we must recognize that the common law did not work perfectly, nor have modern river basin associations. Indeed, it is unlikely that we will find a water quality management program that is perfect. At the same time, we can take the list of characteristics and observe just how closely they fit currently evolving institutions that might lend themselves to permit trading and the evolution of a market.

Permit Trading under Current Conditions

The Current Picture

At present, the U.S. system for controlling water pollution motivates industrial sources to seek lower cost alternatives. The system of command-and-control they face is tied to higher water quality goals. Their motivation is dictated by regulation, not by a rule of property. In a sense, the EPA holds the property rights to water quality and is insisting the industrial sources reduce discharge. But the system goes beyond mere insistence. Industrial dischargers are required to reduce their discharge in specified ways. Command-and-control is the baseline.

Agricultural users of environmental quality do not face a binding water quality constraint; they are not bound by EPA technology based standards. In that sense, agricultural users may first be viewed as passive players in a potential permit market. As passive players, they have the property rights to their current use of the environment, but their property rights are threatened by pending rules.

Nonetheless, industrial sources of pollution can reduce their cost of reducing discharge by enticing agricultural interests to transfer some of their discharge rights. How can the transfer take place?

Permit Trading in the Current Regulatory Environment

At present, agricultural users of the environment are viewed generally as nonpoint sources of pollution. Seen that way, they cannot readily install a piece of capital equipment at the end of a pipe and reduce their environmental loadings. Instead, they must change the way they cultivate land; modify their dairy operations; find substitutes for chemical fertilizers, and take other continuing management steps.

However, technology has a way of transforming nonpoint problems to point sources. A search for sources of agricultural discharge will lead to identification of particular pastures, feedlots, and concentrated dairy operations where waste treatment facilities can be developed in conjunction with sediment basins.[14] Alternately, an entire farm can be named a point source.[14]

Command-and-control will either dictate methods of operation or installation of treatment facilities, which will likely take on the form of technology-based standards. All of this can be achieved easier if farmers are paid by the operators of industrial point source systems. Still, a middle man is needed. An institutional arrangement has to exist.

Since the burden of control is on industrial sources, they are motivated to organize and fund a community of dischargers so as to minimizing control costs, which means finding low cost pollution control. A river basin or watershed association is a natural outcome, where a manager/broker becomes the intermediary between farmers and industrial dischargers. Once the association is formed and gains from trade are witnessed, farmers will be motivated to offer discharge reductions, to sell permits. They will be active participants in the market. Currently, farmers are unlike their industrial counterparts; they will not face penalties for not achieving specified pollution reduction goals. Of course, that condition will change if federal law specifies goals and penalties for agriculture.

The characteristics of a permit trading system, described above, tell us some of the functions of the association manager. The association must develop baseline data, identify the water quality goal to be met for specific pollutants, and document current activities and their impact on achieving the water quality goal. Of course, that is where current uncertainty is largest. The impact of agriculture on water quality is highly uncertain and quite variable. Still, with the baseline identified, the manager must monitor water quality and the behavior of all users.

If an industrial discharger finds a farmer who can reduce his discharge at lower cost, the industrial discharger will be willing to pay up to his alternative cost for the farmer's reductions. The association manager must monitor the trade and enforce the actions of the farmer, who reduces his discharge. The offsetting increase from the industrial source must also be measured and monitored.

Permit Trading among Nonpoint Sources

Gains from trade and the binding constraint faced by industrial point sources can motivate trade among industrial point sources and agricultural nonpoint sources of pollution. A change in the agricultural legal environment could motivate trade among nonpoint sources. If a binding constraint is imposed on nonpoint sources of pollution, which means their current rights to discharge are confiscated, then nonpoint sources will be motivated to minimize cost. The market for permits will expand to include farmers as buyers, not just sellers of permits. The binding constraint will have to specify levels of discharge to be achieved in a stated period of time.

Consider two farmers who face a sediment control constraint. Assume their operations have differing terrain and soil characteristics; their crops are different, as are their tillage and harvest methods. Further assume that a unit of runoff from the two farms has equal impact on the quality of a receiving stream. Both farmers are required by law to reduce their current levels of expected runoff. If farmer A can alter his crops and tillage methods at a lower cost than farmer B, there are potential gains from trade. Now, add to the market an industrial discharger of suspended solids who also seeks to reduce community discharge, his or someone else's. If the industrial discharger faces a higher opportunity cost than either farmer, he may purchase permits from both farmers.

The expanded situation contains binding quality constraints that may differ for all parties but are binding for each of them. The system may include technology-based standards for industrial dischargers and best management practices for farmers. That is, a regulatory baseline sets certain conditions that define alternatives for the trading parties. Even so, there can be gains from trade that result from differences in costs and differences in the value of product.

What Do Case Studies Tell Us?

At this point, it is safe to say that there have been no permits traded among nonpoint sources in the United States.[15] However, budding institutions for accommodating trade appear to be emerging. Whether or not they are ready to function is an open question. The EPA has documented the institutional characteristics, potential gains from trade, and the possibilities for point source/nonpoint source transactions (EPA Office of Water 1992); the regulatory constraints that motivate trade have not become binding, and in some cases there is a subsidized alternative for agriculture that should reduce interest in entering the market for permits.[16] However, a combination of continued economic growth, tighter regulatory constraints, and increased demand for water quality can combine to cause a market to emerge. Scarcity can be contrived by regulation.

As current systems stand, the motivation for trade comes largely from industrial sources. Baseline conditions are defined by management of river basin associations, state regulatory authorities, or the U.S. Geological Survey. Generally speaking, a team of specialists that include faculty from land grant universities and the U.S. Soil Conversation Service participate in baseline identification.

Since there have been no trades, nothing can be said about the form and enforcement of contracts. However, efforts have been made to develop modeling techniques that enable water quality managers to identify the water quality impact of nonpoint source modifications (EPA 1990). In addition, the EPA has developed proposed guidance for nonpoint sources that must meet the requirements of the Coastal Zone Act of 1990 (EPA 1991). This regulatory step is supplemented by a memorandum of understanding that addresses a joint effort to reduce agricultural pollution (EPA 1992b). Simply put, the locomotive of change is on the track and moving.

Final Thoughts on the Evolving System

The evolving system of water quality in the nation has now reached the point where agricultural firms and other nonpoint sources of discharge are a part of the pollution control scheme. The regulatory path followed to this point predicts that command-and-control, technology-based regulation will continue to play a fundamental role in the overall process. That is particularly the case for industrial sources of pollution and for municipal treatment works. However, the inherent difficulties associated with specifying technology for nonpoint sources raise the possibilities for a property rights system and enhanced ability to minimize costs.

In some cases, subsidy schemes will reduce the supply of pollution reduction permits from agriculture and work against achieving environmental goals; the potential benefit of gains from trade will be reduced. In other instances, the bureaucratic process involved in permit trading will be so burdensome that firms will be discouraged from attempting to enter the constrained market. However, encouragement can still be mustered when a community of interest develops in a watershed area and the people directly concerned take it upon themselves to organize a water quality management system based on flexible market forces.

At this point, the best possible outcome is for numerous experiments to develop where different approaches and different institutional arrangements emerge. Our best hope lies in the discovery process that always tends to emerge when scarcity beckons.

There is no doubt that scarcity will beckon. The EPA has recently released a draft study of the economic effects on the agricultural sector of meeting the requirements of the Coastal Zone Act Amendments of 1990, which affects 13 percent of all American farms, and 45 percent of all horticultural producers, including 48 percent of vegetable production.[17] Many of the management practices being discussed for all of agriculture are now a part of the requirements of the Coastal Zone Act. The projected impacts are large and significant, especially for smaller agricultural units. The EPA documents the number of vulnerable farms, the expected number of units that will exit the industry and the related price effects. In short, costs are high. The effects on water quality are still speculative.

Some Specific Recommendations

Given the high costs and disruptions expected from efforts to control nonpoint sources, it is important that communities, states, and regions be encouraged to find water quality management systems that match their particular soil, water, farming, and other characteristics. Permit trading is one option that will likely emerge in the experiments. It raises community issues that go beyond the notion of experimentation. The following recommendations address some of the issues:

- On a case-by-case basis, a set of scientifically determined baseline data must be obtained. These include determinations of the linkages between agricultural activity, discharge and runoff, and ambient water quality of affected streams. Water quality improvement, not pollution prevention, should be the goal for any trading community.

- Once an environmental constraint is set, it should not be changed arbitrarily. The constraint forms a property definition. Those who wish to reduce pollution beyond the total constraint should be required to purchase reductions from members of the affected permit trading community.

- A credible monitor/broker must be identified to maintain a set of baseline data, manage transactions, and monitor environmental conditions and activities across permit traders. The monitor/broker's services can be funded through a system of brokerage and membership fees.

- Farmers who achieve reductions in discharge beyond the requirements of an environmental constraint should be allowed to "bank" their reductions for future trade. Expanding members of a trading community will be required to purchase allowances from existing farmers.

- Trading communities should be encouraged to establish water courts of law that specialize in settling contract disputes and in handling suits that relate to abuses of the water law.

- Proposed changes in agricultural policy that affect production, commodity prices, and subsidy programs should be evaluated first to determine their impact on the environmental property rights formed by permit trading communities. If permits are effectively confiscated, the affected parties should be paid the market value of their lost assets.

This chapter has focused on institutions that have evolved for managing water quality and has described some changes that have occurred in the regulatory pageant. Property rights and the possibilities for gains from trade have been the focal points of the discussion.

The development of institutions for managing environmental quality is a study in community action; the environment, whether it be air or water quality, is still a common access resource that is made private through the design of legal arrangements, which is a community activity. If there are to be river basin associations or trade of pollution permits, it will be with the cooperation of members of an affected community.

If trade evolves, we can be certain that the resulting market will be highly regulated. However, given regulation, we can be confident that trading parties will be better off with the right to trade than without it. With property rights protection, we can also be assured that trade will improve the well-being of the larger community.

Notes

1. See Testimony of William K. Reilly. Reilly is not alone in his persuasion regarding the merits of the market. After almost 20 years of history using other approaches, the OECD has concluded that "economic instruments provide more flexibility, efficiency and cost-effectiveness." The multinational organization reports that "declarations at [the] highest political level call for a wider and more consistent use of these instruments." (See Organization for Economic Cooperation and Development 1991.)

2. The story sketched here is certainly not novel; details for such a scheme were described in 1968 by J. H. Dales. The fact that the United States has not chosen to follow the scheme reflects a deliberate choice, not a lack of knowledge.

3. A much documented and analyzed situation comes to mind here. The Fox River of Wisconsin is a case where a permit trading system was developed. Because of bureaucratic inertia and heavy regulation of technologies, the scope for trade finally vanished. For the optimistic story on the possibilities offered, see Joeres and David. For a description of what has not happened, see Yandle 1991a. Also see Maloney and Yandle.

4. The trading analysis here assumes that discharge from the industrial source is a perfect substitute for discharge reduction from the agricultural source. In a geographic sense, one can imagine a farm and industrial plant operating in close proximity. Trading ratios may be established to cause discharge from different locations to be equivalent. That is, one unit of waste reduction from a farm may be equal to two units from an industrial source, if the effect of industrial waste on water quality is half that of farm-generated waste.

5. See Segerson; her analysis recommends a reward/penalty scheme that deals with the problem on a collective basis.

6. EPA's document on the rural clean water program effectively describes the nonpoint source problem and management practices that can reduce discharge. However, in the extensive discussion of specific cases, the report generally fails to give solid, unambiguous evidence that the reductions in agricultural discharge translate into improvements in water quality. This scientific weakness is obviously a comment on the complex nature of the problem being addressed. See U.S. Department of Agriculture and U.S. Environmental Protection Agency.

7. For relevant discussion, see Yandle 1978; Hahn; and Hahn and Hester. For a useful recent survey of literature, see American Petroleum Institute.

8. See Pashigian 1984, Pashigian 1985, and Maloney and McCormick 1982.

9. The research on air pollution control is rather extensive. For a survey of findings, see Yandle 1991.

10. See Magat et al. A survey of studies of air pollution control costs by Yandle (1991a) indicates similar opportunities for reducing costs. He calculated the ratio of command-and-control to least cost controls (which assumes marketable

permits) and found the ratio to be as high as 22. The typical ratio was in the order of 4 to 5 to one.

11. For example, see U.S. EPA, *Managing Nonpoint Source Pollution*. For a survey of state programs, see National Water Quality Evaluation Project. For discussion of activity underway in North Carolina, see Division of Soil and Water Conservation. In general, these and other reports speak of and rely on "best management practices," which are technology based, as the basis for regulation.

12. For the theoretical insight, see Buchanan and Tullock.

13. Ibid., pp. 30-31. The report suggests that point source polluters can obtain the right to increase pollution by financing the expansion of "best available agricultural practices." (Ibid., 30.)

14. Both these ideas have been suggested by Alm.

15. This statement is based on the EPA 1992b report on the topic.

16. The North Carolina Department of Natural Resources and Community Development administers a state-funded program that provides 75 percent of the cost of adopting improved management practices in agriculture. The remaining 25 percent can be paid in cash or in kind.

17. The related EPA documents are: EPA 1992b, EPA 1992c, EPA 1992d, and EPA 1992e. The latter two items are a part of the draft reports. All are from EPA's Nonpoint Source Control Branch, Washington, D.C.

References

Alm, Alvin L. 1991. Nonpoint Source Pollution. *Environmental Science and Technology* 25: 1369.

American Petroleum Institute. 1990. *The Use of Economic IncentiveMechanisms in Environmental Management*. Research Paper #051. Washington, DC: American Petroleum Institute.

Buchanan, James M., and Gordon Tullock. 1975. Polluter's "Profit" and Political Response. *American Economic Review* 65 (March): 139-47.

Conservation Foundation. 1987. *State of the Environment: A View Toward the Nineties*. Washington, DC: Conservation Foundation.

Council on Environmental Quality. 1989. *Environmental Trends*. Washington, DC: Council on Environmental Quality.

Crowder, Bradley M., Marc Ribaudo, and C. Edwin Young. 1988. *Agriculture and Water Quality*. Washington, DC: U.S. Department of Agriculture.

Dales, J. H. 1968. *Pollution, Property and Prices*. Toronto: University of Toronto Press.

Davis, Erroll B. 1992. Cleaning Up Pollution. *New York Times* (May 17): 12F.

206   *Taking the Environment Seriously*

Division of Soil and Water Conservation, North Carolina Department of Natural Resources and Community Development. 1987. *North Carolina Agriculture Cost Share Program for Nonpoint Source Pollution Control*. Raleigh, NC: Division of Soil and Water Conservation (May).

Environmental Protection Agency. 1990. *Biological Criteria*. Washington, DC: EPA (April).

_____. 1991. *Proposed Guidance Specifying Management Measures for Sources of Nonpoint Pollution in Coastal Waters*. Washington, DC: EPA (May).

_____. Office of Water. 1992. *Managing Nonpoint Source Pollution*. EPA 506/9-90. Washington, DC: EPA (January).

_____. Office of Water and Office of Policy. 1992. *Incentive Analysis for Clean Water Act Reauthorization: Point Source/Nonpoint Source Discharge Reductions*. Washington, DC: EPA, April.

_____. 1992a. *Fact Sheet: Agriculture and Pollution Control*. Washington, DC: EPA, April.

_____. 1992b. *Draft: Economic Impact Analysis of Coastal Zone Management Measures Affecting Confined Animal Facilities*. Washington, DC: EPA (June 11).

_____. 1992c. *Preliminary Economic Achievability Analysis: Agricultural Management Measures*. Washington, DC: EPA, (June 12).

_____. 1992d. *Agricultural Impacts of Erosion Management Measures in Coastal Zone Drainage Basins*. Washington, DC: EPA.

_____. 1992e. *Agricultural Impacts of Requiring Alternative Conservation Systems in Coastal Zone Drainage Basins*. Washington, DC: EPA.

Hahn, Robert W. 1989. Economic Prescriptions for Environmental Problems: How the Patient Followed the Doctor's Orders. *The Journal of Economic Perspectives* (Spring): 95-114.

Hahn, Robert W., and Gordon L. Hester. 1989. Marketable Permits: Lessons from Theory and Practice. *Ecology Law Quarterly* 16:361-406.

Joeres, Erhard F., and Martin H. David. 1983. *Buying a Better Environment*. Land Economics Monograph No. 6. Madison: University of Wisconsin Press.

Loigu, E. 1989. Evaluation of the Impact of Non-Point Source Pollution on the Chemical Composition of Water in Small Streams and Measures for the Enhancement of Water Quality. In *Advances in Water Pollution Control*, ed. by H. Laikari.

McSweeny, William T., and Randall A. Kramer. 1986. The Integration of Farm Programs for Achieving Soil Conservation and Nonpoint Pollution Control Objectives. *Land Economics* 62 (May): 159-73.

McSweeny, William T., and James S. Shortle. 1990. Probablistic Cost Effectiveness in Agricultural Nonpoint Pollution Control. *Southern Journal of Agricultural Economics* 22 (July): 95-104.

Magat, Wesley A., Alan Krupnick, and Winston Harrington. 1986. *Rules in the Making: A Statistical Analysis of Regulatory Agency Behavior.* Washington, DC: Resources for the Future.

Maloney, Michael T., and Robert E. McCormick. 1982. A Positive Theory of Environmental Quality Regulation. *Journal of Law and Economics.* 25: 99-124.

Maloney, Michael T., and Bruce Yandle. 1983. Building Markets for Tradable Pollution Permits. In *Water Rights,* ed. by Terry Anderson. San Francisco: Pacific Institute for Public Policy Research.

Meiners, Roger E., and Bruce Yandle. 1992. Constitutional Choice in the Control of Water Pollution. *Constitutional Political Economy* 3 (Fall): 359-80.

Milon, J. Walter. 1987. Optimizing Nonpoint Source Controls in Water Quality Regulation. *Water Resources Bulletin* 23 (June): 387-95.

National Water Quality Evaluation Project. 1989. *NWQEP 1988 Annual Report: Status of Agricultural Nonpoint Source Projects.* Raleigh, NC: Biological and Agricultural Engineering Department, North Carolina State University, May.

Organization for Economic Cooperation and Development. 1991. *Environmental Policy: How to Apply Economic Instruments.* Paris: OECD.

Pashigian, Peter. 1984. The Effects of Environmental Regulation on Optimal Plant Size and Factor Shares. *Journal of Law and Economics* 27 (April): 1-28.

_____. 1985. Environmental Regulation: Whose Interests Are Being Protected? *Economic Inquiry* 23 (October): 551-84.

Sergerson, Kathleen. 1988. Uncertainty and Incentives for Nonpoint Pollution Control. *Journal of Environmental Economics and Management* 15: 87-98.

Testimony of William K. Reilly, U.S. Environmental Protection Agency. 1991. Presented before the U.S. House of Representatives, March 20, Washington, DC, 32-33.

U.S. Department of Agriculture and U.S. Environmental Protection Agency. 1991. *The Rural Clean Water Program: A Report.* Washington, DC.

Yandle, Bruce. 1978. The Emerging Market in Air Pollution Rights. *Regulation* (July/August): 21-29.

_____. 1989. *Political Limits of Environmental Regulation.* Westport, CT: Quorum Books, Inc.

_____. 1991a. A Primer on Marketable Permits. *Journal of Regulation and Social Costs* 1: 25-41.

_____. 1991b. *Why Environmentalists Should Be Efficiency Lovers.* St. Louis: Washington University Center for the Study of American Business (April).

_____. 1992. Escaping Environmental Feudalism. *Harvard Journal of Law and Public Policy* 15 (March): 601-23.

Chapter 9

Risky Business: Rational Ignorance in Assessing Environmental Hazards

Daniel K. Benjamin

Introduction

Life is both dangerous and uncertain. Faced with hazards, we must assess their magnitudes and choose among them. Risk assessment, as it has come to be known, is the process of acquiring and evaluating information about hazards, to establish an estimate of their magnitudes. At its best, the process of risk assessment enables us to transform the uncertainties of what *might be* into the reality of what *is*. Electric power, for example, may be generated by either nuclear fuel or fossil fuel; one poses the menace of radioactive contamination, while the other threatens air pollution and acid rain. Which fuel is more hazardous?

Equipped with assessments of the risks, we may then undertake risk management—the process of deciding which hazards are acceptable and which are not. Risk management involves the formulation of policies—and thus choices—that transform what *is* into what *will be*. For example, motorcycles are more dangerous than automobiles; should we ban motorcycles, require cyclists to wear helmets, or simply inform people of the hazards and allow them to make their own choices?

Much of the debate over environmental policymaking implicitly assumes that the process of hazard assessment has been completed successfully. Once we know, for example, that the regulation of airborne asbestos would save ten lives per year at a cost of $104.2 million per life saved, the risk management issue is quite clear: Is a human life worth $100 million or not (Morrall, 1986)? But suppose the estimate of lives saved is off by a factor of 10 or 100, thereby distorting the cost per life saved by the same multiple. The risk management issue—do the benefits warrant the costs—would remain the same, but only by chance would the regulatory *decision* remain unchanged.

Ultimately, the environmental policy choices we make are no better than the hazard assessment process that antecedes those choices. If we err in the risk assessment process, then the chances rise that we shall err in the risk management process. This in turn increases the likelihood that our choices will make us worse off rather than better off—and may ultimately lead to more rather than less environmental destruction.

Over the past 25 years, Americans have delegated much of the risk assessment process to government agencies. While there are many reasons for development, there is little doubt that one of the reasons is the growing belief that individuals may be unable to accurately make accurate hazard assessments on their own. Indeed, there exists a body of literature which argues that individuals are subject to systematic errors when assessing the hazards they confront.[1] Specifically, it seems, individuals regularly tend to overestimate the risks of relatively safe activities and underestimate the hazards of relatively dangerous activities. Given such a pattern, it would appear sensible to redirect hazard assessment from individuals and into the hands of the experts at government agencies.

Yet there also is evidence that the experts are prone to error—or at least prone to assess hazards in such a way that subsequent risk management decisions cannot help but be in error (National Academy of Sciences 1983; Nichols and Zeckhauser 1986). In particular, the drive for prudence in risk assessment has evolved into a degree of conservatism that can only be viewed as extremism: At every point in the process, the most conservative (i.e., worst case) assumptions are made, so that at the end of the process, the compound effect may be to overstate the true risks by a factor of 10 or even 100—without saying so. The result is not merely inappropriate (and excessively expensive) attempts to reduce environmental hazards that are far less dangerous than advertised; along the way, the *relative* hazards of different threats may be so severely distorted that we end up attacking the less serious risks, leaving the more deadly to wreak their havoc.[2]

If it is true that perfect judgment is unlikely on the part either of the individuals exposed to risks or of the public servants charged with regulating risks, it becomes prudent to ask the question, How serious are the errors that individuals make when they assess hazards? In search of an answer to this question, I address three key issues. First, I reexamine the risk perception data that has been the springboard for the literature arguing that individuals are prone to serious biases in hazard assessment. I find that the actual biases in hazard assessment are far smaller than they appear to be; indeed, when I examine hazards most relevant to the individuals involved, their assessments are strikingly accurate. Second, I examine a growing body of literature that deals with the ability of individuals to learn about the risks present in their environment. I find that there is increasingly strong evidence that as the rewards to being unbiased rise, the extent of bias diminishes. In effect, accuracy (of which bias is a component) is a matter of choice for individuals; their refusal to choose perfection in risk assessment is thus little different from their refusal to constrain their automobile portfolios to Rolls-Royces—which is to say, worthy of lament only in a world without scarcity. Third, and only briefly, I touch upon the growing dissatisfaction with the science and politics of risk assessment as undertaken by the experts. My overall assessment from this exercise thus comprises three elements: (1) individuals are much better at assessing risks than might be expected; (2) when the rewards to being right are high, people become better at it; and (3) there is little reason to believe the so-called experts could do much better.

Background

Over the past 20 years researchers in both economics and psychology have identified numerous seeming anomalies in the way individuals make assessments about uncertain outcomes.[3] There are many phenomena that are not yet well understood. For example, most individuals appear to be grossly overconfident in their ability to judge the likelihood of uncertain outcomes; people rely too heavily on small samples and on the "availability" of evidence (i.e., on their ability to readily recall events); and they tend to "anchor" their estimates, under-adjusting probabilities in response to new information. I do not attempt to resolve all of these behavior patterns. Instead I seek to understand a narrow but important type of apparent error on the part of individuals: their inclination to overestimate the probability of low-risk hazards and underestimate the probability of high-risk hazards.

One example of the propensity for such biases is evident in Figure 9.1, prepared with data presented (Lichtenstein et al. 1978). Two separate groups of college students were told the annual death toll from one of two causes (motor vehicle accidents or electrocutions) in the United States, and then asked to estimate the frequency of 40 other causes, ranging from smallpox to heart disease. The actual and estimated death rates are plotted on logarithmic scales in Figure 9.1, together with a 45-degree line, along which the data would fall if estimated and actual frequencies were equal. It is apparent from this figure (and may readily be confirmed statistically) that the student responses do not match the actual frequencies. Indeed, the student responses are biased in a specific manner: They markedly overestimate the frequency of death for infrequent causes of death (such as botulism), and underestimate frequencies for common causes

Taking the Environment Seriously

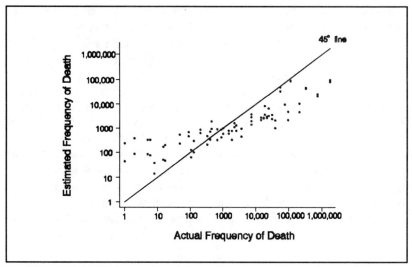

Figure 9.1 Estimated and Actual Frequencies of Death, 1973

of death (such as heart disease). The original discoverers of this apparent bias offered no explanation for its existence, but were led to conclude that "People do not have accurate knowledge of the risks they face" (Lichtenstein et al. 1978, 578). I begin by showing that despite its existence, this bias has little do with the risks people face, and—by inference—little to do with the decisions they make. I then inquire into the relevance of my findings for environmental policy.

Salience

The numbers behind Figure 9.1 were stimulated by a request that experimental subjects (college students) estimate "the frequency of deaths in the U.S. due to ... [these] lethal events...." It is apparent that the students were not very good at answering the question that was asked. Yet it is not obvious why they (or anyone else except a statistician at the Centers for Disease Control) might have the slightest interest in knowing what the true numbers might be. This seems a peculiar contention, so I must be clear about what is meant.

Lichtenstein et al. interpret the data on frequencies of death by cause as being "the risks [people] face." In effect, these frequencies are viewed as being the outcome of multiplying the U.S. population by the true probabilities of dying from each of those causes. Thus, with a population of 205,000,000 at the time of the study, and 1,025 deaths from electrocution, Lichtenstein et al. treat (1,025/205,000,000) as being the probability that their respondents will die of electrocution. Thus, accidents involving motor vehicles and trains (which caused

1,517 deaths) are viewed as being approximately 50 percent more hazardous than electrocution for the survey respondents, while lightning strikes (which killed 107 people) are only about one-tenth as dangerous. Oddly, Lichtenstein et al. adopt this interpretation despite the fact that they did *not* ask any of the following questions:

(1) What is the probability that a representative person will die during the next year due to each of these causes?
(2) What is the probability that you (the respondent) will die next year due to each of these causes?
(3) What is the probability that you or a representative person will die over the course of a lifetime due to each of these causes?

Just as strangely, the entire literature that has expanded upon Lichtenstein et al. has followed their original interpretation of the numbers, despite the fact that the data itself may have (almost) nothing to do with such judgments by individuals (Arrow 1982; Slovic et al. 1982; Viscusi 1985).

To see the distinction, consider the following. Imagine asking a group of people how many people die as a result of (1) gunshot wounds and (2) lung cancer. Now imagine *interpreting* the replies as being responses to these questions: (1) What is the probability that you will die of a gunshot wound if you put a loaded handgun to your temple and pull the trigger? (2) What is the probability that you will die of lung cancer if you smoke a cigarette? For any remotely plausible set of answers to the questions actually asked, one would surely conclude—given the interpretations of the questions—that the respondents had no clear idea of the hazards of life that they faced. As absurd as this example might seem, I hope to show that it is nevertheless a useful approximation of the approach and subsequent interpretation of the work by Lichtenstein et al.

Like Parent, Like Child?

The causes of death examined by Lichtenstein et al., and the frequencies of death for each cause, are shown in Table 9.1. There are two attributes of these causes that are worthy of note. First, the latency of the causes—the delay between onset and death—varies enormously. For example, emphysema, syphilis, and lung cancer are all long latency causes, for the delay between the action that initiated the death and the death itself is typically measured in terms of decades. Conversely, measles, drowning, and falls are all short latency causes, for the delay between onset and death usually only ranges from minutes to a few days at most. The second significant attribute of these causes is that the age at which they kill varies enormously. The youngest killer is measles (at 8.7 years), while the oldest killer is strokes (at 78.4 years).[4]

The average death rates for these causes are the *ex post* outcomes of a variety of processes, some of which go back fifty years or more. The fatalities produced by long latency causes, such as cancer, stroke, and heart disease, are the result of past exposure rates, latency, lethality, and so on that are surely relevant for the parents and grandparents of the respondent students but may have little to do with the future likelihood of death for the students.

Even if one were buying or selling life insurance, for example, the gross mortality statistics utilized by Lichtenstein et al. might do little more than establish the orders of magnitudes of the deaths due to various causes. Thus, between 1973 and 1988 the fatality rates for both emphysema and automobile accidents fell sharply (by 45 and 16 percent, respectively), while the rates for lung cancer and suicide both rose sharply (by 70 and 21 percent, respectively).

Since insurance contracts cover *future* hazards, the fatality rates for 1988 would seem at least as relevant to students in 1973 as were 1973 fatality rates. So, I would argue, it is not surprising that the students would know little about 1973 fatality frequencies for many of the causes in Table 9.1, simply because such numbers would be of little relevance to them.[5]

Table 9.1 Frequencies of Death, 1973

Cause	Deaths
Smallpox	0
Vitamin poisoning	1
Botulism	2
Measles	5
Fireworks	6
Smallpox vaccine	8
Whooping cough	15
Polio	17
Venomous bite	48
Tornado	90
Lightning	107
Nonvenomous bite	129
Flood	205
Hypothermia	334
Syphilis	410
Pregnancy	451
Hepatitis	677
Appendicitis	902
Electrocution	1025
Motor vehicle/train	1517
Asthma	1886
Firearms	2255
Poisoning (other)	2563
Tuberculosis	3690
Drowning	7380
Fire and flames	7380
Leukemia	14555
Falls	17425
Homicide	18860
Emphysema	21730
Suicide	24600
Breast cancer	31160
Diabetes	38950
Motor vehicle crash	55350
Lung cancer	75850
Stomach cancer	95120
All accidents	112750
Stroke	209100
All cancer	328000
Heart disease	738000
All disease	1740450

Is All Ignorance Bad?

Should we be concerned that the students (or any respondents) have no idea how many people died of a particular cause, such as lung cancer? For individuals to make correct decisions, they should know something about the hazard rates of the activities *they* will be undertaking. Consider bungee jumping and cigarette smoking. The adverse consequences of bungee jumping are immediate, and the observed frequency of jumping deaths will equal the probability of dying from it (*conditional* upon engaging in it) multiplied by the number of people who engage in the activity. We would expect bungee jumpers to be able to correctly assess the probability of dying or being injured while engaging in their sport. We might even question their rationality (or at least their intelligence) if they erred seriously in making this assessment. Yet even if a bungee jumper has an un-biased estimate of the probability of dying from her activity, she may not be very good at estimating the incidence of bungee deaths in the entire population, unless she also is good at estimating the population exposure rate for bungee jumping.

The contrast between individual hazard rates and population death frequencies is even more striking in the case of cigarette smoking. Most life-threatening adverse effects of smoking emerge only after about 20 pack-years of exposure.[6] So I ask, what is the hazard associated with smoking? "The" hazard depends on what is meant by "smoking." If we mean smoking one cigarette (the equivalent of one bungee jump?), then the answer is approximately zero (which is to say, only slightly higher that the risk of igniting the match used to light the cigarette.) If we mean smoking a pack per day for a year, then aside from immolation considerations, the risk remains about zero. And even if we mean the risk of smoking for 20 or 30 pack-years, the answer still may bear only tangentially on the observed death rate in the population as a whole—which depends on the actual exposure rate (how many people smoke and how long they smoke), the adverse effects of that amount of smoking, and the probability that something *else* will kill them before they die of smoking-related causes. In general, then, for long latency causes, I would expect an even lower ability of the individual to predict death rates in the population as a whole, and rightly so, because death rates for the population as a whole are even further removed from anything relevant to the individual.

The Relevance of Hazard Rates

For any potential cause of death, the actual probability of death (what I call the *hazard rate*) is equal to the probability of death conditional on exposure (or *lethality*), multiplied by the probability of exposure: $p = p_d \cdot p_e$. Thus, causes of death may differ from one another both in terms of their exposure rates (p_e) and their lethality (p_d). To take but one simple example: People of all ages fall down, yet falling is rarely lethal, *except* for the elderly. As people age, protective reflexes slow, bones become more brittle, and so on, so that the probability of dying from a fall begins to rise sharply at around age 65, because it is at that point that p_d begins to rise. As a result, the average age of death conditional upon dying from a fall is approximately 73 years.[7] Toward the other end of the spectrum, driving an automobile into a concrete bridge abutment at 85 miles an hour is almost always fatal ($p_d \approx 1$) to the occupants of the vehicle. Yet deaths by this cause are relatively rare, except among the young, who are prone to drive fast and to drive under the influence of alcohol and drugs. Since the probability of an 85 mph exposure to a bridge abutment (p_e) is relatively high for young persons, the average age of death due to automobile accidents is but 38.

Thus, due to variations in both p_d and p_e, the age profiles of the hazard rate can differ dramatically from one cause of death to another. Neither Lichtenstein et al. nor any of the subsequent work on risk assessment has accounted for this possibility. Instead, the standard method has been to treat the population death rate as the true hazard rate relevant for all individuals. In general, however, the hazard rate for any given segment of the population will not equal the population death rate, a fact that readily may be illustrated by simply examining the data.

In Figure 9.2, I show the distribution of deaths by age of death for two specific causes of death: stroke and homicide. The pattern for strokes is very much like that observed for other long latency killers such as heart disease, most cancers and so forth. The pattern for homicides is also representative of many other sudden killers, including motor vehicle accidents, electrocution, firearm accidents, and the like. By definition, $p_d = 1$ for homicides, so that the time pattern of deaths for this cause also illustrates the fact that, in general, rates of exposure to those activities that cause sudden death are not fully independent of age. In fact, for such causes of death, the hazard rate for young people is typically substantially greater than the population death rate, while for older people, the hazard rate is well below the population death rate (except, of course, for falls). Clearly, the deviation of a person's hazard rate from the population death rate for a given cause of death will depend on the age profile of the hazard rate and the age of the person in question. In the case of college students (the source of the data used in Figure 9.1), the hazard rate of things that tend to kill the young (such as motor vehicle accidents) will be greater than the population death rate for that cause, while the hazard rate for things that kill the elderly will be substantially lower than the population death rate.

Thus, if respondents base their estimates of *population death frequencies* on their own *hazard rates* (data with which they have some reason to be familiar), there will be a systematic effect of the age profile of a given cause of death on the deviation of the respondents' estimates from the actual population death rate: Respondents will offer up higher estimates (relative to population frequencies) for those causes that tend to kill earlier in life, and lower estimates for those causes that tend to kill later in life. If the age at which death occurs is not taken into account, the result will be exactly the sort of bias reported by Lichtenstein et al.: Low frequency events will be overestimated, while high frequency events will be underestimated.

This inference can be tested by explicitly allowing the effect of the population death rate to depend on the age of death. Doing so yields some striking conclusions (Benjamin and Dougan 1992). First, as predicted by the preceding students' estimates of the hazard rate; for any given population death rate, discussion, the age at which a cause kills has a strong negative effect on causes that kill earlier are viewed as more hazardous than causes that kill late in life.

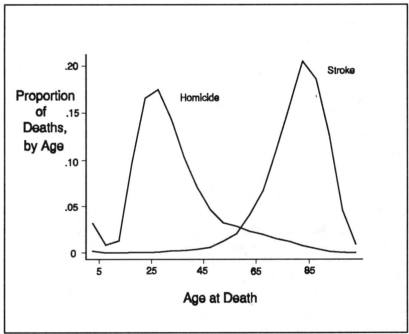

Figure 9.2 Incidence of Death by Age of Death

In effect, the student-respondents are (quite sensibly) discounting the hazards associated with causes of death that kill chiefly the elderly. Second, accounting for age of death dramatically increases predictability of the students' responses. Following the Lichtenstein et al. method, which considers only the population death rate, only about 20 percent of the students' responses can be explained statistically. Once the age of death is accounted for, nearly 80 percent of the student responses can be explained. Third, even for causes of death that are the least frequent, and thus most overestimated according to Lichtenstein et al., accounting for age of death brings the students' responses into close conformity with the facts. For example, there were no fatalities from smallpox in the Lichtenstein et al. sample; the student estimates that take age into account imply a fatality rate of 0.82 deaths per million. That is, when the true probability is zero, the students respond "the probability is one in a million." Finally, the estimates I have developed enable me to infer the accuracy of the students in estimating the hazard rates most relevant to them—those that apply to causes that kill people their age. Thus, consider a hypothetical cause with an average age of death equal to the age of the respondent students. One might ask, what is the implied difference between the estimated death rate and the true death rate? If I assume the average age of the students to be 20, this difference is about 4 percent, a number that is small arithmetically, and is also not statistically different from zero. Of course the assumption that the students are 20 years old is arbitrary. One might alternatively ask, what age would the students have to be for their estimated death rate to be *exactly* equal to the true death rate? The answer is 17.5—which is not far from the average age of incoming college freshman.

Taken together, these findings suggest that for causes with an average age of death equal to the age of respondents, there is virtually no tendency for people to overestimate low-probability events or underestimate high-probability events. Apparent biases such as those reported by Lichtenstein et al. are due to the fact that in the United States, causes that kill large numbers of people also tend to kill older people disproportionately.

My interpretation of these results may be summarized quite simply: Lichtenstein et al. asked the students an irrelevant question. For most causes of death, the observed population death frequency is at most only slightly related to the hazard rate facing the respondents to the question. My findings strongly suggest that the students responded to this question with answers that look remarkably like the hazard rates relevant for individuals in their age bracket. As it turns out, there is additional evidence that enables me to subject this inference to even more demanding tests.

More on Hazard Rates

The same study that produced the numbers I have been using thus far also produced another set of numbers which confirm the basic hypotheses I have laid out thus far. Lichtenstein et al. surveyed two additional groups of subjects—one again comprising students, the other consisting of members of the League of Women Voters. The latter group was chosen as being "representative of the best-informed citizens in the community." The researchers utilized the same 41 causes of death discussed above, but placed them together in 106 pairs of causes. Subjects were asked, regarding each pair:

"Which cause of death is more likely? We do not mean more likely *for you*, we mean more likely *in general*, in the United States.

Consider all the people living in the United States—children, adults, *everyone*. Now supposing we randomly picked just one of those people. Will the person more likely die next year from cause A or cause B?" (Lichtenstein et al., 554, emphasis in the original)

There are several key aspects of this experiment. First, the subjects were asked explicitly to estimate ratios of *hazard rates* (not population frequencies); this eliminates any possible ambiguities in interpreting the subjects' responses. Second, two different subject groups were asked to evaluate hazards for the same *representative* individual; if both groups independently make the same assessment, this would add to our confidence that the nature of their responses is not merely the result of chance. Finally, the fact that the respondents were asked to make pairwise *comparisons* of hazard rates across causes means that this experiment provides a slightly different specification against which to test hypotheses.

Despite having explicitly asked about hazard rates, Lichtenstein et al. once again used population frequencies of death when computing "true" ratios against which the subjects' responses were compared. Once again, the researchers conclude that the respondents were biased in their hazard assessments, particularly in underestimating the hazards associated with the most common causes of death. Yet the age at which a cause kills is crucial in assessing how hazardous that cause is to the *representative* individual. Consider falls and homicides. Both killed about the same number of people in the sample period, yet the average age of death of homicide victims was 37.9, while the average age of death for persons who died in falls was 73.8. Because people who died from homicides were 35 years closer to the median age than were the people who died from falls, then for the representative individual, homicides should have been viewed as more hazardous. In effect, any failure to control for the ages of death of the causes will once again distort one's conclusions, with the magnitude and direction of the distortion depending upon (1) the correlation between average ages of death and frequencies of death, and (2) the correlation between ages of death and hazard rates.

For the United States, the first of these correlations is positive: Causes that kill many people (such as strokes, cancer, and heart disease) tend to kill them late in life. Table 9.2 illustrates the number of fatalities per cause and the average age of death for the least and most common causes of death. The average age of death among the 10 biggest killers is 20 years greater than the average age of death among the 10 smallest killers.

The second determinant of potential distortion is the correlation between ages of death and hazard rates. As I noted in the preceding section, this correlation is

Table 9.1   Ages of Death for the Least and Most Common Causes of Death

The Incidence of Death and the Average Age of Death		
	Ten Least Common Causes of Death	*Ten Most Common Causes of Death*
Fatalities per cause	690	156,830
Average age of death	42.3	63.2

negative: Causes that kill later tend to be less hazardous to an individual of any given age. The reason for this negative correlation is simple: As the age at which a cause kills increases, the probability that some *other* cause of death will intercede rises. Thus, the probability of dying from the first cause decreases. For example, although falls (age of death = 73.8) and homicides (age of death 37.9) kill about the same number of people each year, falls are much less hazardous to the representative individual, because of the higher probability that something other than a fall will kill that individual before he or she becomes old enough to die of a fall.

Once the ages at which the causes kill are taken into account, I find that the apparent bias reported by Lichtenstein et al. completely disappears for all practical purposes (Benjamin and Dougan 1992). Thus, for example, if we consider two causes of death that have the same age of death, both the League of Women Voters and the students estimate hazard rate ratios that differ only trivially from population death frequencies. Not only do the estimates of the two groups accord with the facts, they accord with each other. Moreover, for pairs of causes for which the ages of death differ, the voters and the students agree that, holding population death frequencies constant, each year sooner that a cause kills raises the implied hazard of that cause by about 5 percent.

Taken in conjunction with the earlier results, these findings suggest three general conclusions. First population death frequencies and hazard rates are conceptually different, and at the level of the individual may bear little relationship to one another; any failure to recognize these differences is likely to lead to nonsensical conclusions. Second, the same data that have been interpreted as showing that people are poor at assessing the hazards they face actually reveal that people are remarkably accurate at estimating hazards. Third, two activities that have the same impact on life expectancies may pose markedly different hazards to individuals, and thus produce markedly different behavioral responses by individuals.

A Bayesian View

Based on the evidence assembled thus far, it appears that when individuals are asked the right question, they reply with remarkably accurate responses. Of course these responses are arguably less than perfect, and so one might ask what determines their proximity to the truth? There are two strands of research that bear on this question.

The first of these, which was also the first systematic attempt to explain the existence of the apparent bias in risk assessment, has been pioneered by Viscusi (1984, 1985).[8] He argues that the existence and direction of any apparent bias in risk assessment is consistent with a Bayesian view of the world in which individuals have a set of prior beliefs about risks, beliefs that are updated in response to new information. The general nature of Viscusi's argument can be illustrated with a simple example.

Imagine asking an interplanetary visitor to estimate the risk of injury associated with activities one might engage in while sailing. For concreteness, let these activities be called gybing, tacking, and luffing. Suppose the visitor has never been sailing and has no knowledge of sailing terminology. Upon observing a variety of sailboats in action, the number of individuals on the boats, and the number of injuries inflicted upon them, the visitor would be able to formulate an estimate of the overall risk of sailing, but distinguishing among the hazards associated with each of the activities would be impossible. If compelled to produce estimates of these hazards, one approach for the visitor would be to attribute the average injury rate to each of the three activities, even if he knew that there were in fact differences among them.[9] If the visitor's judgments (perceived risk) were plotted as a function of the truth (actual risk), the result would be something like that shown in Figure 9.3.

Here the actual risks of the activities are shown as A_1, A_2, and A_3, where $\Sigma A_i/n = \mu$ is the (average) true risk of sailing. The visitor's estimates of these risks are given by $P_1 = P_2 = P_3 = \mu$. It is evident that the visitor's lack of knowledge about sailing produces a large and systematic bias in his estimates (perceptions) of risk:[10] Despite being correct on average ($\Sigma P_i/n = \Sigma A_i/n$), the visitor overestimates the hazards associated with relatively safe activities ($P_1 > A_1$), while he underestimates the risks of relatively hazardous activities ($P_3 < A_3$).

Clearly, through some combination of sailing lessons and careful observation, the visitor could improve on these estimates in a Bayesian manner. As learning occurred and the visitor's prior beliefs were revised, P_1 would presumably decline toward A_1 and P_3 would rise toward A_3. But to engage in such learning would require that the visitor devote some resources to the task—resources that

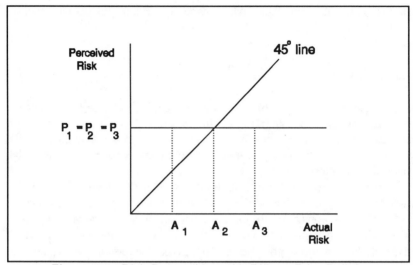

Figure 9.3 Risk Perceptions with Diffuse Prior Beliefs

would be worth expending only if the rewards were great enough. The general points are that (1) as long as information is costly, hazards will be estimated only with error; and (2) the existence of this error will produce systematic biases in perceived risks. I would add a third point: The extent of the error and thus the magnitude of the bias will be negatively related to the rewards to being accurate.

To investigate these issues, Viscusi and O'Connor (1984) examine the responses of workers to job-related risks, seeking to determine whether workers behave in this sort of Bayesian manner. There are three key findings. First, the compensating wage differentials earned by workers are consistent with the hypothesis that workers are aware of and respond to risk differentials across different environment.[11] Second, when workers are given new information about risks, they revise their prior beliefs accordingly, demanding higher risk premia, for example, when on-the-job risks rise. Third, the arrival of new information does *not* cause workers to discard their prior information; instead they formulate revised estimates in a manner that reflects the relative precision and importance of the information sets. The net effect is that workers behave in a distinctly Bayesian manner, apparently incorporating a broad array of information into their decisionmaking—information that *includes* their prior beliefs. In such a setting, any attempt to determine whether individuals "accurately" assess environmental risks will almost surely conclude (for spurious reasons) that they do not.

To see this, suppose that one obtained a measure of "true" job risks and also estimated worker estimates of those risks. Further suppose that this data suggests the existence of bias. Viscusi and O'Connor's results imply that, even though Bayesian workers are distinguishable from non-Bayesians, they are observationally equivalent to biased workers. To successfully disentangle (1) biased workers from (2) Bayesian workers with nontrivial priors, one must know the unknowable—an exact enumeration of the information taken into account by workers.[12] Absent such knowledge, one might well argue that there are potential benefits from providing workers (or consumers) with new information about the risks they face, but there is no basis for claiming that the decisions they make based on existing information are somehow inferior.

The Viscusi and O'Connor results ignore a point subsequently raised by Harrison (1989, 1990) in a different context. In general, the finders of bias have relied on the results of surveys, in which respondents have little incentive to tell the truth, nor to learn the truth if they do not initially know it. Following the Bayesian approach suggested by Viscusi, one might imagine that survey respondents begin by simply classifying the causes of death presented by researchers as being nothing more than that—which is to say, clearly distinct from things that do *not* cause death, but otherwise indistinguishable from one another. Clearly, this is an overstatement of any plausible starting point for respondents, since the actual number of deaths associated with the various causes on Lichtenstein et al.'s list range from 0 to 1.7 million; one must surely presume that (almost) everyone knows that the fatality rate from heart attacks is higher than from measles. Nevertheless, by the earlier discussion it should be clear that even people who know *exactly* the conditional probability of being killed in a bungee jump may know almost nothing about the unconditional probability, simply because they lack the (largely irrelevant to them) information about how many people engage in bungee jumping each year. Thus, the mere fact that these "things" are lumped together as "causes of death" would be expected to upgrade the frequency of low frequency causes and downgrade that of high frequency causes.[13]

If there is a tendency for people to behave in this way, then the survey venue—in which the penalty for such behavior is nil—is where it should be exhibited most clearly. Conversely, when the rewards for discriminating more finely are greater, there should be less of this behavior, and thus less bias in ranking the relative frequencies. Direct evidence on the role of rewards in reducing decisionmaking errors dates back at least to Siegel and Fouraker (1960). They found that in multiperson bargaining situations, increasing the opportunity cost of missing the optimum induced a tighter clustering of the observed outcomes in the neighborhood of the optimum outcome. Siegel et al. (1964) obtained similar results in the context of individual decision making: Raising the monetary rewards to correct decision making moved individual decisions closer to the optimum, and also reduced mean square decision errors. Indeed, in an experimental setting well known (from prior research) to induce extreme bias in decision making, Siegel et al. found that modest monetary payoffs were sufficient to eliminate entirely all biases among many of the experimental subjects. More recently, Bull et al. (1987) and Drago and Heywood (1989) find that when payoff functions are more sharply peaked, the variance of the outcomes in tournaments is reduced markedly—exactly what one would expect if high rewards reduce decision making errors. Even more to the point, Smith and Walker (1992a) directly test for the influence of reward structure on decision-making. They find that as the rewards to being correct increase, decision error decreases.[14] Smith and Walker also find that, holding payoffs constant, experience on the part of the experimental subjects also decreases decision errors. These findings reinforce the work of Viscusi and O'Connor, for they not only mean that the experimental subjects were Bayesian, they also imply that the weight assigned to prior information in arriving at a posterior assessment depends on the rewards to being correct. Thus, while Viscusi and O'Conner note that the decisions of individuals may be improved by providing them with new information about their environment, the findings of Smith and Walker imply that individuals *will themselves* seek this information out if given the incentive to do so. The point, of course, is not that everyone will always correctly assess risk. It is rather that when the rewards for being right are smaller, people will invest little in being correct and thus will likely be wrong. On the other hand, as the rewards for being correct rise, so too will accuracy. Hand-in-hand with this result is that ultimately it is incentives that are the key to efficient risk assessment.

Expertise

It is tempting to conclude, as some have done, that because people may be prone to error in risk assessment, experts should make assessments on behalf of people who would otherwise err. In my view, such a conclusion not only has things wrong; it has things backward. If anything, the possibility of bias suggests that, to the extent that experts play a role in the process of risk assessment, they should appear as tools rather than arbiters in the decision-making process. Two recent but entirely characteristic episodes illustrate this point.

At the micro level, consider cadmium, a toxic industrial metal used to coat metals and to make batteries and pigments. There is general agreement that at high doses, cadmium can damage kidneys and possibly cause lung cancer. There is less agreement on what to do as a result. During the early 1980s, the Occupational Safety and Health Administration (OSHA) began investigating the possibility of imposing stringent controls on workplace exposure to cadmium. OSHA's review of the evidence led it to propose rules that would have reduced exposure levels hundredfold, thereby (in the expert view of OSHA) saving the lives of 14 workers each year. The Office of Management and Budget (OMB) subsequently reviewed the same body of evidence relied upon by OSHA and concluded (in its expert view) that the proposed regulations—far from saving 14 lives each year—would actually kill at least 25 additional individuals because the regulations would reduce our wealth and so reduce the demand for safety throughout the country (Davis 1992).

On the one hand, say the experts, the proposed regulations are an improvement; on the other hand, say the other experts, they are not. I do not know who is correct, and indeed that point may be unknowable. The issue is that the experts disagree, as is perhaps inevitable in risk assessment, for uncertainty is inherent in the process.[15] Despite this disagreement, a decision must be made. If the expert is to make the decision, we must still decide: *Which expert*?

At the macro level, consider the "Greenhouse Effect"—the apparent tendency of carbon dioxide (CO_2) and other gases to accumulate in the atmosphere, acting like a blanket that traps radiated heat, thereby increasing the earth's temperature. There seems little doubt that humankind is producing greenhouse gases at a record rate, and that they are steadily accumulating in the atmosphere. Airborne concentrations of CO_2, for example, are increasing at the rate of about 0.5 percent per year, and over the past 50 years, the amount of CO_2 in the atmosphere has risen a total of about 25 percent (National Academy of Sciences 1991). In principle, higher CO_2 levels should lead to higher global temperatures;[16] despite this, it is considerably less apparent what is actually happening to the earth's temperature, and why it is happening.

The National Academy of Sciences (1991) recently has suggested that by the middle of the twenty-first century, greenhouse gases could be double their levels of 1860, and that global temperatures could rise by as much as 2° to 9°—global warming on such a scale that much of today's temperate climes would become arid dust bowls. Such a view seems consistent with the fact that, on average over the past century, greenhouse gases have been rising and so has the average global temperature. Yet almost all of the temperature rise occurred *before* 1940, while most of the increase in greenhouse gases has occurred *after* 1940. In fact, global average temperatures fell about 0.5° between 1940 and 1970; this cooling actually led many prominent scientists during the 1970s to forecast a coming *ice age*! We thus find ourselves in the position that, less than 20 years after the experts assured us the evidence pointed directly at falling temperatures, we are now assured the evidence points toward rising temperatures. That the evidence may point in different directions is perhaps inevitable in risk assessment, for uncertainty is inherent in the process.[17] Despite this, a decision must be made. If our decision is to be made on the basis of the best available evidence, we must still decide: *Which evidence*?

Once we admit the possibility that experts err (or at least disagree) and that evidence is sometimes ambiguous (or at least arguable), then we are forced to recognize that experts' judgments—and our choices among those judgments—

depend on the incentives at hand. If it is true that rewards influence the quality of the decisions that people (expert or otherwise) make, then if we ignore this fact by simply abdicating to the experts, we are doomed to suffer higher costs and capture lower benefits than are actually feasible.

It is commonplace to think of "experts" as being as interchangeable as the units of labor or capital encountered in the standard textbook discourse on the theory of the firm: One can have more or less of them, but once one has one, one has all, save for a scalar multiplicative factor. This mode of thought is both incorrect and dangerous, and the cadmium episode reveals quite clearly one dimension along which experts may differ substantively—and the issues thereby raised. As reflected in its name, OSHA is charged with protecting worker safety, and one must presume that the rewards facing its employees are structured accordingly. Similarly, both the name and mission statement of OMB emphasize managerial efficiency and the cost implications of government actions. The positive safety implications of the proposed cadmium regulations stem from the physical protections offered workers employed in handling cadmium; it was the evidence on these effects that OSHA's experts found most compelling. The adverse implications of the regulations—so compelling to the OMB experts— arise from their negative impact on our standard of living and the resulting decline in the demand for safety. It may be sheer coincidence that the respective experts' conclusions dovetailed so closely with the mandates of their respective agencies. In fact, I think it far more likely that these experts—like all experts —responded to the incentives they faced. They chose to evaluate the evidence not in a vacuum, but in accord with the perceived costs and benefits that would accrue to *them* as a result of their decisions. Given this, I am compelled to ask: How shall the incentives facing the experts be determined?

I would argue that only people who bear the consequences of decisions can fully know the advantages and disadvantages of each expert decision, including decisions that include, exclude, or assign weights to particular bodies of evidence. Consider the global warming (or cooling) issue: one body of evidence suggests that we act now to avoid further atmospheric warming; other evidence suggests that we adopt a wait-and-see attitude. Does action now commit us to a major, irretrievable investment? Does inaction now commit us to inescapable losses in the future if we are wrong today? Absent knowledge of the loss function associated with different alternatives, the physics and chemistry of the issue are insufficient to determine which body of physical and chemical evidence should be acted upon. And the ultimate "experts" on that loss function are the individuals who will gain or lose as a result of the decisions that are made.

It will also do no good simply to suppose that we might instruct the experts to behave in a manner that is consistent with the wishes of those affected by their decisions. First, such a plan assumes that the experts are already *in situ*. Second, it assumes that the experts can know what other people know as well as those people know it. Although both assumptions are commonplace (at least implicitly), neither is tenable, for each amounts to assuming away a pivotal aspect of the risk assessment problem. To suppose, implicitly or explicitly, that we may rely on experts who are already "in place" requires that one of two conditions be satisfied: Either there must exist some *deus ex machina* who has anointed experts on our behalf, or—in a world in which uncertainty is the essence of the discussion—we are somehow endowed with *certain* knowledge of the best expert in each case. The second assumption—that the appointed experts are endowed with full information of the preferences and endowments of the people affected by their decisions—is even more extraordinary, for it assumes that these experts are *endowed* with the information that is *produced* by the price system (Hayek 1945). Given these inferences, I conclude that both the experts and the instructions under which they operate must be chosen by the people who will bear the costs and benefits of the experts' assessments.

The flip side of this, of course, is that those who are choosing the experts (or choosing to do without them) and are structuring the experts' incentives must themselves *bear* the full range of costs and benefits associated with their choices. Thus, it will do no good to allow a firm to enjoy all of the benefits of, say, a particular production process, while at the same time limiting its liability on the cost side in the event something goes wrong:[18] There is simply no presumption that the decisions that result would be any better than what would result if the firm bore *none* of the consequences of its decisions.

Ultimately, then, the uncertainty inherent in the process of risk assessment reinforces rather than obviates the need for individual resource owners to be the final arbiters of the risk assessment and decision-making process. There is simply no other way to choose (or choose to ignore) the experts, nor any way to weigh their findings. The consequences of risk assessment decisions will be borne by someone, whether that someone is the decision maker or not. Those consequences will be the best possible only if the individuals that have the greatest incentive to decide among the unknowns—and the unknowable—are making the decisions.

Conclusions

People err. But sometimes by less than we would have them. Frank Knight once observed, "We are so built that what seems reasonable to us is likely to be confirmed by experience or we could not live in the world at all" (Knight 1921, 227). The evidence I have found is consistent with Knight's view—at least as it applies to risk assessment undertaken by the individuals who must confront those risks.

Knight's observation was made at a time (1921) that, except for the Food and Drug Administration, the regulatory agencies that so predominate hazard assessment today were not in existence. Whether an assertion similar to Knight's would apply to the experts at these agencies remains an unswered question—but one that is surely worthy of further research.

Notes

1. See Tversky et al. (1974), Lichtenstein et al. (1978), Arrow (1982), Kahneman et al. (1982), Viscusi and O'Connor (1984), Viscusi (1985), Slovic (1987), and Zeckhauser and Viscusi (1990).
2. See Nichols and Zeckhauser (1986) for a more complete development of this argument, particularly as it relates to the Environmental Protection Agency. See also Freudenberg (1988) and Slovic et al. (1991).
3. For an extensive compilation of the psychology literature, see Kahnerman, Slovic, and Tversky (1982). Zeckhauser and Viscusi (1990) and Machina (1987) summarize much of the salient economic literature.
4. See note 7, below for a discussion of the sources and methods of constructing average age at death.
5. Although as I shall show below, there are other numbers that might be relevant to them, and it is about these that the students seemingly *do* know a great deal.
6. One pack-year of smoking is equivalent to smoking one pack of cigarettes per day for one year. Thus, 20 pack-years could consist of two packs per day for 10 years or one pack per day for 20 years.
7. Average age of death computed based on Center for Disease Control (CDC) data for deaths by cause for various ages. CDC reports deaths by five year age ranges. At the top end, the CDC's last category includes everyone over the age of 100. I use the upper end of the range (and 105 for the >100 group) in computing average age of death by cause, thus probably overstating by about 2.5 years the true average ages.
8. Slovic et al. (1982) offer ad hoc explanations for some of the outliers observed by Lichtenstein et al., but no systematic explanations. Arrow (1982) simply accepts the apparent biases as facts.
9. If the visitor seeks to minimize the quadratic loss function of the form
$$L = E(\hat{\mu} - \mu)^2$$
where E designates the expectations operator, μ is the true injury rate and $\hat{\mu}$ is the estimated injury rate, then as long as the visitor is willing to make *some* estimate of the risk of a particular activity, that estimate $(\hat{\mu})$ will be set equal to μ.

10. For diagrammatic and expository convenience I let $A_2 = \mu$, but nothing in the argument hinges on this assumption.

11. This finding is consistent with a broad body of literature on compensating wage differentials. See, for example, Thaler and Rosen (1976), Smith (1979), Viscusi (1979), and Brown (1980).

12. Alternatively, the observer might actually know the true risks, in which case *any* deviation—Bayesian or otherwise—is bias. One can only wonder how the observer obtained the data on true risk without market participants—arguably the highest-valued users of such information—being able to get their hands on it.

13. One implication of this argument is that the breadth of the frequencies presented to any given group will influence in a predictable way the extent of the apparent bias in the responses. The broader the range of frequencies, the greater will be the group's degree of overstatement of low frequency causes and understatement of high frequency causes.

14. These findings are consistent with the finding that weather forecasters are impressively unbiased in their forecasts of precipitation probabilities. See Camerer (1992) and Winkler and Murphy (1977). See also Harrison (1990).

15. In terms of Figure 1, we may think of the measurements recorded along the horizontal axis as being the "truth," but to do so is to deceive ourselves: Experts A and B are likely to write down two completely different sets of numbers along that very same axis.

16. Laboratory analysis of glacial ice dating back at least 160,000 years indicates that global temperatures and CO_2 levels in the atmosphere do in fact tend to move together, suggesting that the impact of today's rising CO_2 levels will be higher global temperatures in the future. See National Academy of Sciences (1991).

17. Indeed, Charlson et al. (1992) argue that the warming effects of greenhouse gases are currently being offset by the cooling effect of additional particulate matter produced by the same forces (chiefly hydrocarbon combustion) that generate the greenhouse gases. The net impact on global temperatures--for the moment--thus appears to be *nil*.

18. This is *not* to say that the firm should be prohibited from purchasing insurance on the open market. The point is that insurance should not be subsidized by the legal system.

This paper draws heavily on my work with William R. Dougan (1992), and I have benefited greatly from discussions with him and with Tim O. Ozenne. Bruce Yandle's comments on an earlier draft improved the present product.

230   *Taking the Environment Seriously*

References

Arrow, Kenneth. 1982. Risk Perception in Psychology and Economics. *Economic Inquiry*, (January): 1-9.
Benjamin, Daniel K., and William R. Dougan. 1992. The Hazards of Risk Assessment, Clemson University Discussion Paper, November.
Bull, Clive, Andrew Schotter, and Keith Weigalt. 1987. Tournaments and Piece Rates: An Experimental Study. *Journal of Political Economy*. (February): 1-33.
Camerer, Colin F. 1992. Individual Decision Making. In J. Kagel and A. Roth, *Handbook of Experimental Economics*. Princeton: Princeton University Press.
Charlson, Robert J., et al. 1992. Climate Forcing by Anthropogenic Aerosols. *Science*, 252 (January): 423-30.
Davis, Bob. 1992. Risk Analysis Measures Need for Regulation, but It's No Science, *The Wall Street Journal* (August 6): A1.
Drago, Robert, and John S. Heywood. 1989. Tournaments, Piece Rates, and the Shape of the Payoff Function. *Journal of Political Economy*, August.
Freudenberg, William R. 1988. Perceived Risk, Real Risk: Social Science and the Art of Probabilistic Risk Assessment. *Science*, 242 (October): 44-49.
Harrison, Glenn. 1989. The Payoff Dominance Critique of Experimental Economics. University of New Mexico Discussion Paper.
_____. 1990. Expected Utility Theory and the Experimentalists. University of South Carolina. Working Paper B-90-04.
Hayek, Friedrich A. 1945. The Use of Knowledge in Society. *American Economic Review*, (September): 519-30.
Knight, Frank H. 1921. *Risk, Uncertainty, and Profit*, New York: Houghton-Mifflin.
Lichtenstein, Sarah, Paul Slovic, Baruch Fischoff, Mark Layman, and Barbara Combs. 1978. Judged Frequency of Lethal Events. *Journal of Experimental Psychology: Human Learning and Memory*, 4: 551-78.
Machina, Mark J. 1987. Choice Under Uncertainty: Problems Solved and Unsolved. *Journal of Economic Perspectives*, (Summer): 121-54.
Morrall, John F. III. 1986. A Review of the Record, *Regulation* (November/December): 25-34.
Murphy, A. H., and Winkler, R. L. 1977. Can Weather Forecasters Formulate Reliable Probability Forecasts of Precipitation and Temperature? *National Weather Digest*, 2: 2-9.
National Academy of Sciences. 1991. *Policy Implications of Greenhouse Warming*. Washington, DC.
_____. 1983. *Risk Assessment in the Federal Government: Managing the Process*. Washington, DC.

Nichols, Albert L., and Richard J. Zeckhauser. 1986. The Perils of Prudence: How Conservative Risk Assessments Distort Regulation. *Regulation* (November/December): 13-24.

Siegel, Sidney, and Lawrence Fouraker. 1960. *Bargaining and Group Decision Making: Experiments in Bilateral Monopoly.* New York: McGraw Hill.

Siegel, Sidney, Alberta Siegel, and Julia Andrews. 1964. *Choice, Strategy, and Utility,* New York: McGraw Hill.

Slovic, Paul. 1987. Perception of Risk. *Science* 236 (April): 280-85.

Slovic, Paul, James H. Flynn, and Mark Layman. 1991. Perceived Risk, Trust, and the Politics of Nuclear Waste. *Science* 254 (December): 1603-07.

Slovic, Paul, Baruch Fischoff, and Sarah Lichtenstein. 1982. Facts versus Fears: Understanding Perceived Risk. In *Judgment Under Uncertainty: Heuristics and Biases,* ed. by D. Kahneman, P. Slovic, and A. Tversky. Cambridge: Cambridge University Press.

Smith, Vernon L., and James M. Walker. 1992. Monetary Rewards and Decision Costs. University of Arizona Discussion Paper.

_____. 1992. Rewards, Experience, and Decision Costs in First Price Auctions. University of Arizona Discussion Paper.

Thaler, Richard, and Sherwin Rosen. 1976. The Value of Saving a Life: Evidence from the Labor Market. In *Household Production and Consumption,* ed. by N. Terleckyz. New York: Columbia University Press.

Viscusi, W. Kip., 1979. *Employment Hazards: An Investigation of Market Performance,* Cambridge: Harvard University Press.

_____. 1985. A Bayesian Perspective on Biases in Risk Perception. *Economics Letters* 17: 59-62.

_____. 1989. Prospective Reference Theory: Toward an Explanation of the Paradoxes. *Journal of Risk and Uncertainty* (September): 235-64.

Viscusi, W. Kip, and Charles O'Connor. 1984. Adaptive Responses to Chemical Labeling: Are Workers Bayesian Decision Makers? *American Economic Review* (December): 942-56.

Zeckhauser, Richard J., and W. Kip Viscusi. 1990. Risk within Reason. *Science* 248 (May): 559-64.

Chapter 10

Environmental Calvinism: The Judeo-Christian Roots of Eco-Theology

Robert H. Nelson

Introduction

In June 1992 more than 200 scientists, including 27 U.S. Nobel prize winners, presented an appeal to the heads of state attending the Earth Summit in Rio de Janiero. Their joint statement declared that "we are worried, at the dawn of the 21st century, at the emergence of an irrational ideology which is opposed to scientific and industrial progress and impedes economic and social development" (*Wall Street Journal* 1992). These scientists were recognizing a growing religious element in the contemporary environmental movement that is hostile to science, to technology, and to economic growth—all historically associated with "progress." Conflicts between science and religion have been going on for a long time; although the religion in this case is a secular one, the increasing tensions between science and environmentalism represent yet another installment in this long-running saga.

To be sure, the environmental movement is very diverse. Any broad generalization is likely to fail with respect to at least some portion of environmentalism. There are probably at least several different varieties of religion within the environmental movement. And many environmentalists are concerned mainly with utilitarian matters such as cleaner air, more parks and recreation, and less cancer, matters that have little to do with religion.

Nevertheless, in this chapter I will argue that environmentalism is giving an important new voice in American public life to a particular religious message. Important parts of the environmental movement are offering in a secular form a view of the human condition that, although found throughout the history of Christianity, played an especially important role in the theology of Martin Luther, John Calvin, and the Protestant Reformation (Tillich 1967). This view sees mankind as deeply sinful and the world as filled with evil—the result of the basic corruption of human nature since the fall of man in the Garden of Eden. Environmentalism today often portrays a similarly corrupt and sinful world, brought to this fallen state in the modern era through the misguided attempt to remake the world in the name of "progress."

In England, the Puritans were the leading Calvinists. The environmental movement is helping to revive what might be called a secular puritanism. This newly puritanical outlook ironically is today often found in secular creeds that outwardly proclaim their liberation from traditional attitudes and beliefs. The new puritans warn that alcohol, beef, and other foods, rather than a source of pleasure, are filled with dangers—potentially even lethal. Pornography is not titillating but contemptible; normal sexual intercourse can even resemble "rape" —suggesting that for some perhaps a new celibacy is the proper course for the truly virtuous. Politically incorrect speech provokes the moral outrage of new defenders of righteousness. Environmentalism is playing a part in what is apparently yet another revival of the puritanism that has been deeply ingrained in the American character since the earliest days of European settlement.

The Study of Environmental Theology

Many environmentalists describe their own efforts in terms of spreading new values and spiritual beliefs. They argue explicitly that new religious directions are needed in American life. In *The Voice of the Earth*, a leading environmental thinker, Theodore Roszak, recently stated that "the emerging worldview of our day will have to address questions of a frankly religious character." Environmental theology will have to give answers to "ethical conduct, moral purpose, and the meaning of life"; it will thereby be "seeking to heal the soul of its wounds and guide it to salvation" (1992, 101, 51). Arguing for a reduction in the human presence in National Parks, Joseph Sax stated that he and fellow preservationists are "secular prophets, preaching a message of secular salvation" (1980, 104).

In this chapter I thus propose to take seriously the religious content of the environmental movement. That is to say, I intend to study environmentalism as an exercise in theology. As will also be examined below, environmental theology is playing a significant—if often unremarked—role in shaping environmental policies. There is a set of theological premises and a theological logic that yields environmental policy conclusions. By studying this underlying theology, many features of government policy and matters relating to environmental issues come into better focus. The problems of American environmental policies today are, in significant part, problems of the theological underpinnings for these policies.

I will argue in a later section that, even taken on its own terms, environmental theology contains significant internal tensions and even some outright contradictions. On some matters, the underlying assumptions of environmental theology seem to reflect more the wish than the fact. The full implementation of government policies based on this theology would yield results that in some areas many environnmentalists themselves would probably regard as unfortunate. Although most social scientists in their professional capacities have sought to avoid theological discussions, it may be that a necessary step—conceivably the most important step—in achieving significant improvements in government policies for the environment will be to move the theological discussion forward.

Some people may wonder whether it can be appropriate to regard a belief system that does not mention a god as an actual religion—as this chapter does. Yet, many theologians and other leading thinkers have responded affirmatively. One theologian, Willis Glover, wrote that to describe a secular belief system as a religion "is no mere figure of speech. One's religion is whatever serves as one's ultimate source of meaning" (1984, 150). Peter Drucker stated recently that since the Enlightenment the set of secular beliefs promising "salvation" here on earth has been "the dominant creed of Western Man. And however much it pretends to be 'anti-religious,' it is a religious belief" (1992, 97).

Secular Calvinism

In the Calvinist and Puritan view, the presence of evil in the world is pervasive. The human condition, as Calvin wrote in his classic of theology, *Institutes of the Christian Religion*, is characterized by "ignorance, vanity, poverty, infirmity, and—what is more—depravity and corruption" (Calvin 1989, 17). One authority explains that Calvin taught "the total depravity of man.... It is ridiculous to think of pleading our good works before Almighty God because they are hopelessly trivial in view of the condemnation of our sin which divine justice demands; they themselves are, without exception, stained with our corruption and wickedness" (Calvin 1989, 17).

In a new secular form, the echo of this Calvinist outlook can be heard in many recent environmental statements. At the extreme, Dave Foreman, founder of the radical environmental organization Earth First, states that "humans are a disease, a cancer on nature."[1] Paul Watson, a founder of Greenpeace and later of a second environmental organization, Sea Shepherd, believes that "we, the human species, have become a viral epidemic to the earth"—in truth the "AIDS of the earth." Such statements are heard with increasing frequency among the more radical members of the environmental movement, that mankind in its present state is so infected with evil as to be a plague upon the earth.

To be sure, mainstream environmentalism avoids such strong condemnations of the human presence on earth. Nevertheless, it offers an unremitting stream of moralistic descriptions of nature being raped, assaulted, murdered, pillaged, destroyed. Contemporary society is an immoral place, filled with corporate profiteers, callous government bureaucrats, and other sinful types. By their evil actions, these people brutalize nature and may even be setting mankind on a path of destruction. The Calvinist outlook of "doom and gloom" is today being redirected to the impacts of modern civilization on the world, as widely portrayed in environmental writings (Nelson 1990a).

In seeking to mobilize public support to resist a recent government plan for greater energy development, the Sierra Club thus declared that the Nation's "wilderness faces environmental disaster." There was a "scandalous plan" in the works, involving "rampant oil and gas development," that would yield an "outrageous all-out assault on our precious environment." In Alaska the wilderness would be "pillaged" and the "beautiful shores" would be "ravaged." Part of the plan was to "desecrate the wondrous Arctic National Wildlife Refuge." And what was the driving force behind all these sacrileges and moral offenses? It was greed, selfishness, and the desire for more and more—the same temptations that so many Christian preachers have seen corrupting man since the fall.[2]

So what is required to reverse this baneful direction of events? For many environmentalists the answer is that people must be environmentally "born again." They must experience a spiritual reawakening, turning away from their current false values and sinful activities. Indeed, the environmental message often sounds remarkably similar to that of preachers such as Billy Graham. In *How to Be Born Again*, Graham explains that "something has gone wrong with our jet age." He offers a litany of evils to show the spiritual failings and the moral decline of our time (including the fact that "the atmosphere [is filled] with waste products that nearly obscure the sunset"). In a Graham sermon we hear of terrible statistics such as that "in the U.S. in the past 14 years, the rate of robberies has increased 255%, forcible rape 143%, aggravated assault 153% and murder 106%.... There is no longer a safety zone in any city" (1979, 76-77). Our environmental preachers use different examples and different numbers but to the same effect—to emphasize the current fallen condition of humanity and the necessity of a spiritual renewal.

Divine Retribution Is Looming

Calvin warned that, if humanity did not turn away from its evil ways, God's plan for sinners was "wrath, judgment and terror": their future he "would devote to destruction" (1989, 100, 115). Environmental doomsdayers today see human iniquity bringing on great future suffering and destruction. Some foresee floods covering the earth, perhaps due to global warming. Or maybe drought will parch the land. Environmentalism raises the spectre of a long list of possible disasters reminiscent of biblical warnings of catastrophe brought on by evil ways. Paul Ehrlich predicted in 1968 that famine would spread over the earth in the 1970s; recently he suggests the date has only been postponed for this ancient retribution for the sins of mankind (Ehrlich 1968; Ehrlich and Ehrlich 1991).

At times environmentalism uses the old Puritan language. The Puritans, it may be recalled, placed a great emphasis on the idea of a calling. The Sierra Club recently wrote to enlist help from those who were being "called to action" to deal with the problem of global warming.[3]

Calvin preached that "our nature, wicked and deformed, is always opposing his [God's] uprightness; and our capacity, weak and feeble to do good, lies far from his perfection." Indeed, it is man's misplaced "pride" in his knowledge, skills and power that is "the beginning of all evils" (1989, 65, 56). In Calvin's view any grand efforts at human improvement must be undermined by the pervasiveness of human depravity owing to original sin; to aim too high for Calvin is almost certain to be to sink very low. Similarly, many in the environmental movement today see the great optimism and expectations for progress in the modern era as yet another example of how human pride and high hopes will always be subverted by human weakness and corruption. Science is not the savoir of mankind that so many have portrayed; instead, it is a snare, leading us astray, destroying the natural world and spreading a false set of values. Rather than progress, science has created instruments of mass destruction and a technocratic world of mass alienation.

In an essay "Beyond Ecology," biologist Neil Everndon (1978) thus writes that ecology is subversive of "not only the growth addict and the chronic developer, but science itself." In one of the leading statements of environmental theology, George Sessions and Bill DeVall contend in *Deep Ecology* that:

> Technological society not only alienates humans from the rest of Nature but also alienates humans from themselves and from each other. It necessarily promotes destructive values and goals which often destroy the basis for stable viable human communities interacting with the natural world.... The ultimate value judgment upon which technological society rests—progress conceived as the further development and expansion of the artificial environment necessarily at the expense of the natural world—must be looked upon from the ecological perspective as unequivocal regress. (1985, 48)

Nature as the Messenger of God

Calvin taught that for many people "the knowledge of God [is] sown in their minds out of the wonderful workmanship of nature." For those able to turn away from the "prodigious trifles" and "superfluous wealth" that occupy the attention of so many, it will be possible for them to be "instructed by this bare and simple testimony which the [animal] creatures render splendidly to the glory of God." Humanity must show great respect for the natural world because it is especially in the presence of nature that men can find "burning lamps" that "shine for us ... the glory of its Author" above. Indeed, Calvin preaches that God intends for "the preservation of each species until the Last Day" (1989, 26-27, 99, 41).

The source of spiritual inspiration in nature, the preservation of the species, and many other Calvinist themes are found in secular form in environmental theology today. In American history the roots of contemporary environmentalism can be traced back 150 years to New England transcendentalism. Even then, much closer to Calvin's day, philosophers such as Henry David Thoreau and Ralph Waldo Emerson were offering secular versions of Puritan and Calvinist themes. One authority reports that in transcendentalist thinking "nature was the connecting link between God and man"; thus, "God spoke to man through nature" (Ekirch 1963, 51-52). In his recent book, *The True and Only Heaven*, Christopher Lasch comments that "Calvinist theologians spoke of God's 'vindictive' justice.... Emerson restores the older conception in all its uncompromising severity" when he attacks the crass materialism and simplistic pieties of his time. In other respects as well, Emerson secularizes "his Calvinist forebears.... Our fallen nature, 'our lapsed estate,' discloses itself precisely in our blindness to the 'deep remedial force' in nature" (1991, 269-70). Later in the nineteenth century John Muir—the leading advocate for setting aside Yosemite National Park and other wild areas, as well as founder of the Sierra Club—was in turn a devoted follower of Emerson.

The Environmental Heaven on Earth

In Calvin's theology, the prospects in this world were bleak but there lay in store—at least for those elect who were among the chosen—a glorious and heavenly future in the hereafter. However, most environmentalists do not mention God or heaven in their writings. As a secular system of belief, environmental theology can offer no such consolation. Indeed, the environmental gospel might seem to offer a message of extreme pessimism—nothing more than a story of a world of sinners moving inexorably toward their own destruction and that of the other species of the earth as well.

However, there may be another possibility. Perhaps there is a path to heaven that can be discovered here on earth. Perhaps the salvation of mankind can be a matter for human action in this world. Indeed, many secular religions throughout the modern era have preached messages of just this kind (Nelson 1991). Following the triumph of the proletariat, Marx saw the end of class struggle and the arrival of a world of perfect harmony among all people—a world in which all material needs would be satisfied as well. It was such a compelling vision that the distinguished theologian Paul Tillich once rated Marx in terms of impact as "the most successful theologian since the Reformation." (1967, 476).

For many followers, environmental religion in fact does offer the hope of heaven on earth. The environmental path of salvation differs, however, from most secular faiths of the past 300 years. In the typical secular creed of this period, it is economic growth and scientific progress that are the key factors in eliminating social conflict, meeting all material needs, and arriving at an earthly paradise. However, environmental theology now turns all this on its head; the salvation of mankind now is to require a turning away from science, economic progress, and indeed many of the characteristics outlooks of the modern period. Environmental theology adopts a view of the world more commonly found in Calvin's time, but it does depart sharply from Calvin—who no doubt would have condemned all of modern secular theology as a vile heresy—in following the modern propensity to find its heaven here on earth.

The tenets of environmental theology are most likely to be fully and explicitly developed among environmental thinkers who do not feel constrained by political acceptability and mainstream opinion. They are able to speak views that others may more or less share but cannot afford to advocate freely. For obvious practical reasons, religion is best left unspoken among those who must seek political alliances in many directions. For others, they may have an implicit belief in environmental theology but, even in their own minds, they may not have come fully to terms with all the theological assumptions, logic, and conclusions.

Radical Environmentalism

One person who understands his own mind clearly and feels few constraints is Dave Foreman, as noted above, the founder of the radical environmental organization Earth First. Foreman (1991) offers a full-fledged theology of sin and salvation. As he sees matters, the world was a blissful place until about 10,000 years ago. It was then that the beginnings of organized agriculture commenced the corruption of the human condition, leading to the current evils of "city, bureaucracy, patriarchy, war" and many others. Foreman describes the growing separation of man and nature, the environmental version of the Biblical rift between God and man followed the expulsion from the Garden of Eden:

> Before agriculture was midwifed in the Middle East, humans were in the wilderness. We had no concept of "wilderness" because everything was wilderness and we were a part of it. But with irrigation ditches, crop surpluses, and permanent villages, we became apart from the natural world and substituted our fields, habitations, temples and storehouses. Between the wilderness that created us and the civilization created by us, grew an ever-widening rift. (1989, 20)

In Christianity, salvation restores a natural harmony and innocence that was originally found in the Garden of Eden before the fall. For Foreman, the environmental path of salvation similarly requires the recovery of natural conditions found long ago, before the arrival of organized society plunged mankind into such deep alienation. The whole world—or at least as much as is at all possible—should be returned to the original wilderness, the secular equivalent of recovering the biblical paradise. Other prominent environmental writers such as Bill McKibben thus explain that "it is not utter silliness to talk about ending—or, at least, transforming—industrial civilization." McKibben is prepared at least to hope for "a different world, where roads are torn out to create vast new wildernesses, where most development ceases, and where much of man's imprint on the earth is slowly erased." This would bring humanity back to the "blooming, humming, fertile paradise" that existed before the earth was corrupted by the spread of civilization (1989, 186, 180, 50).

Another environmental writer refers to "the harmony that once existed between precivilized people and their habitat." There was once an "intimately enveloping environment" in which "the young are born to the sky, the songs of birds, the textures and odors of the wild." Children grew up in a way that they could flow "gracefully into a lifelong sense of kinship with the natural world." Unfortunately, however, all this changed beginning "with the practice of agriculture some ten thousand years ago"—the moment of "original sin" for environmental theology. Following this disastrous event, the disruption of the natural world yielded "ontogenetic crippling"—the environmental "fall of man." As human beings were corrupted by civilization, "they had begun to manhandle their environment in ways that broke the bond that had for so long kept them connected to nature. The result has been 'chronic madness'" (Shepard 1982; Roszak 1992).

Bringing Heaven to Earth

Within Christianity, there has been a long running theological debate concerning the timing and the mechanism for the arrival of the millennium—and eventually the kingdom of heaven on earth. Some Christian theologians have believed that mankind must simply await an act of divine intervention that will occur at some future date. But others have argued that the millennium will arrive gradually and that the process may have already begun. Similarly, some environmentalists are hopeful that mankind is already beginning the process of returning to a wilderness existence and the recovery of the original harmony and innocence of uncorrupted nature. As one environmental group describes this development:

> Everywhere, all over the earth, human beings have gathered in small groups, laying down their differences and focusing on their common wisdom. They call themselves communities ... coming into unity ... for a new age on earth which

shall be the embodiment of every positive thought we hold in our minds, just as the old age embodied our fears. The construction has begun, of a new reality, where the mysteries are revealed within each human being as s/he comes into harmony with the planet as a whole. We celebrate this sunrise ... and the building of one earth nation.[4]

Ed Marston is the editor of the biweekly *High Country News*, a leading news source for information on environmental developments in the western United States. He is well positioned to understand the ideas and concerns of the contemporary environmental movement. As Marston summarizes matters,

> Environmentalism is still and never more than today, a moral movement: It is telling humanity, with a thousand voices, that we are destroying what we should be cherishing, that we must change our ways, and that unless we change, we will make of the earth a hell for all living things. And like any moral movement, environmentalism holds out a paradise. In our paradise, the air is clear, the water pure, and the wildlife plentiful. (1989, 15)

In 1951 Eric Voegelin delivered an influential series of lectures at the University of Chicago in which he argued for a "general theory of religious phenomena" that would recognize the ideologies of "totalitarian movements" and other secular systems of belief as also belonging to the category of "religion." Moreover, contrary to a common opinion, it would be a mistake to think that such beliefs were "neopagan." Although there was a "superficial resemblance" to pagan faiths, the reality was that the leading ideologies of the modern era tended to have "origins rather in Christianity itself." Indeed, Marxism, socialism and many other secular belief systems were a "Christian derivative" (1987, 25, 107, 163).

Voegelin thus found that modern thinking still followed Christianity in promising "salvation," although the redemption of mankind was now seen as occurring in this world. In this manner, traditional religious energies could be "diverted into the more appealing, more tangible, ... creation of the terrestrial paradise." Indeed, Voegelin located the origins of this immensely important development before the modern era and in a surprising place. Although Calvin would have condemned secular religion, the beginnings of the modern drive for salvation here on earth could actually be found in "the work of Calvin" (1987).

There were in fact some major tensions within Calvinism that parallel tensions today also found in environmentalism. The harsh Calvinist condemnations of the sinfulness of the world, combined with a fierce righteousness, yielded in many later Puritans a radical determination to improve the world —despite the deep Calvinist skepticism about the capacities of fallen men to do good in any way. It would not, however, be a perfection of the world through rational and scientific "progress"; the proper means were religious, through the moral and spiritual conversion of mankind. The Puritan goal was to bring together new communities of the Puritan saints of true faith. In this way, it would be possible to recover a valid Christian existence as it had been found centuries ago, before the many corruptions introduced by the Roman Catholic church.

With radical environmental theology in the current period, the Puritan impulse to save the world continues unabated. And this impulse now abandons the modern religions of scientific and economic progress and reverts to the Puritan view that the the real answers must be religious. The fallen and depraved order found in existing American and other western societies must be renounced as corrupted beyond hope of redemption. There must be whole new values and a turn to—many leading environmental thinkers now state explicitly—new religious (if secular) foundations for society. What is required is to turn back to recover a far better and more innocent world that did once exist long ago. In a final similarity, much as the Calvinist revolutionaries faced a basic paradox, this new secular salvation is today said by environmental theology to be possible even for the deeply alienated and crassly materialistic men and women that dominate our current time.

Policy Impacts

As the history of secular religion in the modern period has amply demonstrated, the theologies laying out an environmental path to heaven on earth should not be dismissed as the mere utopian plans of idle dreamers. The hopes once invested by so many Marxist faithful in the future triumph of the proletariat today appear a utopian fantasy, but no one can doubt their practical significance for the history of the world. Indeed, the goal to recover an original environmental paradise is today having substantial impacts on policymaking in American government (Nelson 1990b). At a minimum such visions motivate activists who then turn their zeal to more limited objectives that are seen as serving the long run Edenic goal. In *Green Rage* environmental activist Christopher Manes reports that, although often implicitly and indirectly, "radical environmentalists now exert a growing influence on public land decisions and environmental policy." Manes finds that "increasingly, grass-roots activist groups like Earth First! are setting the environmental agenda" (1990, 8). In one importance instance, the members of Earth First played a major role in the spotted owl controversy in the Pacific Northwest, helping to move the issue from the margins of public attention to the center of policy debate.

But it is not only the radical camp of environmentalism that is injecting new theological elements into the policy process. Over large areas of environmental policy making, there is an underlying, if mostly left unspoken, theological content. This is not to say, of course, that there is any one environmental theology that is driving all environmental policy. Indeed, it is worth repeating that the environmental movement is filled with all kinds of beliefs, religious and nonreligious. Some ground their commitment to protect the environment in traditional Judaic and Christian tenets of faith. Other people regard environmental policy making as a matter merely of doing economics better, using market forces to achieve environmental goals, and taking full account of all environmental benefits and costs in government decision making.

However, amidst the great diversity of views within the environmental movement, the closest thing to a constant is the strong moral judgment that environmental policy should do that which is "natural" and avoid that which is "unnatural." This is the basic environmental criterion of good and evil, being applied widely in government policy making today. Underlying this moral judgment is the theological message of the need to recover the innocence of the original creation, to return to the state of nature as it existed before being altered (corrupted) by the many works of man. Another powerful influence is the Calvinist (and now environmentalist) conviction that it is in itself a grave sin— as well as doomed to failure—to seek to assume the place of God through remaking the world by human action and according to a man-made plan. For both Calvinist theology and contemporary environmentalism, humanity can find a greater spiritual awareness by living in closer harmony with nature.

Environmental Theology in Practice

In the 1970s Senator John Culver (Democrat from Iowa) was a leading supporter of the Endangered Species Act of 1973—the modern legislative version of God's injunction in the Bible to Noah to save two of every species. Speaking on the floor of the U.S. Senate during the 1978 debate over renewal of the Act, Senator Culver stated that "we have the ethical and moral responsibility to pass on to future generations, in as pristine a state as possible, what we in turn have inherited" (1978, S10973). He told his fellow Senators that they were addressing a question of basic religious significance:

> Those questions, Mr. President, are very fundamental ones. They go to the nature of our universe. They go to the nature of our ecosystems, and our biosphere. They go to basic questions of "What does it all mean" and whether one is intellectually and spiritually persuaded that what we experience in life is the result of some divine creation and guiding hand. (1978, S10973)

The Endangered Species Act is by no means the only instance in which theology has been invoked to shape government policy. The supporters of the national system of wilderness areas frequently explain the need for such a system in spiritual terms resembling those used by Senator Culver. Harking back to

Calvin's argument that man can encounter the presence of God in nature, John Muir spoke 100 years ago of primitive areas as "temples" and trees as "psalm-singing" (Nash 1967, 125). More recently, the Wilderness Society explained that it is necessary to preserve wilderness areas because "destroy them and we destroy our spirit ... destroy them and we destroy our sense of values."[5] In 1964, Congress enacted the Wilderness Act which specified that a wilderness area must be a place "where the earth and its community of life are untrammeled by man" and which should still exhibit a "primeval character and influence." In effect, in establishing the criteria for wilderness designation, Congress was setting the government standard for an adequate sacred quality in order for an area to be included in a national system of environmental churches. The key factor was that the impact of man—and thus the presence of sin—should be minimized in these places.

Sacred Forests

It is hard to find a more powerful symbol of human assault on nature than the clear cutting of a forest—a harvesting method employed in order to remove the timber more efficiently. Today, under strong pressure from the environmental movement, the federal government is eliminating timber harvesting over large areas of "ancient forest" in the Pacific Northwest. The government has determined that this policy is necessary to preserve the spotted owl, as required by the Endangered Species Act. The strong support of the American public for an action with such large costs—quite possibly 30,000 workers displaced and $15 billion of net timber value foregone in the long run—shows the growing power of environmental morality in American life. For many people, to cut an old growth forest—a forest never harvested before and where the trees may be 200, 300, or more years old—is to commit an evil act, an act really of desecration.

Over the course of the spotted owl controversy, thousands of letters from ordinary citizens around the United States were sent to the Department of the Interior. One woman in Florida wrote to Interior Secretary Manuel Lujan to say that "I want to go to Oregon someday and walk among these living cathedrals with my grandchildren." A second woman in North Carolina wrote: "Do not allow another ancient tree to be sacrificed on the sham altar of employment.... The spotted owl is only a visible symbol of the soul of the planet. Please don't take another step toward the death of the Earth."[6] From New Mexico, a writer lamented that "economic considerations are being used as a lever against preserving an endangered species.... It is morally and ethically wrong." What is notable in the many such letters received is the moral terminology and the religious framework. They speak of preserving forest "cathedrals," the "immoral" destruction of nature, and offenses against the "soul of the earth."[7] Reflecting what is seen by many as a godlike task, the government committee assembled to decide whether some Oregon forest areas might be exempted from the Endangered Species Act is widely known as the "God committee."

Keeping Out Evil

Similar moral issues are central to the current debate over the fate of the Arctic National Wildlife Refuge (ANWR) in northeast Alaska. ANWR is a rather featureless plain, cold and dark most of the year, and so remote that hardly anyone is likely to visit it. Any recreational benefits will be small, while oil exploration—which could well discover the largest new oil field in the United States—has a potentially very large value. So by any ordinary utilitarian test of benefits and costs, oil exploration will win out. However, the application of environmental theology yields a much different conclusion. ANWR is exceptional precisely because it is so unattractive to most people for any direct use. Indeed, it is a virgin land, nature little touched in the past by human impacts and one of the few such places left on earth. And oil companies now want to use their drilling rigs and their other crude equipment to "rape" and "defile" this virtuous place. So far, with respect to ANWR, the new puritanism has been winning out over the old utilitarianism.

One of the most graphic illustrations of the power of environmental theology involves Yellowstone National Park. Going back to the 1960s, the National Park Service adopted a policy to destroy mountain goats coming in from the northeast and south sides of the park. Mountain goats coming in from the west side, however, were to be welcomed and protected. One might wonder, what is the difference, since the goats from any side are the same species and would have the same impacts on the park? The answer is that the mountain goats on the west are a natural population, while the goats on the northeast and south sides were introduced some years ago by hunters. Hence, environmental theology decreed that the western goats were permissible in the park, while the northeastern and southern goats would introduce an "unnatural" presence that demanded their elimination. Such theological distinctions are reminiscent of medieval scholastic reasoning to determine which financial arrangements are permissible and which must be prohibited because they commit the sin of "usury" (Noonan 1957).

Many environmentalists also seek the removal of yet another artificial and unnatural presence, the cattle which have long grazed on the public rangelands managed by the Bureau of Land Management (BLM). The BLM has been dominated over the years by graduates of western schools of natural resource management who often specialized in rangeland science. In essence, the BLM view of proper management has been to apply science to maximize the amount of forage production from the rangelands for the benefit of livestock, wildlife and other users (Nelson 1984). In the past decade or so, however, BLM increasingly has been encountering a different vision. Cattle for many environmentalists are offensive because they originally had no place in the natural ecology of the rangeland. Thus, a popular slogan in the environmental movement has been that the western public rangelands must be "cattle free by 93."

The application of a moral criterion of naturalness to drive government policies is in fact pervasive in the environmental and natural resource areas. In the area of global warming, for instance, the public and government response would undoubtedly differ sharply if the warming were deemed a natural event, as opposed to the identical warming claimed to have been caused by human actions. Government regulatory agencies spend billions of dollars to eliminate minute traees of potential cancer causing agents that are deemed "unnatural," but if the agent is considered "natural" they ignore larger exposures for which the potential hazards are much greater. In general, the perception that higher economic outputs are likely to cause still greater intrusions on the natural world leads to an indifference in much environmental thinking to the policy consequences for economic growth—and in some cases to even an outright preference that rates of economic development are reduced.

A Theological Assessment

So what do we make of all this? What kind of environmental policies emerge from our process of disguised theological controversy? The answer depends, of course, partly on the perspective. From an economic perspective, environmental policies are often clearly inefficient and irrational. However, it is also important to examine environmental policy as a matter of theology. Indeed, based on the record of history, it could well be that theological considerations will prove decisive in determining the ultimate outcome.

Of course, many people will reject the environmental gospel out of hand as inconsistent with the message of the Bible—as a crude and heretical caricature of a valid Jewish or Christian faith. It is also important to recognize that there are basic contradictions and failings on secular grounds alone (Douglas and Wildavsky 1983; Wildavsky 1988).

One such failing is that the vision of primitive nature does not square with the available knowledge concerning previous history. The environmental view of the world long ago is the Garden of Eden, but the historical record suggests more the jungle world of competitive survival described by Charles Darwin—of "nature, red in tooth and claw." Historian Arthur Schlesinger recently complained of the romanticizing of Indian societies in the Americas by those who now lament the arrival of Columbus and European settlement. As Schlesinger comments, the true record seems to show that:

> The more developed Aztecs brought the processes of ritual torture and human sacrifice to exalted heights. Thousands of captives won in war or exacted in tribute would line up before the 114 steps of the great pyramid waiting for priests

to plunge in the obsidian knife and tear out their bleeding hearts—a ceremony no doubt laudably designed to propitiate the sun god, but not easy to reconcile with the revisionist myth of prelapsarian harmony and innocence. (1992, 22)

Theological Contradictions

A second failing of environmental theology is that, while preaching that people should behave naturally, it simultaneously exhibits an attitude toward the world that is in itself very unnatural. Environmental theology argues that mankind should assume special burdens for other species, sometimes at its own expense. But no other species is expected to do this. In the real world, the lion has little sympathy for its prey. The Endangered Species Act is not "natural." There is a contradiction here from which there seems no escape.

Environmentalism in fact proposes a special moral responsibility for the world that is similar to the unique role prescribed for humanity in the Bible. There, man alone among species shares in the divine responsibility for the world. The Bible asserts a special obligation of "stewardship" for mankind. But for the most part environmentalism does not acknowledge the Bible as the authority for its views. Nor does environmentalism offer another moral standard beyond doing what is in accord with "nature." And a literal application of this standard, as noted, is more likely to defeat than to support environmental purposes.

Environmental theology offers a negative outlook on the human species that takes an extreme form in the environmentalist references, seemingly becoming more frequent, to the human species as the cancer, AIDS, or other plague upon the earth. As noted above, there is an echo of Calvinism here, but for Calvin the human presence was part of the grand design of God. Lacking this element, environmental theology raises the question of whether there is any real and positive role for mankind whatsoever. What is the argument for the existence of the human species on earth? At times environmental theology seems to have difficulty answering this question. Environmental historian Roderick Nash remarked recently that "I'm sorry people are starving but I'm much more concerned with members of the species smaller than Homo sapiens" (*High Country News* 1991, 16). A few people have even carried the premises of environmental theology to their ultimate extreme, to the conclusion that the human presence on earth may now deserve to be ended. Writing in the *Los Angeles Times*, a biologist for the National Park Service stated a while ago that "until such time as Homo sapiens should decide to rejoin Nature, some of us can only hope for the right virus to come along" (Graber 1989; National Center for Policy Analysis 1991, 3).

Mainstream environmental groups have made a number of less radical proposals that would still aim to reduce sharply the human population. The question of how this will be accomplished is unclear. One outcome is likely, however, if matters ever get that far. It will in practice be the poorest and weakest who will be sacrificed first. Prominent environmental spokesmen have suggested that we should not do anything about starvation in Bangladesh and other impoverished areas around the globe (Neuhaus 1971). It is still another reminder of Calvinist theology, which regarded the poor as properly afflicted because they were sinners—and thus whether they arrived in hell sooner or arrived later was not a matter of great moment.

Economic Ignorance

While environmental theology makes strong moral judgments about economic life, it is often uninformed and unrealistic when it comes simply to understanding the basic mechanics of an economic system. Environmental theology aspires to a natural utopia in which there will be no economic problem. In this regard it is a lot like Marxism. The human condition will be transformed, the economic problem abolished, and humanity will live in happy innocence and harmony forever after without having to face any problems of production and consumption. For Marx, this heavenly condition was to follow the triumph of the proletariat, the culminating event in the salvation of mankind through the economic workings of history. For environmental theology today, it is to follow the recovery of a natural condition around the world, as the culminating rejection of economic progress.

Environmental groups often resist even the concept that there is a necessity to trade off environmental goals against other social needs. This allows them to avoid dealing at all with messy matters such as efficiency. Environmental theology thus is often opposed to using benefit-cost measures to help to decide the appropriate level of environmental protection. Instead, protection of the environment is said to be priceless; in a number of legislative enactments, Congress has in fact prohibited administrative agencies from considering costs. In truth, if this principle were actually put into practice fully and literally, the ultimate consequence would be the exhaustion of all social resources in the service of environmental purposes alone.

Similarly, there is often an antagonism to the market. Many environmentalists thus are opposed to creating markets in rights to pollute. They take the view that to sell pollution rights, as one critic wrote recently, would be the moral equivalent of having government sell permits to commit "felonies" (Gitlin 1989, A27). Such attitudes have led some people to conclude that environmentalism is bearing the message of socialism in a new form. The two in fact differ in fundamental ways—as in their sharply contrasting views of "progress"—but do share an antagonism to the market and a common utopian aspiration to heaven on earth.

Partly as a result of the lack of economic understanding and the substitution of moral righteousness, the environmental movement tends to win a lot of symbolic victories but often there is not much real environmental gain

(Samuelson 1989, A25; Portney 1990). Yet, there is still a large social cost. If the level of funding now being devoted to environmental objectives were spent more wisely, the potential for further reducing pollution, improving public health, and achieving other practical benefits in the quality of the environment would be very large.

Finally, the actual result of any genuine attempt to follow the utopian hopes found commonly in environmental theology would be not only economic chaos but in all likelihood a widespread loss of personal freedoms. In this century there have already been many cases where the highest ideals were in a sense too high for the current condition of humanity. They led instead to a new hell on earth. Radical environmentalism would probably have similar consequences for individual liberties if anyone ever actually sought to organize a whole society on this basis (which fortunately is a very slim possibility in at least the United States).

Is Environmental Theology Pantheism?

Although a number of people have by now addressed the religious elements in the environmental movement, the most common view has been that environmental religion is an animistic or pantheistic faith—that environmentalism is the worship of nature. Both leading supporters and critics have taken this position. In a much discussed 1967 article in *Science*, historian Lynn White blamed Christianity for the environmental destructiveness of western civilization and argued that it might be necessary to return to some type of pre-Christian and pagan religion (White 1967). In *Playing God in Yellowstone*, Alston Chase asserted that environmentalism had in fact taken this route, that it offered a blend of "non-Western and non-modern theories," drawing upon "Buddhism, Taoism, inhumanism, organicism, mysticism, transcendentalism, animism." At its heart, there was a "vast, impersonal pantheism" preaching a message that "the universe is one inter-connected whole and that every atom in creation is part of the sacred being of God" (1986, 304).

Although some pantheistic elements may well be present, such characterizations probably do more to inhibit than to advance understanding of the environmental movement. They make it too easy, for example, for critics to dismiss environmental theology as some sort of aberration or radical departure from the main lines of religion in the west. If that were true, however, the great popular appeal that the environmental movement is today demonstrating in American life would be inexplicable. By contrast, the source of attraction is readily comprehended when the roots of environmentalism are located within the Judeo-Christian tradition—when environmentalism is seen as yet another manifestation of the Calvinist judgment on the human condition, when it is seen as a secular reassertion of the Puritan moralism that has been such a powerful force in this nation from its earliest days.

Of course, it is also true that many members of the environmental movement are happy as well to regard environmental theology as a kind of pantheistic or pagan faith. Seen in this light, the environmental faithful can regard themselves as contributing to the development of new religious truths for our time, proselytizers for an innovative and exciting new spiritual message. It is less inspiring to think that the message may actually be an old and familiar one in the Judeo-Christian tradition. It might be even less appealing to think that the message follows in the line of what is often characterized as the harsh, pessimistic, dour thinking of "doom and gloom" Calvinism—a set of ideas against which the Enlightment faith in progress and the whole modern age to some degree were a reaction. In short, there are some practical reasons why both many critics and supporters thus far have been slow to investigate the deep roots that environmental theology has in the western religious heritage.

The Max Weber Thesis

It is now approaching 100 years since Max Weber published *The Protestant Ethic and the Spirit of Capitalism*, developing the famous thesis that Calvinism was significantly responsible for the emergence of capitalism in the west. Since then, the overall judgment of historians has been that Weber's thesis was considerably overstated. Capitalist institutions, for example, were already well developed in some Catholic areas long before the Protestant Reformation. Nevertheless, Calvinism did encourage a commitment to hard work, promoted a highly rational approach to life, and favored a life lived for a business or other worldly "calling." Historians generally agree that these and other elements in fact contributed from the sixteenth century onward to the eventual spread and acceptance of market economies in the western world.

Can this role of Calvinism in promoting capitalism be squared with the argument in this chapter that important segments of environmentalism exhibit a secular form of Calvinism? After all, environmental theology today is often hostile not only to the market but to the very idea of economic progress. In addressing this matter, it is important first to recognize that Calvin did not regard earning a high income or maintaining a high level of consumption as an acceptable goal in itself. The importance of the calling lay not in the resulting goods and services and the wealth obtained, but in the doing of the work itself.

The real purpose of a calling was the "disciplining [of] their own character by patient labor, and of devoting themselves to a service acceptable to God" (Tawney 1926, 105). In the Calvinist view, as Weber states, "you may labor to be rich for God, though not for the flesh and sin" (Weber 1958, 163). Indeed, God must mean to test human resolve, because the greater the success in the calling, the greater are likely to be the temptations to sinfulness—further emphasizing the necessity of a strong will and tight rational self-control among the Calvinist faithful. This is hardly the utilitarian attitude that has characterized much of the modern emphasis on economic progress.

In his classic, *Protestantism and Progress*, the German theologian Ernst Troeltsch observed that the theologies of both Luther and Calvin were in truth attempts to turn back the economic and other forces of modernization which even in the sixteenth century could be seen looming. Luther and Calvin sought a greater piety and a truer Christianity—a "revival of the [true] Catholic idea," as it had existed in earlier and much simpler times before the devil had taken over the Roman church. Indeed, in Troeltsch's judgment, the actual consequence of the "revolutionary conservatism" of the Protestant Reformation had been that "Europe had to experience two centuries more of the medieval spirit." Yet, it was also undoubtedly true that the Reformation—especially its Calvinist branches— played a "conspicuous part in the production of the modern world" (1958, 86-7).

The seeming paradox could be explained by recognizing that the modernizing impacts of Protestantism were "mainly indirect and unconsciously produced effects ... even in accidental side-influences, and again in influences produced against its will" (Troeltsch 1958). For example, one of the most important impacts was simply the removal of the authority of the Roman Catholic church over wide areas of Europe, thereby opening a new latitude for experimentation in all kinds of social and intellectual matters. Calvin would very likely have been disturbed—horrified might be the better word—at many of the features of modernity that today are attributed partly to the legacy of Calvinism. In this distaste for modern developments, Calvin would now be able to find some surprising new compatriots—an apparently growing number of people who believe that the Americas before Columbus, other primitive societies around the world, the "natural" relations among the creatures of the animal world, and it seems virtually any premodern and/or animal existence is possessed of a higher moral standing than our current civilization.

Conclusion

At the end of the twentieth century we seem to be in a period of religious ferment. At least in terms of their impact on society, the most powerful religions of the twentieth century have been secular faiths of economic progress. The American welfare state, for example, was significantly shaped by the "gospel of efficiency" of the American progressive movement early in this century (Nelson 1991). Yet, although environmental theology may exaggerate the problems of progress, it is also true that the prophesies of heaven on earth have hardly been realized. The historical record of the twentieth century—replete with genocide, warfare, and other inhumanity to man—tends to undermine the earlier assurance that growing material prosperity alone will solve the age-old problems of the human condition. It thus should be no great surprise that many people are turning away from the modern religions that have placed such great faith in economic progress. Yet, to turn simply from exalting progress to exalting its absence in the wilderness is not likely to help matters.

The current wide sense of disillusionment does not demonstrate that there is a lack of idealism in American life today but in many cases the opposite. Many people have a set of ideals so high that in comparison the current behavior of their fellow men and the general state of the world seem mean-spirited and even contemptible. It is understandable that a gospel offering the prospect of finding a more innocent and happier world holds a strong attraction. In Calvinism, although current existence must be sinful, there lay in store the prospect of a glorious and heavenly future. But in Calvinism this final outcome was predetermined and to be brought about by God. In environmental theology, there is no such transforming agent presented or explained; there is only a deep and for most people it would seem sincerely felt desire that the world should become a much better place than they find it. Yet, the history of the twentieth century has amply shown that in building a new world sincerity and good intentions are not enough (Johnson 1983).

Partly because of the great religious diversity in the United States, and the fear that any strong religious disagreements might prove irreconcilable or even provoke outbreaks of violence, Americans are uncomfortable with religious debates in public concerning matters of government policy. Nevertheless, it is time to face two important facts: (1) that religion is already exerting a large influence on government policy in the environmental area, and (2) that all religions are not equal. Americans may not be able to agree on any one correct theology, but they must also recognize that to follow the wrong theology can lead to missteps on a grand scale. Theological discussion and debate have become both unavoidable and necessary in at least some policy areas such as the environment.

Moreover, there is no problem in America today in getting agreement on the practical importance of maintaining a clean and attractive environment; Americans of very widely varying faiths and convictions can readily agree on this matter. The problem is that we are currently being prevented from developing sound policies to achieve this widely shared goal by an underlying set of assumptions and attitudes of a fundamentalist environmental theology. It is time for Americans to move beyond this barrier presently standing in the way of more practical and effective policies to attain a healthy, clean and attractive American environment. If there is perhaps no such thing as a policy that is entirely "value-free," it can be said that the core values in the improved environmental policies sought here are those of greater peace and greater economic prosperity for the nation and for the world.

Notes

1. Interview with Foreman, quoted in Douglas S. Looney, "Protection or Provocateur?" *Sports Illustrated* (May 27, 1991), 54.
2. Memorandum to Sierra Club Members for Carl Pope, Conservation Director, "Administration's Shameful Energy Plan," undated. Solicitations of funding and other support such as this one are particularly useful in illustrating the public mood and attitudes to which environment organizations are appealing.
3. Letter from President Richard Cellarius to fellow Sierra Club members, "Year-end Report," November 1988, 6.
4. Statement of the "Church of the Earth Nation," quoted in Catherine L. Albanese, *Nature Religion in America: From the Algonkian Indians to the New Age* (Chicago: University of Chicago Press, 1900), 153.
5. Letter from Wilderness Society President George Frampton Jr. to potential supporters, undated, 3.
6. Letters sent to Interior Secretary Manuel Lujan and directed to the Office of Program Analysis for reply.
7. Ibid.

This chapter is adapted from a speech delivered at a Cato Institute Conference on "Global Environmental Crises: Science or Politics," Washington, D.C., June 5, 1991.

References

Albanese, Catherine L. 1990. *Nature Religion in America: From the Algonkian Indians to the New Age*. Chicago: University of Chicago Press.

Calvin, John. 1989. Institutes of the Christian Religion. In *Calvin's Institutes: A New Compend*, edited by Hugh T. Kerr. Louisville, KY: Westminster/John Knox Press.

Chase, Alston. 1986. *Playing God in Yellowstone: The Destruction of America's First National Park*. Boston: Atlantic Monthly Press.

Culver, John. 1978. Comments. *Congressional Record-Senate*. July 18.

Devall, Bill, and George Sessions. 1985. *Deep Ecology*, Salt Lake City, UT: Peregine Smith Books.

Douglas, Mary, and Aaron Wildavsky. 1983. *Risk and Culture*. Berkeley, CA: University of California Press.

Drucker, Peter F. 1992. The Post-Capitalist World. *The Public Interest* (Fall 109: 89-100).

Ehrlich, Paul R. 1968. *The Population Bomb*. New York: Ballantine Books.

Ehrlich, Paul R., and Anne H. Ehrlich. 1991. *The Population Explosion.* New York: Simon and Schuster.

Ekirch, Arthur A. 1963. *Man and Nature in America.* New York: Columbia University Press.

Everndon, Neil. 1978. Beyond Ecology. *North American Review* 263.

Foreman, Dave. 1989. The Destruction of Wilderness. *Earth First—The Radical Environmental Journal* (December 21): 20.

Foreman, Dave. 1991. *Confessions of an Eco-Warrior.* New York: Harmony Books.

Gitlin, Todd. 1989. Buying the Right to Pollute, What's Next? *New York Times* (July 18): A27.

Glover, Willis B. 1984. *Biblical Origins of Modern Secular Culture: An Essay in the Interpretation of Western History.* Macon, GA: Mercer University Press.

Graber, David M. 1989. Mother Nature as a Hothouse Flower. *Los Angeles Times Book Review* (October 22).

Graham, Billy. 1979. *How to Be Born Again.* New York: Warner Books. *High Country News.* 1991. Bulletin Board. (September 23): 16.

Johnson, Paul. 1983. *Modern Times: The World from the Twenties to the Eighties.* New York: Harper and Row.

Lasch, Christopher. 1991. *The True and Only Heaven: Progress and Its Critics.* New York: Norton.

Looney, Douglas S. 1991. Protection or Provocateur? *Sports Illustrated* (May 27): 54-58.

McKibben, Bill. 1989. *The End of Nature.* New York: Random House.

Manes, Christopher. 1990. *Green Rage: Radical Environmentalism and the Unmaking of Civilization.* Boston: Little Brown.

Marston, Ed. 1989. Ecotage Isn't a Solution, It's Part of the Problem. *High Country News* (June 19).

Nash, Roberick. 1967. *Wilderness and the American Mind.* New Haven: Yale University Press.

Nelson, Robert H. 1984. Economic Analysis in Public Rangeland Management. In *Western Public Lands,* edited by John Francis and Richard Ganzel. Totowa, NJ: Rowman and Allanheld.

————. 1990a. Should Policy Analysts Study Theology? The Case of Environmental and Natural Resource Policy Making. Paper prepared for the 12th Annual Conference of the Association for Public Policy Analysis and Management, October 18-20, San Francisco, CA.

————. 1990b. Unoriginal Sin: The Judeo-Christian Roots of Ecotheology. *Policy Review* 53 (Summer): 52-59.

————. 1991. *Reaching for Heaven on Earth: The Theological Meaning of Economics.* Lanham, MD: Rowman and Littlefield.

Neuhaus, Richard. 1971. *In Defense of People: Ecology and the Seduction of Radicalism.* New York: Macmillan.

Noonan, John T. Jr. 1957. *The Scholastic Analysis of Usury.* Cambridge, MA: Harvard University Press.

Portney, Paul R. 1990. *Public Policies for Environmental Protection.* Washington, DC: Resources for the Future.

Progressive Environmentalism: A Pro-Human, Pro-Science, Pro-Free Enterprise Agenda for Change. 1991. National Center for Policy Analysis (April).

Roszak, Theodore. 1992. *The Voice of the Earth.* New York: Simon and Schuster.

Samuelson, Robert J. 1990. Environmental Delusions. *Washington Post* (May 25): A25.

Sax, Joseph L. 1980. *Mountains without Handrails: Reflections on the National Parks.* Ann Arbor: University of Michigan Press.

Schlesinger, Arthur Jr. 1992. Was America a Mistake? *Atlantic Monthly* (September): 22.

Shepard, Paul. 1982. *Nature and Madness.* San Francisco: Sierra Club Books.

Tawney, R. H. 1926. *Religion and the Rise of Capitalism: A Historical Study.* New York: Harcourt Brace.

Tillich, Paul. 1967. *A History of Christian Thought: From Its Judaic and Hellenistic Origins to Existentialism.* New York: Simon and Schuster.

Troeltsch, Ernst. 1958. *Protestantism and Progress: A Historical Study of the Relation of Protestantism to the Modern World.* Boston: Beacon Press.

Voegelin, Eric. 1987. *The New Science of Politics: An Introduction.* Chicago: University of Chicago Press.

Weber, Max. 1958. *The Protestant Ethic and the Spirit of Capitalism.* New York: Charles Scribner.

Wildavsky, Aaron. 1988. *Searching for Safety.* New Brunswick, NJ: Transaction Publishers.

White, Lynn Jr. 1967. The Historical Roots of Our Ecologic Crisis. *Science,* (March 10).

Index

About the Political Economy Forum and the Authors

The Political Economy Research Center (PERC) is a nonprofit think tank in Bozeman, Montana. For over a decade, PERC has pioneered recognizing the value of the market, individual initiative, the importance of property rights, and voluntary activity. This approach is known as the New Resource Economics or free market environmentalism. PERC associates have applied this approach to a variety of issues, including resource development, water marketing, chemical risk, private provision of environmental amenities, global warming, ozone depletion, and endangered species protection.

In 1989, PERC first organized a forum aimed at applying the principles of political economy to important policy issues. The purpose of this forum is to bring together scholars in economics, law, political science, anthropology, history, and other disciplines to discuss and refine academic papers that explore new applications of political economy. It is increasingly evident that the interface between government and individuals in society is vital in determining the rate and direction of economic progress. Political economy analyzes this interface.

This volume is the third in PERC's Political Economy Forum. While *Taking the Environment Seriously* is not based on a specific PERC meeting, its goal, like that of the others, is the application of the principles of political economy. Most of the contributors to this volume are affiliated with PERC and share a respect for the principles underlying the New Resource Economics.

We believe that books of this type can integrate "cutting-edge" academic work with crucial policy issues of the day. We anticipate that future books in the series will provide stimulating ideas for other important policy issues.

Terry L. Anderson

Terry Anderson is Senior Associate of the Political Economy Research Center in Bozeman, Montana, and Professor of Economics at Montana State University. In addition to this volume, other books in the Rowman & Littlefield Political Economy Forum series edited by Anderson include *Property Rights and Indian Economies* (1992) and *The Political Economy of Customs and Culture* (1993). He is editor of *NAFTA and the Environment* (Pacific Research Institute, 1993) and has been a visiting scholar at Stanford University and Clemson University and has lectured extensively and taught in England, Europe, Africa, and New Zealand.

Daniel K. Benjamin

Dan Benjamin is a Professor of Economics at Clemson University and was a Visiting Scholar at the Political Economy Research Center in 1993. Author of numerous articles in professional journals, prior to joining the Clemson faculty in 1985, Benjamin served as Chief of Staff at the U.S. Department of Labor. He received his Ph.D. in Economics from the University of California, Los Angeles. His most recent book, coauthored with Roger LeRoy Miller and Douglass C. North, is *The Economics of Public Issues* (HarperCollins, 9th ed., 1993).

Brett A. Dalton

Brett Dalton is Director of Financial Planning for Clemson University, where he received his M.A. in economics. During 1991-92, Dalton led a research project that focused on Superfund activities in South Carolina. His current research examines the financial markets effects of Superfund legislation.

Paul Heyne

Paul Heyne is a Senior Lecturer in the Economics Department at the University of Washington in Seattle, where he has taught since 1976. He holds his masters degrees in theology and in economics and a Ph.D. in ethics and society from the University of Chicago Divinity School. The author of *The Economic Way of Thinking* (SRA, 7th ed., 1992), which has been translated into numerous languages, Heyne's research and teaching focus on the areas in which economics, law, and ethics intersect.

Donald R. Leal

Don Leal, Senior Research Associate at the Political Economy Research Center, is coauthor of *Free Market Environmentalism* (Pacific Research Institute and Westview Press, 1991) and coeditor of *The Yellowstone Primer* (Pacific Research Institute). Widely published on natural resources topics, Leal received his M.S. in statistics from California State University at Hayward.

Roger E. Meiners

Roger Meiners is Professor of Law and Economics at the University of Texas at Arlington and is a member of the Political Economy Research Center's Board of Advisors. Author of numerous books and articles on law and economics, Meiners' recent work focuses on common law and its influence on environmental law and policy. He is coeditor of *The Economic Consequences of Liability Rules* (Quorum, 1991). He received his Ph.D. in economics from Virginia Polytechnic Institute and his J.D. from the University of Miami.

Robert H. Nelson

Robert Nelson is a senior policy analyst with the U.S. Department of the Interior and a frequent participant in conferences at the Political Economy Research Center. Author of numerous articles in professional journals on natural resources and other policy topics, his most recent book is *Reaching for Heaven on Earth: The Theological Meaning of Economics* (Rowman and Littlefield, 1991). Nelson received his Ph.D. in economics from Princeton University.

David W. Riggs

David Riggs is a doctoral candidate in economics at Clemson University. His research agenda includes work on the evolution of pollution permit trading and the political economy of the 1990 Clean Air Act. In 1991, Riggs was a research fellow at the Political Economy Research Center in Bozeman, Montana.

Jane S. Shaw

Jane Shaw is a Senior Associate of the Political Economy Research Center where she directs the center's editorial outreach program for the popular and non-academic press. Widely published in major newspapers and magazines throughout the United States, Shaw is Senior Editor of *Liberty* and a member of the editorial advisory board of *Regulation*. From 1981 to 1984, Shaw was Associate Economics Editor of *Business Week*.

Richard L. Stroup

Richard Stroup is a Professor of Economics at Montana State University and a Senior Associate of the Political Economy Research Center. Widely published in areas of natural resources and environmental economics, Stroup is coauthor with James Gwartney of *Economics: Private and Public Choice* (HBJ, 6th ed., 1992). Stroup received his Ph.D. in economics from the University of Washington and served as Director of the Office of Policy Analysis at the U.S. Department of Interior from 1982 to 1984.

Bruce Yandle

Bruce Yandle is Alumni Professor of Economics and Legal Studies at Clemson University and is a member of the Political Economic Research Center's Board of Advisors. His writings on environmental policy include many journal articles, special reports, and monographs. He is author of *The Political Limits of Environmental Regulation* (Quorum, 1989). Yandle's current research focuses on the rise of markets for environmental goods. Yandle received his Ph.D. in economics from Georgia State University and served as Executive Director of the Federal Trade Commission from 1982 to 1984.